PETER WILLIAMS

G000126371

Acts: Church on the move

An expositional commentary on the Acts of the Apostles

© Day One Publications 2004
First printed 2004

ISBN 1 903087 65 -1

9 781903 087657

British Library Cataloguing in Publication Data available

Published by Day One Publications
Ryelands Road, Leominster, HR6 8NZ
☎ 01568 613 740 FAX 01568 611 473
email—sales@dayone.co.uk
web site—www.dayone.co.uk

Designed by Steve Devane and printed by CPD

To Betty and Bernard whose Christian fellowship I greatly value

Preface

When writing this commentary I have had the constant feeling of things happening. The early church really was a Church on the move. It was dynamic and exhilarating, and in the record of Acts something seems to be happening on almost every page. They were undoubtedly dangerous and challenging times for those early Christians, but they must also have been exciting times with the power of God so evident in signs and wonders, and the Holy Spirit moving in the lives of both the leaders and the people.

We may look back to that period in the church's history and long for such things to happen in the church today. But God has called us to serve him in our time, and we can do no better than learn from the book of Acts how we can make the gospel known to the men and women of our generation. Our constant prayer should be that God will help us by his Spirit to do that faithfully, and with joyful hearts.

My dear friends Brian and Ruth Kerry have again given considerable time and effort to preparing the manuscript of this book for publication and I am, as always, extremely grateful.

Peter Williams
Bournemouth 2003

Contents

The time of preparation

Read Acts chapter 1

Introducing Acts

Acts has been described in a variety of ways. Calvin describes it as 'a vast treasure', and the Introduction in the New International Version as 'a bridge that ties the church with each succeeding age'. Other descriptions include, 'the keystone' of the New Testament, and 'the most important book in the New Testament' (Barclay). But whilst all these descriptions help us to see that it is a very significant work, it seems to me that the title 'The Acts of the Apostles', which dates back to the second century, is the best of all since it tells us what the apostles did.

Acts is the record of the activity of the apostles in carrying on the work of building the church, which Christ had given them to do. It is a book full of action and movement, which is what we should expect when its purpose, as set out in Acts 1:8, is to fulfil the words of Jesus: '… you shall be witnesses to me in Jerusalem, and in all Judea and Samaria and to the end of the earth'. The movement of Christianity began with the mother church at Jerusalem, spread throughout Palestine, and finally went out to the wider Gentile world. Hence the title of this exposition—Church on the move.

The author

It is widely held among Bible scholars that Luke, who wrote the Gospel named after him, is also the author of Acts. This is a tradition that goes back to the second century, and one very strong piece of evidence for this is the reference to his 'former account' in the opening verse, and the dedication of both books to the person named Theophilus. 'The former account I made, O Theophilus, of all that Jesus began both to do and teach' (Acts 1:1). The name Theophilus means 'lover of God', and he was probably a high Roman official, since Luke in his gospel addresses him with the title 'most excellent', or as we should say, 'your excellency'. Paul uses a similar title when standing trial before Festus, the Roman governor (Acts 26:25).

As a Gentile himself Luke may have written both his gospel and Acts to give Theophilus, who was either a Christian or a seeker after Christian truth, a clearer understanding of the Christian message. But as we said earlier, his main purpose seems to have been to commend Christianity to the Gentile world.

The importance of Acts

Luke's gospel, together with the book of Acts, makes a larger contribution to the writings of the New Testament than the thirteen letters of Paul, and John's gospel, letters, and Revelation combined. Luke is the first church historian, and the importance of his account in Acts of the spread of Christianity cannot be overestimated. The work centres chiefly on the exploits of Peter and Paul, with Peter opening the door of Christianity to both Jews and Gentiles, and Paul travelling far and wide to take the gospel to the pagan world.

It is not difficult to see what we owe to Luke. Without his history we should know little, if anything, of the origin and progress of the church, the outpouring of the Holy Spirit, the organisation of the church and its methods of evangelisation. Also, in a more general way, Acts serves as the link between the gospels and the rest of the New Testament.

Luke looks back

Before beginning on his new history Luke, in the opening verses, looks back to the earthly ministry of Jesus, which he had recorded in his Gospel. 'The former account I made, O Theophilus, of all that Jesus began both to do and teach, until the day in which he was taken up, after he through the Holy Spirit had given commandments to the apostles whom he had chosen' (Acts 1:2).

The words: 'of all that Jesus began both to do and to teach', are significant because they imply that the work and ministry of Christ did not end when his resurrection appearances were over, but that it would continue by the power of the Holy Spirit working through the apostles in the building of the church. His earthly ministry was only the beginning of his eternal purpose, there was much more yet to come.

Christ continued his earthly ministry 'until the day in which he was taken up', meaning his ascension. It is both thrilling and wonderful therefore to think that he did not leave this world and return to the Father's glory without first making arrangements for the on-going work of the gospel here below. What makes it thrilling is that he did not entrust that work to angels or divine beings, but to ordinary men like the apostles, and through them to ordinary people like ourselves. There is a real sense therefore in which we can say that the ministry of Jesus never ends, and is being continued today in the lives and witness of all Christian believers through the power of the Holy Spirit at work in the church. What a great privilege and enormous responsibility we have therefore in being part of the body of Christ in the world.

Christ's works and words

Luke says that his objective, in recording the ministry of Jesus in his Gospel, was to tell us what Jesus began 'both to do and to teach'. His purpose did not go beyond that. We do not know, for example, what Jesus looked like since no description of his physical appearance has come down to us. Indeed, we know practically nothing of the first thirty years of his life which are hidden in obscurity, except for the incident in the temple when he was twelve years old (Luke 2:42). But in his Gospel Luke was not interested in any of these things, he is only concerned to tell us what Jesus did, by way of his miracles and his works of healing and mercy, and what he said, by way of his teaching about the kingdom of God.

And we can easily understand why Luke confined himself in this way. After all, it is the works and words of Jesus that have influenced mankind throughout history. Jesus never wrote a book, or fought a military campaign, or left us any philosophical system of thought, and yet his words are better known, and quoted more often, than those of any other outstanding figure in history. Likewise, what he did in his miracles of healing and works of mercy by his gracious loving manner helped and encouraged many in his own day, and have served to convince vast numbers since that time that he truly was the Son of God with power.

Resurrection appearances

The physical resurrection of Christ would become the cornerstone of the preaching and witness of the church that was about to come into being, hence Luke's emphasis upon the resurrection appearances as infallible proofs. 'To whom he also presented himself alive after his suffering by many infallible proofs, being seen by them during forty days and speaking of the things pertaining to the kingdom of God' (Acts 1:3). There were some ten such appearances in all, to individuals like Mary and the disciples on the Emmaeus road; to the apostles as a group, and on occasion to more than five hundred at the same time (1 Corinthians 15:5–6).

Furthermore, these appearances lasted over a period of forty days and occurred at various times and in various places; in the morning (John 20:1–10), in the evening in a room with a locked door (John 20:19), and on the seashore (John 21:1). Nor were these appearances visionary or insubstantial like some kind of spirit. Thomas actually felt the print of the nails in the hands of Jesus, and felt the wound in his side. He also ate and talked with the disciples to prove to them that, whilst his body was different after his resurrection, it was still recognisably human and could consume food.

Christians therefore need have no doubts about the physical resurrection of Jesus since it is about the best-attested fact in history.

The kingdom of God

What happened during the forty days of the resurrection appearances? It was a period when Jesus gave all his attention to teaching the disciples and preparing them for the work and ministry they were to carry out later. '…during forty days and speaking of the things pertaining to the kingdom of God'. Here was a subject to which Jesus had given great prominence in his own ministry, and is to be found in many of his parables. The Kingdom of God, or Kingdom of Heaven as it is sometimes called, is mentioned over one hundred and fifty times in the New Testament, and yet there is still a lot of confused thinking about it in some quarters. Even the disciples themselves were still a bit fuzzy in their understanding of this important subject. 'Therefore, when they had come together they asked him saying, "Lord, will you at this time restore the kingdom to Israel?"' (Acts 1:6). They still thought of God's kingdom in earthly terms, with nationalistic overtones of freedom from their Roman oppressors. They needed the teaching of Jesus during the forty days, therefore, to clarify their thinking.

If we understand the teaching of Jesus aright, the Kingdom of God is not any kind of political utopia, or social ideal, or blueprint for a better society on earth. He made that perfectly clear when he said to Pilate: 'My kingdom is not of this world. If my kingdom were of this world, my servants would fight so that I should not be delivered to the Jews; but now my kingdom is not from here' (John 18:36). The kingdom Jesus had in mind rests on the relationship a person has with God, by which his Spirit and power rules in the human heart. When he preached: '…the kingdom of God is at hand. Repent, and believe the gospel' (Mark 1:15), he was telling people that through repentance and faith they could enjoy God's forgiveness and salvation and enter his eternal kingdom.

And that is still the kernel of the message we have to preach today, and not be content simply with telling people how they can build God's kingdom on earth by their social ideals, their environmental concerns, and their desire to help the third world. We must present the spiritual aspect of God's kingdom first and foremost, whilst at the same time pointing out its practical implications in today's world. Furthermore, we must help them to understand that the Kingdom of God is not only present, in that we can enter here and now through repentance and faith, but it is also futuristic, since its final fulfilment will only come when Christ returns again and establishes his kingdom for all eternity in the new heaven and the new earth 'in which righteousness dwells' (2 Peter 3:13). In the light of all this we can see why Jesus should have used the forty days to impress these great truths upon the minds of his disciples.

The promise of the Spirit

When it comes to preaching the gospel of the Kingdom of God, it is not enough to have such a great message to proclaim, we also need the power that will give that message its impact on people's minds and hearts. That is exactly what Jesus went on to promise the disciples that God would provide. 'And being assembled together with them, he commanded them not to depart from Jerusalem, but to wait for the Promise of the Father, "which" he said, "you have heard from me; for John truly baptised with water, but you shall be baptised with the Holy Spirit not many days from now"' (Acts 1: 4–5).

We shall learn a lot more about the power of the Holy Spirit when we come to the Pentecost experience in chapter two. For now, it is sufficient to remind ourselves that Jesus told his disciples to 'wait' until the promise of the Spirit should be fulfilled. This tells us that we cannot do God's work without God's power. And all too often the church has attempted to do just that, and has failed in her mission to the world. A preacher may be eloquent, have great knowledge, and be a good communicator, but without the Spirit's power his message will lack the authority to move men's hearts to accept Christ. Our authority is centred in the Bible as the Word of God, and it is when we are faithful in declaring that word, and not our own opinions, that the power of the Spirit is present to honour that Word in making it a blessing to the hearers.

'The Spirit breathes upon the Word,
And brings the truth to sight;
Precepts and promises afford,
A sanctifying sight'
William Cowper.

The ascended Christ

We have already touched on two great biblical doctrines; the resurrection and the Holy Spirit. In these next few verses Luke mentions two others: the ascension of Christ, and his coming again in glory.

'Now when he had spoken these things, while they watched, he was taken up, and a cloud received him out of their sight. And while they looked steadfastly toward heaven as he went up, behold, two men stood by them in white apparel, who also said, "Men of Galilee, why do you stand gazing up into heaven? This same Jesus, who was taken up from you into heaven, will so come in like manner as you saw him go into heaven"' (Acts 1:9–11).

It seems a great pity to my mind that the doctrine of the ascension does not receive the prominence in preaching that it deserves. I am not sure why that is, except that it might be thought that it adds little, if anything, to the truth of the resurrection. But that surely is not so. After all, Christ himself anticipated his ascension as completing his earthly ministry. He told his disciples to expect it. 'What then if you should see the Son of Man ascend where he was before?' (John 6:62). And again, Luke says he resolutely faced the Cross because he anticipated his ascension and exaltation at the Father's side: '…when the time had come for him to be received up, he steadfastly set his face to go to Jerusalem' (Luke 9:51).

An expression closely associated with the ascension and exaltation of Christ is 'seated at the right hand of God'. Which refers to his regal function and authority, and indicates that God the Father had set his seal on Christ's victory and kingship over the world. Paul puts it magnificently: '…according to the working of his mighty power which he worked in Christ when he raised him from the dead and seated him at his right hand in the heavenly places, far above all principality and power and might and dominion, and every name that is named, not only in this age but also in that which is to come' (Ephesians 1:19–21). Today, when there is a distinct lack of firm leadership in the world and in the church, and when uncertainty and confusion seems to be the mark of political and religious life, there is a great need for God's people to re-emphasise this great truth of Christ as the ascended and exalted king ruling over all things. To do so would nerve the church to present the gospel with a new authority, and would breathe new life and exhilaration into the tired hearts of many pastors.

But in addition to what we have said there are practical lessons to be learned from the doctrine of the ascension. In his gospel Luke says that when Christ departed from the disciples they 'returned to Jerusalem with great joy, and were continually in the temple praising and blessing God' (Luke 24:52–53). Why great joy? We should have thought they would have been sad and mournful at losing their leader. But they now understood that although he was passing out of their sight, he was not passing out of their lives. When he was with them physically, their relationship with him was limited, since they could only be with him at one place at one time. But now, through the Holy Spirit, they would know his presence with them constantly. That is what Paul had in mind when he says: 'Even though we have known Christ according to the flesh, yet now we know him thus no longer' (2 Corinthians 5:16). To know the historical Jesus is one thing, but to know him in the heart as the risen and ascended Lord and King is a far greater joy.

Another truth underlying the ascension is that we now have an advocate in heaven who intercedes on our behalf at the throne of grace. Speaking of Christ's intercession the writer to the Hebrews says: 'Therefore he is also able to save to the uttermost those who come to God through him, since he always lives to make intercession for them' (Hebrews 7:25). We may wonder why the believer as a child of God needs an advocate, since his relationship with God is settled. John answers that very clearly: 'My little children, these things I write to you, so that you may not sin. And if anyone sins, we have an Advocate with the Father, Jesus Christ the righteous' (1 John 2:1). He is saying that because we are saved we must not treat sin lightly or think of it as something we need no longer be concerned about. It is still a dreadful reality as long as we live in this sinful world. The difference between the believer when he sins, and the worldly man, is that the believer knows he has an advocate in Christ who pleads his cause and is able to bring him restoration and forgiveness.

A third truth to come out of the ascension is that it fulfils the promise Jesus gave earlier. 'In my Father's house are many mansions; if it were not so, I would have told you. I go to prepare a place for you. And if I go and prepare a place for you, I will come again and receive you to myself; that where I am, there you may be also' (John 14:2–3). What that preparation entails we cannot say. But it is enough to know that Christ ascended in order to get things ready in heaven for our arrival in the father's house. I remember reading somewhere of a little girl who was accustomed to take a short cut on her way home from school through the local cemetery. She was asked if she was at all frightened on the gloomy autumn evenings, to which she replied: 'No, I'm on the way home'. That sums up perfectly the Christian's approach to dying: we are on the way home to the Father's house.

Departure and return

We cannot separate the Christ who ascended into the glory from the Christ who will one day return from that glory to judge the living and the dead, and to gather his own to himself. 'Men of Galilee, why do you stand gazing up into heaven? This same Jesus, who was taken up from you into heaven, will so come in like manner as you saw him go into heaven' (Acts 1:11).

Theologians use the technical term 'Eschatology' from the Greek meaning 'last', to refer to the doctrine of the last things, including death, judgement, heaven, hell and the return of Christ to this earth. Christians may differ among themselves as to some of the details of Christ's second advent, but all are agreed that the New Testament clearly teaches that as time runs down, a day will come when history will reach its consummation with the return of the Lord Jesus Christ in power and glory to finalise his purpose for mankind.

The importance of this teaching may be seen in the fact that it is mentioned all through the New Testament, and the book of Revelation deals with it exclusively. Christ himself dealt with it in great detail, and made it the subject of many of his parables. But it is important for other reasons. It gives shape and meaning to the lives of Christian men and women. Paul describes it as 'the blessed hope' to which we are to look forward, and which inspires and encourages us in our daily lives. It is the central goal for the believer, and is the climax of all our prayers and strivings, and of history itself.

Furthermore, if language means anything at all, then Christ's coming will be literal and physical according to the record. The angels said to the disciples: 'This same Jesus, who was taken up from you into heaven, will so come in like manner as you saw him go into heaven' (Acts 1:11). Nothing could be clearer. And it is important that we stress this physical aspect of Christ's return, for there are those of a liberal persuasion who maintain that it should be interpreted symbolically. They say that Christ came again with the Holy Spirit at Pentecost, or that he is always coming again whenever a person commits his or her life to him in faith. Or take this as another example of the distortion of scripture. 'They knew he would come back because he told them he would. They believed what he said. Truth always comes back … Men have tried hard and tried persistently to eliminate human freedom from the earth … But again and again freedom has come back … One mistake however these early Christian men made. They thought that he would come back the same way he went … The people we love always come back to us, but seldom do they come in exactly the same way they left us. In the glance of a young daughter's eye, a wife lost early may come back to her husband' (*The Interpreter's Bible,* Abingdon Press, 1954, vol. 9, pp. 31–32).

If it were not so serious, such rationalisation would be laughable. The angel's words were this '*same* Jesus'—not some other entity or vision or figment of the imagination. And again: 'will so come in like manner'—not some mystical experience, but the actual physical presence of the Lord. There is a lot more we can say on this subject, but it will come up again in our exposition.

The waiting room

Before his ascension into heaven Jesus instructed his disciples to 'wait' at Jerusalem for the promise of the Holy Spirit to be fulfilled. And that is what they did. 'Then they returned to Jerusalem from the mount called Olivet, which is near Jerusalem a Sabbath's day journey. And when they had entered, they went up into the upper room where they were staying: Peter, James, John, and Andrew; Philip and Thomas, Bartholomew and Matthew; James the son of Alphaeus and Simon the Zealot; and Judas the son of James. These all continued with one accord in prayer and supplication, with the women and Mary the mother of Jesus, and with his brothers' (Acts 1:12–14).

A Sabbath's day journey was approximately three-quarters of a mile, and it must have been with a certain sense of excitement gripping their hearts that the disciples gathered in that upper room. Various suggestions have been made about that room, some say it was in the house of Mary the mother of John Mark (Acts 12:12), others that it was the room where Jesus ate the supper with his disciples (Luke 22:11–12). The fact is we know nothing about that room except that it must have been very large because the number gathered was about one hundred and twenty (Acts 1:15). I doubt myself if it was in a domestic house, but more likely a room in the temple, because Luke says they 'were continually in the temple praising and blessing God' (Luke 24:53).

The disciples were joined by other followers including the women who had ministered to Jesus (Luke 8:2–3), and Mary his mother, who is mentioned here for the last time. There is no suggestion that Mary was treated any differently from the others. It is also encouraging to note that the brothers of Jesus were present, because during his lifetime they were strongly opposed to his ministry (John 7:5). It shows that salvation is not the result of any special privileges such as belonging to a godly family, not even when it contained Jesus, but it must be the work of the Holy Spirit in a person's heart. It also means that we need not despair of the conversion of anyone.

Much more important than speculation about the room in which they were meeting is what they were doing there. They were waiting. But it was not a boring, tired kind of waiting, like standing in a queue, or waiting for a train. It was a positive expectant waiting upon God in prayer. 'These all continued with one accord in prayer and supplication, with the women and Mary the mother of Jesus, and with his brothers'. We note two features of this prayer meeting. They persevered or 'continued' in their praying, and they were united in spirit and purpose—'with one accord'. But why did they have to wait and persevere in praying when the promise of the Holy Spirit had already been given to them? God might easily have sent the Spirit immediately. The reason, I believe, is because God wants to teach perseverance in our praying as good discipline, and so that we can show him that we are in earnest in what we are asking. After all, Jesus gave us the two parables of the Friend at midnight (Luke 11:5–8), and the Persistent Widow (Luke 18:1–8) to teach us that very lesson.

In this next section, verses 15–26, the names of three men are prominent. Peter the leader, Judas the betrayer, and Matthias the new apostle. Let us take them in turn.

Peter the leader

'And in those days Peter stood up in the midst of the disciples (altogether the number of names was about a hundred and twenty), and said, "Men and brethren, this Scripture had to be fulfilled, which the Holy Spirit spoke before by the mouth of David concerning Judas, who became a guide to those who arrested Jesus; for he was numbered with us and obtained a part in this ministry." (Now this man purchased a field with the wages of iniquity; and falling headlong, he burst open in the middle and all his entrails gushed out. And it became known to all those dwelling in Jerusalem; so that the field is called in their own language, Akel Dama, that is, Field of Blood). "For it is written in the Book of Psalms: 'let his dwelling place be desolate. And let no one live in it;' and, 'Let another take his office'"' (Acts 1:15–20).

Here is Peter emerging as the chief spokesman and leader of the apostles. We shall see later that after Pentecost he becomes an outstanding preacher, exercises a healing ministry, administers discipline in the church, and is used of God as the instrument to open the door to the Gentiles into the church. But these leadership qualities did not come all at once, they were the result of a long process of moulding and shaping, of falling and rising, of pressing forward and slipping backward. And it all began when Jesus called him to be his disciple and changed his name.

'And he (Andrew) brought him to Jesus. Now when Jesus looked at him, he said, "You are Simon the son of Jonah, you shall be called Cephas" (which is translated, A Stone)' (John 1:42). That look of Jesus says everything; it was no ordinary look, but a deep penetrating look into the very recesses of Peter's soul, which revealed to the Saviour both Peter's weaknesses, and his potential as a future leader of God's work. The prophetic change of name implies that. At the moment of his calling Peter was his old self, headstrong and impetuous, but the longer he would be in the company of Christ the stronger his faith would become until eventually it would become the rock-like faith that would enable him to emerge as the leader of God's making.

The story of Peter is a wonderful and thrilling story of the power of God to transform the life of a humble fisherman into that of a mighty leader in the early church. But there is a real sense in which God's grace is doing that all the time. Myriads of lives are being transformed all over the world through the spiritual rebirth brought about by the power of the Holy Spirit. And in many instances it is when a life becomes totally committed to God in Christ that a person's true potential in the exercise of their gifts and abilities begins to be fully realised. God moulds and shapes men and women to make them the kind of people he wants them to be and to fit them for the tasks he wants them to do.

Judas the betrayer

Here we are dealing with a totally different kind of person as Luke makes clear in his reference to the tragic suicide of Judas. But what made Judas stoop to such wickedness as to betray the Saviour of the world? We may feel we have no need to look for reasons because it was all part of the inscrutable purpose of a sovereign God, as Peter says in quoting from the Psalms: 'Let their dwelling place be desolate; let no one live in their tents' (Psalm 69:25), and 'Let another take his office' (Psalm 109:8). But looked at from the human side there is such a thing as personal responsibility and personal freedom in the things we do in this life. And that freedom and responsibility carries with it accountability to God.

In Luke 22 we read: 'Then Satan entered Judas' (verse 3). That is an appallingly chilling phrase, since it tells us that Judas did what he did with his eyes wide open, and it makes nonsense of the suggestion by liberal theologians that 'Judas never meant Jesus to die' (Barclay *Acts of the Apostles* p. 9). Judas had arrived at a point in his life when he calculatingly and deliberately sold his soul to the devil. He willingly allowed himself to become the tool and instrument of Satan's purposes. It is a grave warning about the hardening power of sin. Judas had shared in the ministry of Christ, had seen his miracles and witnessed his love and compassion. But as time passed instead of growing closer to Christ, he grew away from him, and sin exerted its hardening power until Satan possessed him completely.

Neither should we overlook the important fact that Judas took money for what he did. He was the victim of his own greed and covetousness. He thought he was selling Christ, but in fact he was selling his own soul to evil, and for the miserable price of thirty pieces of silver (about £100 today). The story of Judas is the story of a shabby sordid tragedy of a covetous soul. No wonder the Bible warns us against the power of greed such as Paul's word to Timothy: 'for the love of money is a root of all kinds of evil' (1 Timothy 6:10). An inordinate love of money makes a person blind to all decency, self-respect, honesty and the fear of God.

One other thing. The price Judas received was miserable, but the price he paid in remorse and revulsion was so enormous he could not live with it, and he went and hanged himself (Matthew 27:5). There is no contradiction in Luke's gruesome description of the body bursting open since it had decomposed and fallen down, or else some one had cut it down. Judas was remorseful but not repentant. Remorse leads to hopelessness and despair, repentance leads to restoration and life.

Matthias the new Apostle

When it came to choosing a new apostle to take the place of Judas the method used seems very strange to our mind. "'Therefore, of these men who have accompanied us all the time that the Lord Jesus went in and out among us, beginning from the baptism of John to that day when he was taken up from us, one of these must become a witness with us of his resurrection". And they proposed two: Joseph called Barsabas, who was surnamed Justus, and Matthias. And they prayed and said, "You O Lord, who know the hearts of all, show which of these two you have chosen to take part in this ministry and apostleship from which Judas by transgression fell, that he might go to his own place". And they cast their lots, and the lot fell on Matthias. And he was numbered with the eleven apostles' (Acts 1:21–26).

Casting lots does not sit easy in our minds when it comes to seeking God's will in decision-making. But that was an acceptable method in Biblical times. What is important is that they also prayed, so that the lot was only the visible expression of God's answer to their prayer. As to Matthias we have many traditions about him, but we know nothing factual within the context of the New Testament. We know nothing of his background or the contribution he may have made to the ministry of the early church. But we are told in these verses that he possessed the two essential qualifications needed to be an apostle.

First, he had been a follower of the Lord Jesus from the time of John the Baptist (Acts 1:22). That tells us something of his faithfulness—a quality all too rare these days, even in evangelicalism. Second, he was a witness to the physical resurrection of the Lord Jesus, and had experienced its power in his own heart and life. With qualifications like that anything else we may like to know about Matthias is of secondary importance.

And that is true of ourselves. If we have these two qualities—are faithful to Christ and his gospel, and if we know his Spirit living in us—we have all we need.

Birth of the Church

Read Acts chapter 2

With this second chapter in Acts the history of the Christian church begins. The forty days of preparation when the risen Lord taught the disciples about the kingdom of God, the appointing of a new apostle in Matthias, and the period of waiting and praying in the upper room were all now over, and the really big thing Jesus had promised—the baptism with the Holy Spirit—was about to happen.

The day of Pentecost

'When the day of Pentecost had fully come, they were all with one accord in one place' (Acts 2:1). Pentecost, which means fiftieth, was one of three great religious festivals held in ancient Israel, the others were Passover and Tabernacles, and it was held on the fiftieth day after the beginning of Passover. It was also called the feast of weeks because it occurred seven weeks after the beginning of the barley harvest. It is important to understand the significance of Pentecost in the history of Israel and its association with Passover, because it explains why Jerusalem was so crowded with visitors 'from every nation under heaven' (Acts 2:5) on the day the church came into being. Josephus, the Jewish historian, tells us that there could be as many as three million people in Jerusalem during the festivals of Passover and Pentecost.

The descent of the Spirit

'And suddenly there came a sound from heaven, as of a rushing mighty wind, and it filled the whole house where they were sitting. Then there appeared to them divided tongues, as of fire, and one sat upon each of them' (Act 2:2–3). Some people make the mistake of thinking that what happened on the day of Pentecost was the Holy Spirit coming into the world for the first time. But that was not so. As the third person of the Trinity the Holy Spirit is eternal and was actively present at the commencement of creation. We read in Genesis: 'In the beginning God created the heavens and the earth. The earth was without form, and void; and darkness was on the face of the deep. And the Spirit of God was hovering over the face of the waters' (Genesis 1:1–2). God is the source and origin of creation, and the Holy Spirit was the life-giving energiser through whom he activated the material world. In the Old Testament we have the progressive revelation of the person and power of the Holy Spirit which reaches its fullness in the outpouring at Pentecost.

The Hebrew word for Spirit is 'ruach', which is also the word for 'wind' and 'breath', as is the Greek word 'pneuma'. This helps us to understand more clearly the description of the Spirit's descent as 'a sound from heaven as of a rushing mighty wind'. There is no mention of an actual wind, only of the 'sound' of a rushing mighty wind to symbolise the Spirit's activity and power. As a symbol of the Spirit's power the wind is used elsewhere in the Bible. In Ezekiel's vision of the dry bones, God commanded him: 'Prophesy to the breath, prophesy, son of man, and say to the breath, "Thus says the Lord God: come from the four winds, O breath, and breathe on these slain, that they may live"' (Ezekiel 37:9). Similarly when Jesus spoke to Nicodemus of the regenerating power of the Holy Spirit in the soul he used the illustration of the wind. 'The wind blows where it wishes, and you hear the sound of it, but cannot tell where it comes from and where it goes. So is everyone who is born of the Spirit' (John 3:8).

The wind is invisible and mysterious and beyond human control, but we hear it and see the effects of its activity. So it is with the work of the Holy Spirit. He is sovereign in the exercise of his power, is not visible in his operations, but the effects of his working in the human soul can be both felt and seen. Furthermore, he came at Pentecost as a 'mighty' wind, suggesting the irresistible power of a hurricane sweeping everything before it. Some conversion experiences are exactly like that, sudden, violent, instantaneous, turning a person's life upside down in an instant. But the wind can also come in the form of a gentle breeze, and some are brought into the kingdom through the quiet operation of the Holy Spirit in their life over a period of time. What this says to us is that we must be careful in our assessment of another's conversion. For one person it can be a hurricane conversion, for another a gentle breeze conversion. Not all conversion experiences are alike.

The descent of the Spirit was also symbolised by fire. 'Then there appeared to them divided tongues, as of fire, and one sat upon each of them' (Acts 2:3). John the Baptist had already prophesied this: 'One mightier than I is coming, … He will baptise you with the Holy Spirit and fire' (Luke 3:16). This is a very fitting symbol of the Holy Spirit since fire cleanses, illuminates, and imparts warmth and comfort. At Pentecost the disciples were inwardly cleansed by the Spirit's presence, their minds illuminated in the understanding of God's truth as never before—witness Peter's sermon—and their hearts were warmed and comforted with the all-pervading sense of Christ's presence with them.

And that happens whenever a person is regenerated by the Spirit's power. He is inwardly cleansed—justified in God's sight—of the polluting effects of sin in the soul; his mind is illumined or enlightened in his grasp of Biblical truth, and his heart is warmed with a deep love for God and comforted by his presence. It is a rebirth of the whole personality: the mind, the spirit, the emotions and the will.

Other Tongues

In all we have said up to this point we can identify with the disciple's experience at Pentecost. But now we come to an effect of the Holy Spirit's power which was unique to the disciples themselves. 'And they were filled with the Holy Spirit and began to speak with other tongues, as the Spirit gave them utterance' (Acts 2:4). By 'tongues' is meant languages. They were miraculously given, by the Holy Spirit, the ability to speak in foreign languages, which they had not previously learned.

Various attempts have been made by commentators to explain this phenomenon without attributing it to the miraculous. According to some, Luke was not an eyewitness of the event and therefore he was simply passing on a story, which he had heard and which had become embellished in the process. Others, whilst accepting the miraculous element, do not accept that other languages were spoken, but that the disciples were giving expression to the ecstatic utterance described in 1 Corinthians 12:10 as a gift of the Spirit.

But it seems to me to make better sense to accept that they did speak in foreign languages, since it fits in better with what we are told in the following verses 5–13 about the vast number of people in Jerusalem from other nations. 'And there were dwelling in Jerusalem Jews, devout men, from every nation under heaven. And when this sound occurred, the multitude came together, and were confused, because everyone heard them speak in his own language. Then they were all amazed and marvelled, saying to one another, "Look, are not all these who speak Galileans? And how is it that we hear, each in our own language in which we were born?"' (Acts 2:5–8). Luke then follows with a list of all the nations represented, sixteen in all, from three continents, Africa, Asia and Europe. At the close of his earthly ministry the Lord Jesus had commanded the disciples: 'Go therefore and make disciples of all the nations' (Matthew 28:19). What better opportunity could there have been for this command to be obeyed than on the very launch day of the church when people were present from so many different nations. They heard the gospel preached, 'the wonderful works of God' (Acts 2:11), and were able to take it back to their respective countries. This was the Holy Spirit preparing the way in those different parts of the world in readiness for the later missionary work of the church.

Response of the people

Among the crowd that gathered to witness the remarkable events of that day the response was twofold. There were those who were clearly affected and knew something unique and supernatural was happening which they simply could not explain. Luke says they were 'confused', 'amazed', 'marvelled' and were 'perplexed'. But some were dismissive and contemptuous and accused the disciples of being drunk. 'Others mocking said, "They are full of new wine"' (Acts 2:13).

We can see from this that, right from the beginning of the church's history, the preaching of the gospel can expect to receive a varied response. For that reason evangelism is never easy, and if we intend engaging in it we must expect successes and failures among those we are seeking to reach for Christ. There will be some, like those on the day of Pentecost, who will be intrigued and perplexed by the message, ready to ask questions, and in general show an openness to the gospel which might lead to full acceptance. But there will also be others, like those who accused the apostles of being drunk, who will close their minds to the message and treat it with derision and contempt.

The important thing is, we must not allow these different reactions by people to lower our spirits, and put us off declaring 'the wonderful works of God' in the gospel. The responsibility for how people respond to the word of God is not ours. By all means let us seek, as Paul says, 'to persuade men' (2 Corinthians 5:11), but it is only the convicting power of the Holy Spirit that can ultimately bring a person to the point of accepting Christ as saviour. Our task is to continue faithfully to preach the word of God, and leave the Spirit to add the anointing that makes it effective. That is what we see happening next on the day of Pentecost.

Peter's preaching

In the second part of this chapter from verse 14 to 47 we have the first sermon of the church preached by Peter, and the reaction of the people. Before beginning his message Peter makes it perfectly clear that the disciples were not drunk, since it was only nine o'clock in the morning. 'But Peter, standing up with the eleven, raised his voice and said to them, "Men of Judea and all who dwell in Jerusalem, let this be known to you, and heed my words. For these are not drunk, as you suppose, since it is only the third hour of the day. But this is what was spoken by the prophet Joel: 'And it shall come to pass in the last days, says God, that I will pour out of my Spirit on all flesh; your sons and your daughters shall prophesy, your young men shall see visions, your old men shall dream dreams. And on my menservants and on my maidservants I will pour out my Spirit in those days; and they shall prophesy'"' (Acts 2:14–18). The sermon itself is extremely important because it contains some of the basic features of the preaching of the early church and which should characterise preaching today.

The use of scripture

The first thing to notice is Peter's dependence upon the Old Testament scriptures. He begins with the quotation from Joel 2:28–32, and follows that with a passage from Psalm 16:8–11, and then gives a further quotation from Psalm 110:1. In other words he does not rely on his own inventiveness as to what he is going to say to the people. He was aware that what he and his fellow-disciples were experiencing was the fulfilment of what God had already revealed and promised in his word, his message was already given, what he had to do was to proclaim it.

And there is a very real sense in which that must be true of preaching today. We do not have to invent our message, nor are we in our pulpits to give our own opinions and ideas on how to change the world. For the evangelical preacher the basics of his message are already present in the Bible, and he will be careful to allow that message to come through in his own exposition of it. He will not be tempted to shape his sermon to fit in with modern thinking and the changes taking place in society, for he knows that the Word of God does not change, and that is what gives authority to what he has to say.

In the quotation from Joel's prophecy there are several things to notice. The expression 'last days' refers to the whole Christian dispensation because it is the age of Messiah and the closing period of history. It does not refer only to the final days immediately before the coming of Christ, else Peter would not have been able to apply it to what was happening at Pentecost. Underlying the promise concerning sons and daughters, young men and old men, visions and dreams, is the truth that in the gospel age the blessing and gifts of the Spirit will be open to everyone, 'all flesh', irrespective of age or sex.

Then comes the second part of the prophecy. 'I will show wonders in heaven above and signs in the earth beneath; blood and fire and vapour of smoke. The sun will be turned into darkness, and the moon into blood, before the coming of the great and awesome day of the Lord. And it shall come to pass that whoever calls on the name of the Lord shall be saved' (Acts 2:19–21). This is more difficult to interpret mainly because of the expression: 'before the coming of the great and awesome day of the Lord'. What does it mean? It cannot refer only to the day of Pentecost, since these dramatic events did not happen. It must mean the same as the 'last days' of verse 17; that is the whole of the gospel age, which would include the wonders of Pentecost itself and the miracles and signs of the New Testament.

But its main reference, I believe, is to the judgement that will accompany the Second Coming of Christ. Mention of blood, fire and vapour of smoke, the sun turning to darkness and the moon to blood, is an apocalyptic picture of the wrath of God in the end time. In Luke, Christ himself gives a similar picture of his return. 'And there will be signs in the sun, in the moon, and in the stars; and on the earth distress of nations, with perplexity, the sea and the waves roaring; men's hearts failing them from fear and the expectation of those things which are coming on the earth, for the powers of the heavens will be shaken' (Luke 21:25–26). The same picture also occurs in 2 Peter. 'But the day of the Lord will come as a thief in the night, in which the heavens will pass away with a great noise, and the elements will melt with fervent heat, both the earth and the works that are in it will be burned up' (2 Peter 3:10).

This presents a fearful prospect for the non-Christian. But in his use of this passage, Peter makes it perfectly clear that, during the gospel age, men and women can avoid that judgement by turning to God for salvation. 'And it shall come to pass that whoever calls on the name of the Lord shall be saved' (Acts 2:21). He then develops this in the next two features of his sermon, the death and resurrection of Christ.

The death of Christ

'Men of Israel, hear these words: Jesus of Nazareth, a man attested by God to you by miracles, wonders, and signs which God did through him in your midst, as you yourselves know—Him, being delivered by the determined purpose and foreknowledge of God, you have taken by lawless hands, have crucified and put to death' (Acts 2:22–23).

The pre-eminent note in the preaching of the early church was 'Christ crucified'. Paul makes that abundantly clear: 'For I determined not to know anything among you except Jesus Christ and him crucified' (1 Corinthians 2:2). Without the atoning sacrifice of Christ for our sins there could be no salvation. The church cannot dispense salvation, nor can it be earned through our good works. It is entirely the gift of God to those who accept that on the Cross, Christ was bearing God's judgement upon our sin that we might be saved.

But the early preachers were also careful to point out that the death of Christ on the Cross was not simply the outcome of powerful religious and political forces, or the martyrdom of a good and holy man, but was part of God's eternal plan. In Revelation Christ is spoken of as 'the lamb slain from the foundation of the world' (Revelation 13:8). Peter in his sermon makes the same point. 'Him, being delivered by the determined purpose and foreknowledge of God, you have taken by lawless hands, have crucified and put to death'. The Cross demonstrates—more fully than anything else—God's love for mankind. 'In this is love, not that we loved God, but that he loved us and sent his Son to be the propitiation for our sins' (1 John 4:10).

The resurrection of Christ

Important though the Cross was in the preaching of the early church, that was not the whole message. Had the story of Christianity ended with the crucifixion of Jesus then the victory would have been with men and the forces of evil in the world. But the last word is never with men and the powers of darkness. The last word is always with God as the resurrection of Christ testifies. Peter stresses this point—'... whom God raised up, having loosed the pains of death, because it was not possible that he should be held by it' (Acts 2:24). He then quotes Psalm 16 to show that David had prophesied Christ's rising from the dead. 'I foresaw the Lord always before my face, for he is at my right hand, that I may not be shaken. Therefore my heart rejoiced, and my tongue was glad; moreover my flesh also will rest in hope. For you will not leave my soul in Hades, nor will you allow your Holy One to see corruption. You have made known to me the ways of life; you will make me full of joy in your presence' (verses 25–28).

Commenting on this prophecy Peter points out that David died and was buried, and that his tomb was honoured by the people of that time. Therefore he must have been speaking of Christ's resurrection, and not his own (Acts 2:29–35). The sermon then ends with the challenging statement: 'Therefore let all the house of Israel know assuredly that God has made this Jesus, whom you crucified, both Lord and Christ' (Acts 2:36).

It is clear from all this that the doctrine of the resurrection was the cornerstone in the ministry of the early church. Indeed the Apostle Paul goes so far as to say that without it the church has nothing worth saying, and the Christian faith is emptied of content: 'And if Christ is not risen, then our preaching is empty and your faith is also empty' (1 Corinthians 15:14). There is a tendency in some modern day preaching to play down the truth of the resurrection, and the other miracles, in order to make the

Christian message more acceptable to modern day thinking. But if we minimise this doctrine in our preaching then we do not have a gospel or Good News to preach, but only a humanistic philosophy. The gospel is a gospel (Good News) precisely because it is the supernatural power of God breaking through into the natural order of life.

Furthermore, as Paul rightly says, if there is no resurrection then our Christian faith is emptied of its real meaning and content. We might just as well believe in the 'power of positive thinking', or 'transcendentalism', or any one of the many 'meditation' techniques to help us face life with confidence. But what a hopeless message that is to preach to a dying world. As Paul says further: 'If in this life only we have hope in Christ, we are of all men the most pitiable' (1 Corinthians 15:19). We know that death is the great unavoidable reality, and therefore the best way to approach it is to destroy the fear of it before it comes to us. And that is what Christ did when he rose from the dead. He robbed death of its sting and power so that we might enjoy the gift of eternal life. That is a message worth preaching.

The sermon's impact

When Peter finished preaching there was a strong reaction from the people. 'Now when they heard this, they were cut to the heart, and said to Peter and the rest of the apostles, "Men and brethren, what shall we do?"' (Acts 2:37). Clearly the effect upon the hearers was electric. Commenting on Peter's sermon Spurgeon says: 'Peter's discourse was not distinguished by any special rhetorical display...He gave his hearers a simple, well-reasoned scriptural discourse, sustained by the facts of experience, and every passage of it pointed to the Lord Jesus...Every word of it was directed to the conscience and the affections. It was plain, practical, personal and persuasive; and in this it was a model of what a sermon ought to be as to its aim and style' (*The Treasury of the New Testament*).

Bearing in mind all that Spurgeon says, we would also add that effective preaching is Spirit endowed preaching. The truly significant feature in the people's response is in the words: 'Now when they heard this they were cut to the heart'. That is, they were stirred in their conscience and convicted of their sin before God. No preacher, not even an apostle, can bring about a response like that, only the Holy Spirit. Peter was faithful, as we have seen, in declaring the truths of the gospel, but it was the Holy Spirit who empowered those truths so that they cut deeply into the hearts and minds of the people. In the letter to the Hebrews we have a marvellous description of that kind of Spirit-filled preaching which compares it with a sword. 'For the word of God is living and powerful, and sharper than any two-edged sword, piercing even to the division of soul and spirit, and of joints and marrow, and is a discerner of the thoughts and intents of the heart' (Hebrews 4:12). As preachers we must pray most earnestly as we enter our pulpits, that the Holy Spirit will empower our message in the same way.

There are two other things we must notice in the people's response. First, they asked the apostles: 'Men and brethren, what shall we do?' That was a vitally important question, indeed it is the most important question anyone can ask in the whole of his or her life. What must we do to get right with God? How can we be saved from the judgement of God because it is our sins that brought God's Son to the Cross? Tell us what to do in order to be forgiven. It was the same question the Philippian jailer asked Paul and Silas: 'Sirs, what must I do to be saved?' (Acts 16:30). I really do wonder what would happen if someone in our congregation should shout out the same question. Would we be embarrassed, or confused, or even unable to give a clear answer as to how that person might get right with God, and receive the gift of salvation? It is worth thinking about.

Second, Peter had no difficulty whatever in giving a clear and precise answer. 'Repent, and let every one of you be baptised in the name of Jesus Christ for the remission of sins; and you shall receive the gift of the Holy Spirit. For the promise is to you and to your children, and to all who are afar off, as many as the Lord your God will call' (Acts 2:38–39). There can be no getting right with God, no salvation without repentance. But what exactly is repentance? It is the recognition that one is a sinner before God, and involves a deep sense of contrition ('cut to the heart') that one had grieved God's Spirit. The Bible teaches that there can be a true and false repentance. Paul puts it like this: 'For godly sorrow produces repentance leading to salvation, not to be regretted; but the sorrow of the world produces death' (2 Corinthians 7:10). False repentance is sorrow over the consequences of sin, but not sorrow over sin itself. Genuine repentance, on the other hand, leads to an inward change of mind toward God, leading to a change of life and behaviour.

Peter urged the people to truly repent, and to follow it through with the outward act of baptism as a sign that their repentance was genuine. Furthermore, he makes it clear that the promise of God's salvation was not only for the Jewish people, but also for 'all who are afar off, as many as the Lord our God will call'. The lesson we must take from this is to preach God's offer of salvation in Christ to everyone.

Before going any further, let us remind ourselves again of the main features in apostolic preaching. (a) The use of Holy Scripture, (b) the substitutionary death of Christ, (c) the resurrection of Christ, (d) dependence on the convicting work of the Holy Spirit, (e) the call to repentance, and (f) outward testimony in baptism.

The Church grows

It is clear from what we are told in these next verses that Peter's sermon was far longer than what we have recorded in this chapter. 'And with many other words he testified and exhorted them, saying, "Be saved from this perverse generation"' (Acts 2:40). But much more significant than the length of the sermon is the number of souls converted as a result of Peter's preaching. 'Then those who gladly received his word were baptised; and that day about three thousand souls were added to them' (Acts 2:41).

Here we have one of these outstanding features of the book of Acts; the phenomenal growth of the church in those first weeks or months after Pentecost. Later, we read of a further five thousand being added to the church, and that refers to men only, apart from women and younger people. It might well have been twice that number. 'However, many of those who heard the word believed; and the number of the men came to be about five thousand' (Acts 4:4). In chapter 6 we are told that it was this rapid growth of the church that necessitated the election of the first officers to sort out certain problems which had arisen. 'Now in those days, when the number of the disciples was multiplying, there arose a complaint against the Hebrews by the Hellentists...' (Acts 6:1–6). With this organisational development the numbers increased even further: 'Then the word of God spread, and the number of the disciples multiplied greatly in Jerusalem, and a great many of the priests were obedient to the faith' (Acts 6:7). As we move through Acts, further progress reports on the church's growth are given in Acts 9:31; 12:24; 16:5; 19:20; and 28:31.

But how do we account for this extraordinary growth in such a short time, and is this something we should be experiencing in the church today? Throughout history there have been periods when the church had experienced revival, and hundreds—even thousands—have been converted and added to the church. But there has never been a revival to equal what happened at Pentecost. That was something quite unique, and can only be accounted for by the fact that it was the launch pad of the church, and God was making a special impact upon the Jewish and pagan world.

But having said that, and whilst recognising that there have been wonderful times of revival in the past, why is it that we are not witnessing any substantial growth in the churches in our country today? And by growth we do not mean those churches that have experienced growth mainly through a sideways movement, as members cross over from one evangelical church to another. Real growth is when outsiders are converted, and brought into the church fellowship. We are not seeing much of that today. Why?

I am not sure what the answer is. I feel certain it cannot be that the gospel is not being faithfully proclaimed. I personally know of many churches where the pastors are preaching with great passion and earnestness, and still they are not getting much success in the way of conversions. One significant fact is that in other parts of the world, Africa, Asia and Eastern Europe, the churches are being wonderfully blessed and number their conversions in hundreds. Can it be that we are partially under God's judgement, and that he has withdrawn his hand of blessing because, as a nation, we have become secularised, and the church in general has lost her spiritual vision? In view of the growing wickedness in our nation I am reminded of Paul's words in his letter to the Romans: 'For the wrath of God is revealed from heaven against all ungodliness and unrighteousness of men, who suppress the truth in unrighteousness' (Romans 1:18). Ungodliness always precedes wickedness. But the apostle goes further and three times in the same chapter repeats the dreadful phrase: 'God gave them over' (Romans 1: 24,26,28).

Chapter 2

I do not believe God has given us over to our own devices totally. That is why I used the expression 'partial judgement' earlier; for there are people being converted, albeit on a small scale, and we must therefore hold on to the promise of the Lord Jesus: 'I will build my church, and the gates of Hades shall not prevail against it' (Matthew 16:18). Let us be even more earnest in praying that God, in great mercy, will again favour our nation with a great outpouring of the Holy Spirit in revival power.

What kind of church?

We have seen how the church started, and how it grew in the weeks and months immediately following. But what kind of church was it? What were its main features? Luke gives us quite a good description of its character.

'And they continued steadfastly in the apostles' doctrine and fellowship, in the breaking of bread, and in prayers. Then fear came upon every soul, and many wonders and signs were done through the apostles. Now all who believed were together, and had all things in common, and sold their possessions and goods, and divided them among all, as anyone had need. So continuing daily with one accord in the temple, and breaking bread from house to house, they ate their food with gladness and simplicity of heart, praising God and having favour with all the people. And the Lord added to the church daily those who were being saved' (Acts 2: 42–47).

It was a church in which the people were eager to learn the great truths of the gospel. 'And they continued steadfastly in the apostles' doctrine'. They were not content only to have been saved from their sins and to be right with God, they wanted to grow in the understanding of their new faith. That is always a healthy sign in any church, when its members are eager to listen to the word of God preached, and to be taught the great doctrines of scripture. It is not enough that a person should be a Christian, he needs to know why he is. As Peter says: '...always be ready to give a defence to everyone who asks you a reason for the hope that is in you, with meekness and fear' (1 Peter 3:15).

Second, it was a church in which the people enjoyed real fellowship in the Lord Jesus Christ. Fellowship (koinonia) means 'unity' or 'togetherness', and is something peculiar to believers. It is unlike friendship or companionship because it arises out of the sense of 'oneness' believers have in acknowledging Christ as saviour, having the same indwelling Holy Spirit, and having the same hope of heaven. It reaches its highest point in the local church in the corporate act of worship, and especially in the 'breaking of bread' or the Lord's Supper. For those early Christians their togetherness manifested itself in their sharing and caring. They 'had all things in common, and sold their possessions and goods, and divided them among all, as anyone had need'.

That kind of communal living is not possible in church life today, but within the church fellowship there should still be that feeling of responsibility for each other's welfare. Furthermore, the togetherness they enjoyed went beyond the normal worship services in the temple and spilled over into their homes. 'So continuing daily with one accord in the temple, and breaking bread from house to house, they ate their food with gladness and simplicity of heart'. This would have been the agape or 'love feast', which was associated with the Lord's Supper or 'breaking of bread' in verse 42, but quite distinct from it. At this early stage in the church's history there were no special buildings set-aside for worship, therefore believers would meet in each other's homes for fellowship and praise. If we have a mind to, there are as many ways as imagination can devise when it comes to using our homes for the work of the gospel. We can offer hospitality to visiting preachers, or invite Christian friends in for fellowship, Bible study and prayer, or make them centres of evangelism in relation to our neighbours.

Third, it was a church in which prayer had a high priority: 'the breaking of bread, and in prayers' (Acts 2:42). As we proceed through Acts we shall see that prayer in the church becomes increasingly evident. In chapter 4:23–31 we have a remarkable prayer of praise when Peter and John are released from prison; and the reason the first church officers were elected was in order that the apostles should give themselves 'continually to prayer and the ministry of the word' (Acts 6:4). More remarkable still is Stephen's prayer for the very people who were stoning him to death (Acts 7:59–60). And in chapter nine Ananias prays for Saul of Tarsus, who had come to Damascus for the very purpose of persecuting people like himself (Acts 9:17). And so it goes on and on. No church can spiritually prosper without fervent believing prayer by its members.

The final impression we are left with is of a church that knew the awesome presence of God—'fear came upon every soul'; was active in displaying God's power—'many wonders and signs were done through the apostles' (Acts 2:43); exhibited to all a spirit of love and joy—'praising God and having favour with all the people'; and was evangelistic in outlook— 'and the Lord added to the church daily those who were being saved' (Acts 2:47).

The Church in action

Read Acts chapter 3:1–4:31

In chapter one we saw the preparation God made for the formation of the church. In chapter two we have the birth of the church on the day of Pentecost. In this third chapter we see the church in action through the activity of Peter and John. Back in chapter 2:43 we were told that 'many wonders and signs were done through the apostles'. In this chapter Luke gives a detailed account of one of those miracles to show the impact the church was having upon society. But first it tells us something about the need for a disciplined devotional life.

Disciplined devotion

'Now Peter and John went up together to the temple at the hour of prayer, the ninth hour' (Acts 3:1). In the Jewish day there were three special times for prayer. The third hour, nine o'clock in the morning; the sixth hour, twelve o'clock; and the ninth hour, three o'clock in the afternoon. The early Christians did not suddenly abandon the discipline of the regular times of devotion they were accustomed to, now that they had come into the new faith. Hence we find Peter and John attending the afternoon prayer session at the temple. We can learn from that.

Prayer is a tremendous privilege and a wonderful gift that God has given to us. But it is also part of a devotional discipline we have to impose on ourselves, if we want it to enhance and strengthen our spiritual life. In the book of Daniel we read of a decree issued by Darius the king forbidding anyone to pray to their god for a period of thirty days. We are then told: 'Now when Daniel knew that the writing was signed, he went home. And in his upper room, with his windows open toward Jerusalem, he knelt down on his knees three times that day, and prayed and gave thanks before his God, as was his custom since early days' (Daniel 6:10). Notice, 'as was his custom since early days'. That tells us that Daniel had a regular, disciplined prayer life, and it was that as much as anything else that enabled him to retain his faith in God during the long years of exile in pagan Babylon.

Prayer, Bible reading and spiritual devotion are not things we should engage in only when we feel like it. They are too important for that. Our devotional time needs to be regular, structured, and disciplined, or else we shall soon find our Christian life becoming dried up and uninspiring.

The church and the world

'And a certain man lame from his mother's womb was carried, whom they laid daily at the gate of the temple which is called Beautiful, to ask alms from those who entered the temple; who, seeing Peter and John about to go into the temple, asked for alms' (Acts 3:2–3). From an expositional point of view what we have here is a picture of the church confronting the world. Peter and John are leading representatives of the new faith in the young church, which has come into being through the power of the Holy Spirit. The beggar, on the other hand, represents the world of humanity in all its brokeness. He may have sat at the gate 'Beautiful', but there was little beauty in his life, which—like the world and society of which he was a part—was crippled and wretched. For make no mistake about it, the world of humanity *is* in many ways in a crippled and broken condition, resulting from the tyranny of sin and evil. It is a fallen world, crippled by hate, paralysed by fear, broken in its disunity. But in what relation does the church stand to that kind of world? For in spite of its godlessness and secularisation our society still expects the church to be in the vanguard when it comes to works of compassion and mercy, just as the beggar expected help from Peter and John in his distress. 'And fixing his eyes on him, with John, Peter said, "Look at us". So he gave them his attention, expecting to receive something from them' (Acts 3:4–5). He expected a few coins to provide material help, and that is society's expectation of the church. It thinks the church's function is to be engaged in social activism, to show compassion for the hungry and homeless, the under-privileged of the third world, to be involved in various humanitarian causes such as fighting drug-addiction and alcoholism, and always to be there in times of natural disaster and world catastrophes.

Now there is nothing wrong with these appeals to the church. But it raises the important question: is it the church's main function to be involved in social activism of this kind, and should we as believers be content only to fulfil these expectations of society? The New Testament is clear that the application of the gospel to social problems and people's practical needs is an outward evidence of the love of Christ. John puts it like this: 'But whoever has this world's goods, and sees his brother in need, and shuts up his heart from him, how does the love of God abide in him?' (1 John 3:17). But we must also keep two other things in mind. First, there are other organisations and government agencies that provide this kind of practical help, and often with greater material resources. Secondly, the church alone, through the gospel, has so much more to give than simply material help.

'Then Peter said, "Silver and gold I do not have, but what I do have I give you: in the name of Jesus Christ of Nazareth, rise up and walk". And he took him by the right hand and lifted him up, and immediately his feet and ankle bones received strength. So he, leaping up, stood and walked and entered the temple with them—walking, leaping, and praising God' (Acts 3:6–8). The beggar received far more than he expected—new life through the power of God. He was taken right out of his broken crippled world, that world of limitation in which he had lived so long, and was able to fulfil his true potential as a human being. A few coins from Peter and John would only have tinkered with his condition; instead, through the power of the risen Lord Jesus they were able to deal with his real need.

It is a wonderful picture of what the church can do for broken humanity when it is true to its calling to preach Christ crucified and to make that its main function. What else but the power of God in the gospel can meet the perennial needs of mankind—the need for forgiveness, for peace with God, and the inward assurance that life is meaningful and leads to the joy of heaven? The evidence of the inward healing in a person's life and personality through the power of the gospel will be as plain as the physical healing was in the man at the gate of the temple. 'And all the people saw him walking and praising God. Then they knew that it was he who sat begging alms at the Beautiful Gate of the temple; and they were filled with wonder and amazement at what had happened to him' (Acts 3:9–10).

To God be the glory

The miracle that had just been witnessed created a sensation among the people, and a crowd quickly gathered. 'Now the lame man who was healed held on to Peter and John, all the people ran together to them in the porch which is called Solomon's, greatly amazed' (Acts 3:11). With a ready-made congregation in front of him Peter takes the opportunity to preach the gospel.

But first, because he could see that the people were ready to give to himself and John the adulation and praise that rightly belongs to God alone, Peter strongly disclaims any personal credit for the miracle. 'So when Peter saw it, he responded to the people: "Men of Israel, why do you marvel at this? Or why look so intently upon us, as though by our own power or godliness we had made this man walk? The God of Abraham, Isaac, and Jacob, the God of our fathers, glorified his servant Jesus, whom you delivered up and denied in the presence of Pilate, when he was determined to let him go. But you denied the Holy One and the Just, and asked for a murderer to be granted to you, and killed the Prince of life, whom God raised from the dead, of which we are witnesses. And his name, through faith in his name, has made this man strong, whom you see and know. Yes, the faith which comes through him has given him this perfect soundness in the presence of you all"' (Acts 3:12–16). 'Give God the glory, not us', that is what Peter is saying.

In a spiritually impoverished age like ours when people have so little to believe in, they are only too ready to focus their praise and adulation on some public figure or other, be it a member of the royal family, a talented footballer, a pop star or a film or television personality. It is both sad and incredulous when this kind of thing happens, because these human 'icons' are sometimes tragic figures in themselves, and it also portrays the emptiness of people's lives. But there is always the danger that it can happen at the spiritual level as well.

In John's gospel we read of certain leaders among the people who 'loved the praise of men more than the praise of God' (John 12:43). That can sometimes be a temptation for the Christian preacher. He may, unintentionally, by his eloquence and vitality draw greater praise to himself than to the Saviour he is proclaiming. In his journal, George Whitfield reports the adulation he received in London when he first began preaching as a young man of twenty-two. 'The tide of popularity began to run very high. In a short time I could no longer walk on foot as usual, but was constrained to go in a coach from place to place, to avoid the hosannas of the multitude. They grew quite extravagant in their applause, and had it not been for my compassionate High Priest, popularity would have destroyed me. I used to plead with him to take me by the hand and lead me unhurt through this fiery furnace. He heard my request and gave me to see the vanity of all commendations but his own' (quoted by Arnold Dallimore *George Whitfield*, Banner of Truth, vol 1, p. 133).

It is a solemn thing to take to oneself the glory and praise that rightly belongs to God. For God has said: 'I am the Lord, that is my name; and my glory will I not give to another' (Isaiah 42:8). Anything we may be enabled to achieve in the Christian life therefore, whether through preaching, personal witness or service, let us be careful to give him the glory and praise.

'Not to us, O Lord, not to us,
but to your name give glory'
(Psalm 115:1).

Peter's sermon

In its substance and content Peter's message in Solomon's porch is strongly similar to the sermon given in chapter 2. The same main notes of the gospel are sounded. He begins with Christ's death on the Cross, as he had done earlier: 'The God of Abraham, Isaac, and Jacob, the God of our fathers, glorified his servant Jesus, whom you delivered up and denied in the presence of Pilate, when he was determined to let him go, but you denied the Holy One and the Just, and asked for a murderer to be granted to you, and killed the Prince of life...' (Acts 3:13–15). He charges them directly with the crime of the crucifixion, thus showing the depths to which sin will go, and the responsibility we all share for the death of the Son of God.

We said earlier that the resurrection of Christ was the cornerstone in the preaching of the early church, and here Peter emphasises it once again: '...whom God raised from the dead, of which we are witnesses' (Acts 3:15). Notice how Peter makes the point that the physical resurrection of Jesus was central to his own personal experience and that of his fellow-apostles.

They were eyewitnesses of Christ's resurrection, but we can claim that it is just as central to our own personal experience. In our witness to people we must make it clear that a Christian is a person who has died to the old life they once lived, outside of God, and they have been raised to a new life through the Spirit of Christ within them. As Paul puts it: 'I have been crucified with Christ; it is no longer I who live, but Christ lives in me; and the life which I now live in the flesh I live by faith in the Son of God, who loved me and gave himself for me' (Galatians 2:20).

Just as he had quoted from the prophet Joel in his first sermon, so Peter again shows that the life and death of Christ had all been foretold in times past by the prophets. 'Yet now, brethren, I know that you did it in ignorance, as did also your rulers. But those things which God foretold by the mouth of all his prophets, that the Christ would suffer, he has thus fulfilled' (Acts 3:17–18). Christ's death on the Cross was no accident, nor was it an afterthought in the mind of God because some other way of bringing about man's salvation had failed. No, it was all in the eternal plan and purpose. Peter develops this theme from verse 20 down to the end of the chapter, thus showing the importance of the prophetic element in our preaching.

Finally, comes the call to repentance. 'Repent therefore and be converted, that your sins may be blotted out, so that times of refreshing may come from the presence of the Lord' (Acts 3:19). When we considered Peter's earlier sermon we looked at the meaning of repentance. But here he speaks of its effect upon a person's past, their sins will be 'blotted out', and also its effect upon their future, 'that times of refreshing may come from the presence of the Lord'. This is a wonderful phrase, but what does it mean? It carries a threefold meaning. First, when a person is converted to Christ, it brings refreshment to his soul and spirit as he enters into a new life of joy and peace. Second, we are now living in the gospel age, which is a refreshing time when God's grace is still available. Third, it looks forward to the future, and the return of the Lord Jesus Christ. For Peter adds: 'and that he may send Jesus Christ, who was preached to you before, whom heaven must receive until the times of restoration of all things, which God has spoken by the mouth of all his prophets since the world began' (Acts 3:20–21). Christ's coming will mean the renewing and refreshing of all things in the new heaven and the new earth.

Opposition to the Church

As we move into chapter 4, it becomes perfectly evident from the opening verses that this is a continuation of the account of the healing of the lame man at the gate of the temple and that there should be no break at this point. 'Now as they spoke to the people, the priests, the captain of the temple, and the Sadducees came upon them, being greatly disturbed that they taught the people and preached in Jesus the resurrection from the dead. And they laid hands on them, and put them in custody until the next day, for it was already evening' (Acts 4:1–3).

It was to be expected that sooner or later the infant church would come into conflict with the Jewish leaders because its message was a direct challenge to their authority and power. Three groups of leaders are mentioned here. The priests were those who officiated at the temple services; the captain was in charge of the temple guard, and responsible for keeping order within the temple precincts where Peter and John were preaching; and the Sadducees were a wealthy priestly sect who exercised great power and influence, including the High Priesthood, and they did not believe in the resurrection or in a personal Messiah. We can understand therefore why Luke says they were 'greatly disturbed', since these were the very truths Peter and John were proclaiming, and which led to their arrest.

We have called this section in our exposition 'The Church in action', and we can see from this passage that when God's people are active in promoting the gospel and doing God's work, that Satan will be equally active in seeking to suppress it. And in doing so he will use every means at his disposal, even those who claim to be worshippers of God such as priests, the temple guard and the Sadducees. But on this occasion Satan failed to achieve his ends, for we read: 'However, many of those who heard the word believed; and the number of the men came to be about five thousand' (Acts 4:4).

This was a time when the church was in its infancy, and the Holy Spirit was especially active in securing its growth so that the forces of evil in the world could do nothing to prevent it. As we study the history of the church through the ages we see this happening again and again. The powers of darkness have attempted time and time again to crush the church and eradicate the gospel message altogether, but in spite of bitter persecution, imprisonment and death, it has not merely survived but has grown in power and influence throughout the world. One reason for that is perfectly clear. The Lord Jesus, even before the church came into being at Pentecost, gave a distinct prophecy concerning its progress. '...I will build my church, and the gates of Hades shall not prevail against it' (Matthew 16:18). As we continue through Acts we shall see how that prophecy was increasingly fulfilled, and it ought to be a great encouragement to us today when the church finds itself pressurised on all sides by the forces of secularisation.

The Church on trial

On the day following their arrest, Peter and John were taken before the Sanhedrin, the supreme Jewish court. 'And it came to pass, on the next day, that their rulers, elders, and scribes, as well as Annas the high priest, Caiaphas, John, and Alexander, and as many as were of the family of the high priest, were gathered at Jerusalem. And when they had set them in the midst, they asked, "By what power or by what name have you done this?"' (Acts 4:5–7).

This was a significant question since Peter had already made it clear (Acts 3:16) that the miracle of healing had been accomplished through the power of the name of the Lord Jesus. But the Sadducees were reluctant to accept that, and were implying that it must have been by some other occult power that the miracle was performed. They had said the same thing earlier when Jesus had healed a man by casting out an evil spirit. 'Now when the Pharisees heard it they said, "This fellow does not cast out demons except by Beelzebub, the ruler of the demons"' (Matthew 12:24). In this way the opposition were hoping to discredit both Jesus and the apostles.

But what they were doing was even more serious than that. In the earlier instance Jesus went on to say that their refusal to accept that he had cast out the evil spirit by the power of God, but had done so by the power of Satan, was a sin against the Holy Spirit and beyond forgiveness (Matthew 12:31–32). They were now doing the same thing by refusing to accept that it was by the power of God in Christ that the lame man had been healed. The sin against the Holy Spirit is the deliberate, wilful rejection of Christ's power and pardon in the light of clear knowledge. The leaders were guilty of that. They knew a miracle had been performed by the power of God in

Christ (Acts 4:16), but deliberately closed their minds to it. In referring to the unpardonable sin Hendricksen puts it like this, 'The blasphemy against the Spirit is the result of gradual progress in sin. Grieving the Spirit (Ephesians 4:30), if unrepented of, leads to resisting the Spirit (Acts 7:51), which if persisted in, develops into quenching the Spirit (1 Thessalonians 5:19) (*Gospel of Matthew*, Banner of Truth, p. 529).

Peter's defence

In replying to the question asked by the court, Peter shows great courage and warns the leaders of the enormity of their sin in rejecting Christ. 'Then Peter, filled with the Holy Spirit, said to them, "Rulers of the people and elders of Israel: if we this day are judged for a good deed done to a helpless man, by what means he has been made well, let it be known to you all, and to all the people of Israel, that by the name of Jesus Christ of Nazareth, whom you crucified, whom God raised from the dead, by him this man stands here before you whole. This is the 'stone which was rejected by you builders, which has become the chief cornerstone'. Nor is there salvation in any other, for there is no other name under heaven given among men by which we must be saved"' (Acts 4:8–12).

The true preaching of the gospel will always seek to combine these two elements of warning of judgement in rejecting Christ, and the offer of salvation through Christ alone. Sin is a radical alienation from God, and brings about the fearful consequence of condemnation and eternal punishment. We must not be hesitant and fearful in warning people of that fact, whilst at the same time pointing out that the only way to avoid that consequence is by accepting Christ as the only saviour. In making the statement that 'there is no other name under heaven given among men by which we must be saved' Peter is saying that Christianity is an exclusive religion. But that is anathema in a day like ours when we are told that the true spirit of Christianity must be love and tolerance towards other faiths. But Peter is only repeating what Christ himself had declared when he said: 'I am the way, the truth, and the life. No one comes to the Father except through me' (John 14:6). That is a totally exclusive statement that closes off every other way of salvation except through Christ. Anyone wishing to study in greater depth the exclusive saviourhood of Christ, based on Peter's statement in verse 4, should read Hywel R Jones, *Only One Way*, Day One Publications, 1996.

The court's response

The members of the Sanhedrin were cultured, educated men, but when they were faced with the apostles they found themselves completely out of their depth, and they were totally bewildered. 'Now when they saw the boldness of Peter and John, and perceived that they were uneducated and untrained men, they marvelled. And they realised that they had been with Jesus. And seeing the man who had been healed standing with them, they could say nothing against it' (Acts 4:13–14).

They were forced, in spite of themselves, to admit that the boldness of Peter and John, and the authority and positiveness with which they spoke, was something out of the ordinary, and they could not understand it, for they were men not professionally trained. But they realised 'that they had been with Jesus', and they knew instinctively that the apostles' boldness arose out of their conviction that he was the Messiah. Furthermore, the presence of the man who had been healed was proof of the truth they were preaching. It was all so bewildering for the members of the Sanhedrin, and they were at a loss what to do next.

There are two main lessons we can learn from this passage. First, our preaching of the gospel, if it is to have impact, must be with Holy Spirit boldness. We must speak with conviction, so that people know that we believe the truth we are preaching. Second, people must, by our manner and sincerity as much as by what we say, see in us the evidence or proof that we have 'been with Jesus'. For the apostles, such evidence was the presence of the man who had been healed, but for us it can only be our knowledge of Christ and his word, and the fervency of our proclamation. And for that to happen it means that we must guard carefully the sanctity of our own inner lives. I recall reading somewhere that the soil out of which all great preaching grows is the preacher's own devotional life. We must spend time to 'be with Jesus'.

What about miracles?

The members of the Sanhedrin were faced with a dilemma. They wanted to punish the apostles, but they could not get around the fact that what had been done was miraculous, and an act of great kindness and mercy. 'But when they had commanded them to go aside out of the council, they conferred among themselves, saying, "What shall we do to these men? For, indeed, that a notable miracle has been done through them is evident to all who dwell in Jerusalem, and we cannot deny it"' (Acts 4:15–16).

Here were the enemies of Jesus being forced to accept the evidence of their own senses. If they could have denied the miraculous, they would have done so. And yet we have modern theologians who deny the miraculous element in the Bible, such as the virgin birth and the Resurrection, and would reduce the gospel to no more than another brand of humanism. In the New Testament, miracles are described as wonders and signs (John 2:11, 3:2, 20:30, Acts 2:22). They are called wonders because they caused people to be amazed by such wonderful things as raising people from the dead, and making blind people see. By signs is meant they pointed in the direction of the Mighty Sovereign all-powerful God who made them possible.

Why then do some people find it difficult to believe in miracles? One argument put forward is that in New Testament times people were less sophisticated and scientifically minded than we are today, and therefore accepted as miraculous what they could not explain. What arrogance! As if the people of Jesus' time were so stupid as not to know that under normal circumstances you cannot feed over five thousand people on five loaves and two fish, or that men cannot walk on water. Or take the disciple Thomas. He was known as the 'doubter', because he was the kind of man who did not believe anything easily, and when told of the resurrection of Jesus he said: 'I will not believe'. But when faced with the risen Lord Jesus he quickly changed his mind. Why? Because the evidence of the resurrection could not be denied.

In answer to the questions: Do miracles happen today, and can miracles happen today? The answer must be yes, if it pleases God to do so. For in the end it all comes down to the kind of God we believe in. If we believe in the God and Father of our Lord Jesus Christ, the God who created the universe, and upholds all things by the word of his power, then we have no problem with miracles. And let us not overlook the greatest miracle of all, which is happening all the time. That is, the miracle of a changed life when the power of the Holy Spirit brings a person out of the kingdom of Satan's darkness and unbelief into the kingdom of God's light and truth. That is the greatest of all miracles because it affects a person's life, not only for time, but also for eternity.

Personal experience

Conscious of their helplessness to do anything to the apostles by way of punishment the members of the Sanhedrin resorted to threats and warnings, and let them go. ' "But so that it spreads no further among the people, let us severely threaten them, that from now on they speak to no man in his name". So they called them and commanded them not to speak at all nor teach in the name of Jesus. But Peter and John answered and said to them, "Whether it is right in the sight of God to listen to you more than to God, you judge. For we cannot but speak the things which we have seen and heard"' (Acts 4:17–20).

In one of his hymns Wesley has the line: 'What we have seen and heard with confidence we tell'. Christian witness, in order to be effective, must be based on personal experience of what God has done in a person's life. That is where our confidence lies, when we know without a shadow of doubt that God, by his power in the Holy Spirit, has invaded the very depths of our personality, and is changing us into the likeness of Christ. It was the confidence with which Peter and John had made their testimony that caused the members of the Sanhedrin to 'marvel' and be impressed.

Sometimes we lack the confidence to speak boldly of Christ to others because the consequences can be so unpleasant. It may invite ridicule, or being isolated and shut out of company. When we feel that way, we must pray earnestly with Paul: 'that utterance may be given to me, that I may open my mouth boldly to make known the mystery of the gospel' (Ephesians 6:19). God will not fail us.

Prayer for boldness

In this final section the apostles on their release pray, with the remainder of the church, that the confidence and boldness they had already shown would continue. 'And being let go, they went to their own companions and reported all that the chief priests and elders had said to them. So when they heard that, they raised their voice to God with one accord...' (Acts 4:23–24). Where would we be without the ministry of prayer and the uplift it gives to our spirits? Especially when it is collective praying with other believers. When Peter and John reported to the church what had happened, and how they were warned not to preach the gospel, we might have expected the believers to have fallen into a mood of deep depression. But that did not happen. But at the same time they realised the seriousness of the threat, and that was why they turned to God in prayer for help and courage and comfort.

The main points of their prayer are these. First, they acknowledge the sovereignty of God as the creator of all things. 'Lord, you are God, who made heaven and earth and the sea, and all that is in them' (Acts 4:24). We must always begin there when faced with a problem or crisis in our lives. For the early church the situation posed by the authorities really was a crisis, but they reminded themselves that God is on the throne and he is greater than any crisis.

Second, they turn to the scriptures for comfort, and quote the second psalm which pictures the rebellious secular powers against the Lord's anointed, a situation similar to their own. 'Why did the nations rage, and the people plot vain things? The kings of the earth took their stand, and the rulers were gathered together against the Lord and against his Christ' (Acts 4:25–26). They understand the psalm as prophetic of the opposition they were presently facing from the Jewish and Gentile authorities. 'For truly against your holy servant Jesus, whom you anointed, both Herod and Pontius Pilate, with the Gentiles and the people of Israel, were gathered together to do whatever your hand and your purpose determined before to be done' (Acts 4:28). The scriptures are meant to bring us comfort and peace in the time of trouble. And if we search the Word of God, we can always find a situation comparable to our own, and how it was handled and dealt with. In this instance the rebellious powers did not win out, neither in David's day nor in the early days of the church.

Third, they ask not that the problem should be removed, but that God will enable them to meet it with courage and boldness. 'Now, Lord, look on their threats, and grant to your servants that with all boldness they may speak your word, by stretching out your hand to heal, and that signs and wonders may be done through the name of your holy servant Jesus' (Acts 4:29–30). In the Christian life we have to guard against the temptation to give way to a victim mentality and always to expect God to remove the crisis facing us. Sometimes, we must do what the apostles did and see the problem or difficulty as a challenge to faith and the need for Holy Spirit boldness. James opens his letter with these words: 'My brethren count it all joy when you fall into various trials, knowing that the testing of your faith produces patience. But let patience have its perfect work, that you may be perfect and complete, lacking nothing' (James 1:2–4).

The church's prayer was answered in a very dramatic fashion. 'And when they had prayed, the place where they were assembled together was shaken; and they were all filled with the Holy Spirit, and they spoke the word of God with boldness' (Acts 4:31). I do not think this means that they were given new powers by the Holy Spirit, but that the shaking was an evidence of God's presence to give them renewed confidence to continue the work he had called them to. We too must believe that God hears our prayers, however he may choose to answer them, since that in itself renews our confidence, along with the reading of the scriptures, to continue in the work of the gospel.

The Church, a mixed company

Read Acts 4:32–5:42

We have given the above title to the passage we are now considering because it presents us with two contrasting pictures of the Christian community. The one is favourable and uplifting, the other is unfavourable and depressing. But that is characteristic of the Bible as a whole. It is God's book and always presents us with the truth as it is, including the failings of his people.

The favourable picture

Back in chapter 2:42–47, we have a picture of the church in its worship and fellowship. And here again, in this passage, we have another little cameo of the corporate life of the Christian community. 'Now the multitude of those who believed were of one heart and soul; neither did anyone say that any of the things he possessed was his own, but they had all things in common. And with great power the apostles gave witness to the resurrection of the Lord Jesus. And great grace was upon them all. Nor was there anyone among them who lacked; for all who were possessors of lands or houses sold them, and brought the proceeds of the things that were sold, and laid them at the apostles' feet; and they distributed to each as anyone had need' (Acts 4:32–35).

This is a picture to gladden our hearts and lift our spirits. Here were the believers experiencing a true sense of spiritual unity, and it sets before us an example of what the local church should be, a loving, caring community. But this picture of the early Christians selling their lands and houses, and giving the proceeds to the Lord's work, is not meant as a model for every church to follow. That would be quite impossible today. But it *is* meant to be a model of the spirit in which the local church should conduct its affairs. It speaks to us of the sense of responsibility we should have for one another within the fellowship. No one should be in need materially. It also says something about the right kind of stewardship where the church's resources are concerned. And it reminds us that, as members of the Body of Christ, we should give as generously as we can to the work of God.

Chapter 4

Barnabas

This picture of the church as a sharing, caring community is further enhanced when special mention is made of Barnabas. 'And Joses, who was also named Barnabas by the apostles (which is translated Son of Encouragement), a Levite of the country of Cyprus having land, sold it, and brought the money and laid it at the apostles feet' (Acts 4:36–37). But why is he singled out in this way, when others in the church also sold their houses and land in the interests of the gospel? I think the answer to that must be because of the important role Barnabas was later to play in the life of the church.

He was a native of Cyprus and probably a Jew of the Diaspora, the dispersion of the Jews following the Exile when many settled in Cyprus. It would also mean that he was a Hellenist or Greek-speaking Jew, and not a Palestinian Jew like Peter and the other apostles. Even at this early stage we get the feeling, from his willingness to give the proceeds of his property to the church, that he was totally committed to Christ. There was nothing half-hearted about his faith, as is so often the case with modern-day Christians. It poses the question: Is ours an easy laid-back Christianity, which makes little demand upon us, rather than an all-consuming commitment and zeal for God?

An Encourager

It is also significant that his original name was Joses (Joseph), but his fellow-believers added the surname Barnabas which means Son of Encouragement. Why did they do that? Was it because they could see that this was a trait in his character? Because we do in fact have instances in Acts when he encouraged others. When Saul of Tarsus wanted to join the apostles after his conversion they were very suspicious of him because of his past, but Barnabas stepped in. 'Barnabas took him and brought him to the apostles. And he declared to them how he had seen the Lord on the road, and that he had spoken to him, and how he had preached boldly in Damascus in the name of Jesus. So he was with them in Jerusalem, coming in and going out' (Acts 9:27–28). Another instance was when the Gentiles began joining the church. 'Then news of these things came to the ears of the church in Jerusalem, and they sent out Barnabas to go as far as Antioch.

When he came and had seen the grace of God, he was glad, and encouraged them all that with purpose of heart they should continue with the Lord' (Acts 11:22–23).

We cannot all be highly gifted in the church fellowship and play an up-front role, but there is no reason why any one of us cannot be an encourager to others. This is a very necessary ministry in the church when it comes to encouraging those whose faith is weak, and speaking the word of help and comfort to those in distress. One does not have to be clever or eloquent or have a dynamic personality in order to be an encourager. What is needed is a loving and gracious nature.

Taking the second place

Barnabas was also greatly used of God in the witness of the church, especially as the companion of the apostle Paul in his missionary journeys. We are told in chapter 11 that 'he was a good man, full of the Holy Spirit and of faith' (verse 24). That was certainly the case when the work at Antioch among the Gentiles was progressing so fast that he was unable to cope alone, and he sent for Saul to work alongside him. 'And when he had found him, he brought him to Antioch. So it was that for a whole year they assembled with the church and taught a great many people. And the disciples were first called Christians at Antioch' (Acts 11:26). In one sense that was a dangerous thing to do, for Barnabas knew well enough that Paul was a man with superior gifts and that he was to become the great apostle to the Gentiles, and that he himself would take second place. And that in fact is what happened, as we shall see.

In chapter 13 both men are set apart by the church at Antioch for missionary work, and from then onwards all the emphasis is upon Paul, and little is said of Barnabas. But being the kind of man he was he would not have minded that since his concern was only for the glory of God. Earlier, when we were considering the miraculous healing of the lame man at the gate of the temple (chapter 3), we saw that Peter and John had the same concern, that God alone should have the glory. That is the best antidote to any jealousy that may arise in our hearts when we see someone else's work being more blessed than our own. Is God being glorified? That is all that matters.

The unfavourable picture

So far, everything in the infant church seems to be sweetness and light. But that was not to last. As we move into chapter 5 the picture changes entirely and we are faced with two members of the church who deliberately set themselves to lie to the Holy Spirit, and who brought God's judgement upon themselves in a terrible way. 'But a certain man named Ananias, with Sapphira his wife, sold a possession. And he kept back part of the proceeds, his wife also being aware of it, and brought a certain part and laid it at the apostles' feet. But Peter said, "Ananias, why has Satan filled your heart to lie to the Holy Spirit and keep back part of the price of the land for yourself? While it remained, was it not your own? And after it was sold, was it not in your own control? Why have you conceived this thing in your heart? You have not lied to men but to God". Then Ananias, hearing these words, fell down and breathed his last. So great fear came upon all those who heard these things. And the young men arose and wrapped him up, carried him out, and buried him' (Acts 5:1–6). What are we meant to learn from a difficult and terrible passage like this?

Wheat and tares

We may wonder what a couple of cheats like Ananias and Sapphira were doing in the church in the first place. But that only raises another question. Is the visible church a community of perfect people, containing no cheats, no liars, no adulterers etc? Of course not, it is a mixed company containing within it not only its Barnabases but also its Ananiases and Sapphiras; true believers and nominal believers. In his parable of the wheat and tares (Matthew 13) Jesus makes this point very clearly. The wheat are the children of the kingdom, and the tares are the children of the evil one. And he concludes the parable by saying: 'The Son of Man will send out his angels, and they will gather out of his kingdom all things that offend, and those who practice lawlessness' (Matthew 13:41). Commenting on this verse Hendriksen makes the valid point: 'How can they be "gathered out", if previously they were not inside, in this case inside the church visible?' (*The Gospel of Matthew*, Banner of Truth, p.573).

We must accept therefore that within the church there will always be lying, cheating, and hypocrisy of all kinds, for we are still in a sinful world, and only God knows in the final analysis those who are truly his. That tells us that we attend God's house not because it is the respectable thing to do, nor because we think that those in church are better than other people. No, we worship at God's house because we are very conscious of our weakness and sinfulness and desire to seek his forgiveness and to know of his grace in our lives. Moreover this passage also teaches that our salvation does not depend upon being part of the visible church on earth. Ananias and Sapphira were part of the early fellowship of believers, and yet God brought a terrible judgement on them because they were not children of his kingdom. We can belong to the church, participate in the sacraments, and share in all that is holy and sacred and still not know the reality of salvation. It is only through repentance and faith in the Lord Jesus Christ that we enter the kingdom.

Cheating God

'Now it was about three hours later when his wife came in, not knowing what had happened. And Peter answered her, "Tell me whether you sold the land for so much?" She said "Yes, for so much". Then Peter said to her, "How is it that you have agreed together to test the Spirit of the Lord? Look, the feet of those who have buried your husband are at the door, and they will carry you out". Then immediately she fell down at his feet and breathed her last. And the young men came in and found her dead, and carrying her out, buried her by her husband. So great fear came upon all the church and upon all who heard these things' (Acts 5:7–11).

What exactly was the sin of this husband and wife that, under the judgement of God, they paid for with their lives? It was not as if they refused to give to God's cause like the other members. Having sold his land we are told that he 'brought a certain part and laid it at the apostles' feet' (Acts 5:2). They were not guilty of selfishness therefore. Nor was it sinful to keep for themselves part of the money they received for their property. It was rightfully their money and, as Peter said, they could have done as they liked with it. 'While it remained, was it not your own? And after it was sold, was it not in your own control?' (Acts 5:4).

Their sin lay in the fact that they deliberately conspired to deceive God. 'Then Peter answered "Tell me whether you sold the land for so much?" She said, "Yes, for so much". Then Peter said to her, "How is it that you have agreed together to test the Spirit of the Lord?"' (Acts 5:8–9). They showed contempt for God and mocked his Spirit by pretending that the money they gave the church was the whole of the amount they received for the land, when in fact it was only a part. That is why God's judgement fell upon them both, because they treated him as if he did not matter, and that is the ultimate blasphemy. It is to treat God as if he does not count, and that he is indifferent to moral wrongdoing and evil in the world.

That is something people are doing all the time. They live and act as if God is not there, or if he is there, he is not wise enough to know what is happening here below. But they are wrong on both counts. One of God's greatest attributes is his omniscience; he is all knowing. The Psalmist says, 'O Lord, you have searched me and known me. You know my sitting down and my rising up; you understand my thought afar off. You comprehend my path and my lying down and are acquainted will all my ways' (Psalm 139:1–3). This must be a frightening thought for anyone who has anything to hide from God, for we shall all have to account on the day of judgement for the life we live here and now. As the writer to the Hebrews puts it, 'And there is no creature hidden from his sight, but all things are naked and open to the eyes of him to whom we must give account' (Hebrews 4:13). The time to expose such hidden things therefore is now, to repent of them, and to receive God's forgiveness.

God's warning

What affect did this dreadful happening have upon the members of the church and upon the general population of Jerusalem? We are told: 'So great fear came upon all the church and upon all who heard these things' (Acts 5:11). In this context by 'fear' is meant a solemn awe, or a deep sense of the awful severity and power of God. We may wonder why God's judgement upon Ananias and Sapphira was so terrible as to cause sudden death. Could it be that in the early days of the church God was giving a warning to all and sundry, both within and without the church, that he is a God not to be trifled with? Men and women need that kind of warning from time to time.

It is one of the basic weaknesses of the church's ministry today that due emphasis is not given to God's majesty and power in our worship and preaching, with the consequence that people no longer have the fear of God in their hearts, and have lost the sense of accountability before the bar of God's judgement. Perhaps this has followed from the honest attempt to make worship more appealing and contemporary through the introduction of dance, mime and loud rhythmic music. Whilst not condemning these efforts out of hand, it must be said that accompanying them is the danger that worship becomes trivialised, and God himself becomes of no consequence. Moreover, it can lead to the faith of Christians becoming soft and flabby, and unequal to the pressures and tensions we all have to face in today's world, because the God they know has been robbed of his greatness, mystery and power.

It is all a matter of keeping the balance between the God who is high and lifted up and 'sits above the circle of the earth' (Isaiah 40:22), and the God who has come 'near by the blood of Christ' (Ephesians 2:13). It is not either or, but both.

The Church goes forward

We might have thought that the sudden and dramatic deaths of Ananias and Sapphira would have been disastrous for the infant church and would have turned people off from having anything to do with it. But instead of that the Christian community experienced a new infilling of spiritual power which enabled it to have a growing impact on the people.

'And through the hands of the apostles many signs and wonders were done among the people. And they were all with one accord in Solomon's Porch. Yet none of the rest dared join them, but the people esteemed them highly. And believers were increasingly added to the Lord, multitudes of both men and women, so that they brought the sick out into the streets and laid them on beds and couches, that at least the shadow of Peter passing by might fall on some of them. Also a multitude gathered from the surrounding cities of Jerusalem, bringing sick people and those who were tormented by unclean spirits, and they were all healed' (Acts 5:12–16).

Sickness and healing

We have already said something about signs and wonders and miracles when dealing with the healing of the lame man at the temple (Acts 3). And here we have the same subject again, except that now it seems as if the healing ministry of the apostles is in the very forefront of the church's witness. The sick were brought out into the streets and they were all healed. People who could not get near Peter for the crowds even laid their sick as near his path as possible, in the hope that even his shadow falling on them might bring healing. What are we to make of all this?

There is no doubt that the apostles were given the power to heal the sick, and that they did so. But why is it that in the apostolic church the healing ministry was fairly common, whereas today it is hardly exercised at all? We must bear in mind that this was a unique time in the history of the church. These were early days when the power of God in signs, wonders and miracles would be seen as an evidence of the truth of the apostles' message, and thus help to establish the church in its beginnings. It must be remembered that today we have the full canon of Holy Scripture to support the message of the gospel, and therefore there is less need of wonders and signs. Furthermore, when it comes to miracles of healing, we have at our disposal today all the advances in medical science which we must make use of, and for which we should give thanks to God. He is still the healer, even when he uses men to do his work for him.

In Bible times, when there was little in the way of medical help, people were nevertheless encouraged to use the means available for healing. Many health and hygiene laws are laid down in the book of Leviticus. King Hezekiah was healed when Isaiah prescribed a poultice of figs (Isaiah 38:21). Luke, the author of Acts, was himself a doctor (Colossians 4:14). The Good Samaritan used a mixture of oil and wine for the wounds of the man mugged on the Jericho road (Luke 10). Paul advised Timothy to drink a little wine for his stomach complaint (1 Timothy 5:23). Although the power of healing was available for the apostles, they were not to use it indiscriminately. Paul himself prayed three times to be delivered from what he calls his 'thorn in the flesh' (possible an eye complaint), but he was not healed (2 Corinthians 12:7–9).

In the light of all we have said, the question still remains: 'Is there direct healing by God's power today?' I am sure there is, although I have never witnessed it myself. If God chooses to heal, that is his sovereign will, and if he chooses not to heal, that too is his sovereign will. We can pray for healing, since prayer always helps, but we must leave the results entirely in his hands.

Demon possession

In the passage we are considering Luke distinguishes between physical illness and possession by unclean spirits. '… Bringing sick people and those who were tormented by unclean spirits, and they were all healed' (Acts 5:16). In the gospels we have numerous instances of Christ delivering men and women from possession by demons or evil spirits, and it is evident that they were aware of who he was, and that he had the power to destroy them. 'Let us alone! What have we to do with you, Jesus of Nazareth? Did you come to destroy us? I know who you are, the Holy One of God!' (Mark 1:24).

If we believe that Satan is a malignant personality, and that evil is not simply an abstract force or power at work in the world, then we will have no difficulty in accepting the belief in demon possession. But liberal theologians attribute such a belief to the primitive thinking of New Testament times. Speaking of Christ's attitude towards demon possession, William Barclay says: 'He knew no more on this matter than the people of his day, and that is a thing we can easily accept for Jesus was not a scientist and did not come to teach science. Or, he knew perfectly well that he could never cure the man in trouble unless he assumed the reality of the disease. It was real to the man and had to be treated as real or it could never be cured at all. In the end we come to the conclusion that there are some answers that we do not know' (*Gospel of Mark,* Saint Andrew Press, 1966, p. 28).

But why do we read so much of demon possession in the gospels and in Acts, and see so little of it today? Satan was probably more active at that time in order to counteract the impact of healing and miracles by Christ and his apostles. Another question sometimes asked is: Are there instances of people being demon possessed today? Yes, undoubtedly, especially in those countries where there is little knowledge of the gospel. After all, Satan is just as active today as he has ever been, perhaps more so as the time of Christ's coming draws ever nearer. Furthermore, where there is an instance of possession by an evil spirit, is there any special act of exorcism that should be applied? It seems to me that there is no suggestion of any special act of exorcism laid down in the gospels or in Acts, other than the preaching of the Word of God. When a person becomes born again through the power of the Holy Spirit it means the total defeat of Satan and the demonic powers. This also answers yet another question people ask: Can a true born again believer be possessed by an evil spirit? The answer must be no. The Holy Spirit and an evil spirit cannot co-exist in the same personality.

A very helpful book on the whole subject of demon possession is Frederick S Leahy's *Satan Cast Out,* Banner of Truth, 1975.

Believers and Unbelievers

We have seen that the judgement upon Ananias and Sapphira led to a new infilling of Spiritual power upon the church, which was reflected in people being healed of physical and demonic illness. But there was also another result. 'Yet none of the rest dared join them, but the people esteemed them highly. And believers were increasingly added to the Lord, multitudes of both men and women' (Acts 5:13–14). Three groups are mentioned here.

First, there were those described as 'the rest', whoever they might have been, but who were hindered, for whatever reason, from believing the gospel and joining the church. They had seen with their own eyes the miracles of healing the apostles had done, and they had heard, like others, the same gospel preached, but they still resisted coming to faith in Christ. Why was that?—since the same thing happens today. Two men can attend the same church, hear the same gospel preached, but one comes to faith in Christ but the other does not. What is it that prevents people from believing? We know no one becomes a believer without the convicting power of the Holy Spirit, but from the human side are there certain things which can hinder a person from coming to personal faith in Christ? I believe there are.

Paul says that when the gospel fails to penetrate the mind and heart of the hearer so as to bring them to faith, it is because of the activity of Satan. 'But even if our gospel is veiled, it is veiled to those who are perishing, whose minds the god of this age has blinded, who do not believe, lest the light of the gospel of the glory of Christ, who is the image of God, should shine on them' (2 Corinthians 4:3–4). Satan exploits the natural weaknesses of people, and thus hinders them from believing. What are those weaknesses?

It might be intellectual pride. An intelligent person hears the gospel preached and is told that he can become a Christian simply by believing that Christ died that he might be forgiven and be reconciled to God. At first he might be inclined to believe, but then Satan's whispering campaign gets to work in his mind. 'You do not believe that, do you, an intelligent person like you? You can not really believe that so much— the forgiveness of sins, life in heaven and peace with God—can be that simple, without any intellectual struggle on your part?' And straight away he dismisses the whole thing. Snatches the word out of his heart just as Jesus warns in his parable of the Sower. 'Those by the wayside are the ones who hear; then the devil comes and takes away the word out of their hearts, lest they should believe and be saved''(Luke 8:12).

It might be the fear of what others might think. A man may feel himself drawn to accept the gospel, but then he wonders what his mates at work might think about it. Will they think he has gone all soft and religious? Will they make fun and say, 'he has seen the light', or 'he has become a Bible puncher'? The fact is we all have a natural fear of what others think of us. We like to have a certain image in their eyes, and we do not want that image spoiled in any way.

It might be the love of their present comfortable life-style. They hear the gospel and are moved by its challenge, but then on further reflection they realise it will revolutionise their life. Certain things they will have to give up, certain places that will no longer be able to go to, certain friends and company they will no longer be able to hang out with. And in addition they will be expected to support the missionary causes, give of their money, read the Bible, attend church regularly, and so on. All this crowds into their minds, and Satan exploits it and snatches the word away.

It might be the sincere feeling that they could never keep up the standard of being a Christian, it is too high. They will have to put God first rather than self, be willing to forgive others when they are wronged, live a disciplined life where sex is concerned. They could never live up to such demands, they feel, because you have to have a certain kind of temperament which theirs is not.

There may be other reasons, at the human level, which hinder people from coming to faith, but whatever it is we can be certain that ultimately Satan is behind it. And therefore we must make it clear to people that whatever the obstacle, God by his power can remove it.

The second group consisted of 'the people who esteemed them (apostles) highly'. They were affected by the Christian message and had a profound regard for the holiness of the apostles, and the obvious sincerity and certainty with which they spoke of the truth of God. But again, they did not come to that point of crossing the line into the kingdom of God through faith in Christ. They remind me strongly of the Scribe to whom Jesus said: 'You are not far from the kingdom of God' (Mark 12:34). He was clearly a man who was seeking the truth and, in his conversation with Jesus, he had come so far in his understanding, but not all the way. Like the people who held the apostles in high esteem, and admired the gospel they preached, he was 'not far' from the kingdom of God, but still outside it. In the end, it makes no difference whether one is not far from the Kingdom, or clearly hostile to it, one is still lost to God's salvation.

The third group was totally different. They took the final step of faith and became firm believers. 'And believers were increasingly added to the Lord, multitudes of both men and women' (Acts 5:14). These were the people represented by the fourth kind of soil in our Lord's parable of the sower. 'But the ones [seeds] that fell on good ground are those who having heard the word with a noble and good heart, keep it and bear fruit with patience' (Luke 8:15). People who hear the word of God and have a real desire to accept it, have their understanding quickened by the Holy Spirit, so that they grasp its truth and enter into salvation.

Arrested yet again

It is not surprising to read that the apostles were arrested for a second time since they had been warned by the authorities not to continue preaching in the name of Jesus. 'Then the high priest rose up, and all those who were with him (which is the sect of the Saducees), and they were filled with indignation, and laid their hands on the apostles and put them in the common prison. But at night an angel of the Lord opened the prison doors and brought them out, and said, "Go, stand in the temple and speak to the people all the words of this life"' (Acts 5:17–20).

The thing that stands out in this passage is the miraculous escape of the apostles from the prison. Not that all students of the Bible necessarily regard it as a miracle. There are those who make great play of the fact that the Greek word 'angglos' can mean 'angel' and also 'messenger'. The escape, they say, might well have been brought about by a human agent and not a divine being. But what human agent would have the authority to command God's apostles: 'Go, stand in the temple and speak to the people all the words of this life'.

Some people, including evangelicals, have difficulty with the idea that angels, in the Bible, come to earth and look and act like ordinary human beings. In Genesis three angels came to Abraham in human form (Genesis 18). An angel appeared to Gideon and sat down under a tree and chatted with him (Judges 6:11). Angels are frequently mentioned in the New Testament—foretelling Christ's birth (Matthew 1:20); in the wilderness temptations (Matthew 4:11); in Gethsemane (Luke 22:43); and at the resurrection John 20:12). Later we shall read of Peter again being let out of prison by an angel (Acts 12); and the writer of Hebrews reminds us: 'Do not forget to entertain strangers, for by so doing some have unwittingly entertained angels' (Hebrews 13:2).

It seems to me that it is no more difficult to accept that angels can appear in human form than it is to believe in Christ's appearance after the resurrection. He too appeared in human likeness and ate and drank with his disciples; and yet his body was different because it was a glorified body. And on the resurrection morning we too will have a glorified body like his (Philippians 3:21). Indeed, Christ said that one day we shall be 'like the angels of God in heaven' (Matthew 22:30). That means we shall be like them in beauty and strength, with bodies no longer subject to disease and pain. And we shall be like them in purity and holiness, living in perfect fellowship and harmony with God. What a glorious prospect!

The new life

When the angel commanded the apostles to go to the temple and preach to the people, the phrase used is most significant: '...speak to the people all the words of THIS life'. In the NIV the phrase is 'this new life'. The word 'this' emphasises the new spiritual life in Christ, in contrast with the secular life of the world. In his letter to the Colossian Christians, Paul makes very clear the contrast between these two interpretations of life. 'Beware lest anyone cheat you through philosophy and empty deceit, according to the tradition of men, according to the basic principles of the world, and not according to Christ. For in him dwells all the fullness of the Godhead bodily; and you are complete in him, who is the head of all principality and power' (Colossians 2:8–10).

Paul is saying that the human interpretation of life is an empty, deceitful philosophy based on human ideas and thinking, or the 'tradition of men', as opposed to the authoritative revelation of God's truth in Christ. Today, that view of life is represented by secular humanism that says, in effect: 'We do not need God, or Christ, or the so-called revelation of the Bible to explain the meaning and purpose of our existence. We ourselves, mankind, have the key to understanding in our own thinking and cleverness'. But, as Paul rightly says, we must not allow ourselves to be 'cheated' or deceived by this thinking, for we see all too clearly where it has got us in the lying, corruption, greed and discontent that pervades modern society.

Our new life in Christ, on the other hand, brings us into the fullness of the very life of God himself. A new life-principle enters into the centre of our being enabling us to interpret our human existence from God's view of things. The Holy Spirit directs our heart, mind and will to new thoughts, conduct and purposes.

Act of daring

It was this 'new life' message that the angel commanded Peter and the other apostles to preach to the people. 'And when they heard that, they entered the temple early in the morning and taught' (Acts 5:21).

The obedience of Peter and the apostles to that command shows an incredible courage, because they were throwing all caution and prudence to the wind. They knew exactly what would happen to them once the Jewish authorities got to hear of it, and yet they went ahead and did it. When I was a boy in Sunday school we used to sing the hymn:

'Dare to be a Daniel,
Dare to stand-alone.
Dare to have a purpose firm,
And dare to make it known'.

What Peter and the others did was an act of daring. Does that speak to us today? Do we ever do anything that is really daring for Christ? Does the principle of caution and prudence always rule Christian lives in every circumstance? I believe that sometimes, just sometimes, God would like us to do something daring for him, something a bit over the top! After all, if safety first is always to be our guide in the Christian life then we would never have had a single missionary in times past to plant the gospel in foreign lands, or thousands of believers today living in countries under the continual threat of persecution.

I am reminded here of that story in John's Gospel (chapter 12) of Mary, who poured a pound of costly spikenard over the feet of Jesus. That was an extravagant and daring thing to have done. Those present might have interpreted it as 'exhibitionism' or 'attention-seeking', but Mary cared nothing for that, she was only interested in expressing her personal love for the Lord. And Jesus commended her for her action.

I sometimes wonder if it would bring joy to the heart of God if occasionally we did something daring and extravagant, just to show our love for him. Instead, we are so often calculating and cautious, giving the acceptable minimum of our time, energy, devotion and service. Peter and the apostles were showing an extravagant, lavish love for the Lord and an almost reckless audacity when they went back into the temple area to preach the gospel. That becomes clear in what happened next.

Trial and witness

From verse 22–32 we have the account of the inevitable re-arrest of the apostles and their second appearance before the Jewish court. 'So one came and told them saying, "Look, the men whom you put in prison are standing in the temple and teaching the people!" Then the captain went with the officers and brought them without violence, for they feared the people, lest they should be stoned. And when they had brought them, they set them before the council' (Acts 5:25–27).

On being questioned by the high priest as to why they had defied the warning of the council not to preach in the name of Jesus, Peter replied: 'We ought to obey God rather than men. The God of our fathers raised up Jesus whom you murdered by hanging on a tree. Him God has exalted to his right hand to be Prince and Saviour, to give repentance to Israel and forgiveness of sins. And we are his witnesses to these things, and so also is the Holy Spirit whom God has given to those who obey him' (Acts 5:29–32).

The important phrase in Peter's defence is the words: 'And we are his witnesses to these things'. In chapter 1 Luke tells us that immediately before his ascension the Lord Jesus spoke to the apostles about the witness they were to make when the church would come into being. 'But you shall receive power when the Holy Spirit has come upon you; and you shall be witnesses to me in Jerusalem, and in all Judea and Samaria, and to the end of the earth' (Acts 1:8). Already, in these early chapters in Acts, we have seen how faithful the church was in its witness through preaching, performing miracles, in prayer, and in fellowship and communion. But beyond the collective witness of the church there must also be the personal witness of believers. This can sometimes be costly and sacrificial as it was for Peter and the apostles. The Greek word for witness (martys) has come down to us in our word 'martyr', showing that for some in history it has meant laying down their lives for the gospel.

In answer to the question: What is a witness?—It is someone who tells what he or she has personally seen and heard. Wesley has in one of his hymns the line: 'What we have seen and heard, with confidence we tell'. That can only apply to the man or woman who has personally experienced the saving power of the Lord Jesus Christ in their own life.

Gamaliel speaks up

Peter's bold defence certainly did nothing to improve their position in the eyes of the council. 'When they heard this, they were furious and plotted to kill them' (Acts 5:33). It was at this critical juncture in the proceedings that Gamaliel spoke up on their behalf. He was a totally unexpected ally since he was a Pharisee. 'Then one in the council stood up, a Pharisee named Gamaliel, a teacher of the law held in respect by all the people, and commanded them to put the apostles outside for a little while' (Acts 5:34).

Gamaliel was clearly a good and godly man, and as a distinguished teacher of the law of God had at one time taught the Apostle Paul, in his pre-Christian student days (Acts 22:3). In Acts 5 35–37 he reminds the court of two earlier instances when popular religious movements led by Theudas and Judas had began with great enthusiasm, but in the end petered out. He then continued: 'And now I say to you, keep away from these men and let them alone; for if this plan or this work is on men, it will come to nothing; but if it is of God, you cannot overthrow it—lest you even be found to fight against God' (Acts 5:38–39).

That was wise advice, since you cannot fight against God and hope to win. History has proved that again and again, where the Christian church and the gospel of Christ are concerned. The forces of evil working through men and governments have attempted all through the ages to destroy the church and obliterate the gospel, but they always failed to do so. And the reason lies in the promise of the Lord Jesus: 'I will build my church, and the gates of Hades shall not prevail against it' (Matthew 16:18). The Jewish rulers made the mistake of thinking that they were opposing a group of ignorant and enthusiastic fishermen. They did not realise that behind them was the eternal God and all the powers of heaven. J C Ryle says, 'the true church never dies. Like the bush Moses saw, it may burn, but shall not be consumed. Every member of it shall be brought safe to glory. In spite of falls, failures, and shortcomings—in spite of the world, the flesh, and the devil—no member of the true church shall ever be cast away' (*Expository Thoughts*, vol. 1, Evangelical Press, p. 198). Gamaliel was absolutely right when he said to the council: 'but if it is of God, you cannot overthrow it'.

Tolerant to all

But whilst Gamaliel was strong in what he said, he was weak in certain other respects. I get the strong feeling that he was a liberally minded man who liked to think of himself as tolerant, broad-minded in all things, including religion. Was this why he asked the apostles to leave the court before making his speech. He did not want them to think that he was identifying with them and their faith, although he would speak on their behalf. He was not convinced that the new movement *was* of God, but 'if it is of God'. What he is saying is something like this: 'Now we must be tolerant in these matters. After all, there might be something in this Christian movement. We have to be big enough to believe that we do not have a monopoly of truth. Let us just wait and see. Toleration in all things, that is my advice.'

It all has a familiar ring today in our 'politically correct' society. Ours is a multi-faith age, and we have church leaders telling us we must be tolerant of one another's faith as part of the total revelation of God to mankind. There are many roads to God. The result of this kind of thinking is that you end up by being tolerant of everything, and believing nothing. Furthermore such a diluted Christianity bears no relation to the gospel Jesus preached and taught when he said: 'I am the way, the truth, and the life. No one comes to the Father except through me' (John 14:6).

The Gamaliel approach of neutrality—sitting on the fence—is not one that people can adopt towards the gospel. For what he was really saying to the council was 'do not oppose these men, but on the other hand, do not support them either. Just do not get involved, but leave things as they are'. That simply will not do where God is concerned, for we already are involved from the moment he created us. He has given us our life, and health and all things, and has even given us the gift of salvation in the death of his Son the Lord Jesus Christ. We cannot afford the luxury of neutrality where that is concerned, for it is a matter of eternal life or eternal death.

Rejoicing in affliction

The result of Gamaliel's intervention was that the apostles were allowed to go free instead of being put to death as was first intended. And that was a good thing for which they would undoubtedly have praised and thanked God. 'And they agreed with him, and when they had called for the apostles and beaten them, they commanded that they should not speak in the name of Jesus, and let them go' (Acts 5:40).

But that was not the end of the matter. Even if they had been put to death it still would not have been the end of the matter. What God begins he always finishes, and there were others he was already raising up to carry on his work. In the meantime the apostles, far from being discouraged or deciding to move elsewhere with their ministry, just carried on as before. 'So they departed from the presence of the council, rejoicing that they were counted worthy to suffer shame for his name. And daily in the temple, and in every house, they did not cease teaching and preaching Jesus as the Christ' (Acts 5: 41–42).

Their courage and positive outlook is breathtaking. How did they do it? I cannot believe for one moment that they were supermen. They were as ordinary as we are, but were enabled by God's grace to do extraordinary things. It puts me in mind of the many Christians today in parts of the world where they are persecuted for their faith. Take this for instance.

'On 15 August the Supreme Court in Islamabad ordered the immediate release of Ayub Masih and concluded: "Ayub Masih is not found guilty of committing blasphemy and allegations against Ayub are baseless and false". Ayub was accused by neighbours of blaspheming against Islam and has spent the last six years in prison with a death sentence hanging over his head. …Following the (original) trial the entire Christian population in the village was evicted' (*Evangelicals Now*, September 2002).

I ask myself, 'Are these Pakistan Christians any different from ourselves that they can endure such trial for the gospel? Are they people of super-holiness?' I do not think so. What is true is that God gives a special grace for special situations. And that is something we must hold on to when we have to face some particularly heavy trial.

The Church gets organised

Read Acts chapters 6 and 7

U p to this point the church has gone steadily forward in spite of the unpleasant and solemn episode involving Ananias and Sapphira, and in spite of the opposition of the Jewish council. The ministry of the apostles in signs and wonders, and in the preaching of God's word, was greatly blessed and the church continued to grow. It now numbered several thousand, and that brought with it certain tensions among the members.

A difficult problem

'Now in those days, when the number of the disciples was multiplying, there arose a complaint against the Hebrews by the Hellenists, because their widows were neglected in the daily distribution' (Acts 6:1). Earlier, when the church was much smaller and its members 'had all things in common' (Acts 4:32), the apostles themselves were able to take charge of the 'social' side of the church's work in the distribution of food, and in providing care and welfare for the poorer members. But as the numbers grew this task became more difficult, and complaints were being made by the Hellenist Jews that their widows were being unfairly treated and discriminated against.

To fully understand this problem we must see it against the clash of culture and language. The Hebrew Jews were those of Palestine and Jerusalem who spoke Aramaic, derived from the ancestral language. They also worshipped at the temple, and saw themselves as the custodians of the oracles of God originally given to their fathers. All this was a matter of great pride. The Hellenist Jews, on the other hand, were those who had lived in Gentile countries for generations, and spoke the Greek language, and studied the Septuagint or Greek translation of the Old Testament in their synagogues. With these differences there was undoubtedly a certain amount of tension between these two classes of Jews with the Hebrews, perhaps, adopting a superior attitude towards the Hellenists, and they in turn accusing the Hebrews of partiality in the daily distribution and the management of social relief.

This again is something that has a familiar ring to it in the light of the problems in our own country in relation to the ethnic minorities. Many of our cities and big towns have witnessed violent race riots between people of different cultures and language. And the churches have not escaped the problems and tensions arising out of this racial mix in our society. I read in a missionary pamphlet recently of a church in Birmingham where twenty-six nationalities are represented. To pastor a church like that calls for great wisdom and much prayer, as attempts are made to introduce multi-cultural worship and to break down the barriers of language. For make no mistake, Satan will quickly get in and exploit that kind of situation, bringing misunderstanding and bitterness. But it is not a new situation, as we can see from this passage we are now studying. It can be handled in the right way where there is much grace and love among the members, and wise guidance from the leaders. This is what we see next.

The first deacons

The apostles in their wisdom took the matter in hand immediately, before the spirit of discontent could escalate. Their solution was the appointment of the first church officers. 'Then the twelve summoned the multitude of the disciples and said, "It is not desirable that we should leave the word of God and serve tables. Therefore, brethren, seek out from among you seven men of good reputation, full of the Holy Spirit and wisdom, whom we may appoint over this business; but we will give ourselves continually to prayer and to the ministry of the word"' (Acts 6:2–4). There are several things to notice here.

We may wonder, in the first place, why the provision for deacons was not made when the church first came into being. But as we have seen, the church was then small in number and there was no necessity for such officers, as the apostles themselves were able to deal with all matters arising in the church's life. But as the numbers grew, and circumstances changed, the apostles had to plan and organise in order to meet the new situation. Does not that speak to us about the changes taking place today, and how the local church must plan and develop ways of meeting those changes? God does not change, the gospel does not change, and people's need of salvation does not change either, but social patterns change from age to age, and each generation brings its own problems.

In God's work prayer, planning, and guidance go together. Today especially with so many changes taking place in society, we must use our ingenuity and initiative in seeking to meet those changes, whilst at the same time asking God's blessing upon them if they are in line with his will. It is very significant that in his parable of the Unjust Steward (Luke 16), Jesus commends his keen-wittedness and foresight in planning for the new situation that had arisen, and ends with the words: 'For the sons of this world are more shrewd in their generation than the sons of light'. He means that we, as God's people, must be as inventive and enterprising in the work of the kingdom as worldly people are in the management of their affairs.

Secondly, there was the order of priorities laid down by the apostles. They were in no doubt that their God-given task was the spiritual leadership of the church through preaching and prayer, and that they should not neglect that ministry for the 'social' side of the church's work. This did not mean that they disparaged in any way the practical service involved in the distribution of food and social relief. But they knew they were called to be under-shepherds of God's people, and to have the care of souls. In order to do that effectively they needed time for prayer and the preaching of God's word, and to be released from other responsibilities.

The same priority applies today in the church's life and ministry. A pastor's main function is to study and preach the word, and to give time to the spiritual and pastoral care of the souls in his charge. That was Paul's advice to Timothy. 'I charge you therefore before God and the Lord Jesus Christ, who will judge the living and the dead at his appearing and his kingdom: Preach the word! Be ready in season and out of season. Convince, rebuke, exhort, with all longsuffering and teaching' (2 Timothy 4:1–2).

It may not always be possible, but a pastor should try to avoid being overloaded with things which other gifted people in the church can do equally well, and perhaps even better—administration, organising events, running the youth club and so on. I appreciate that in a small fellowship where there are few workers this will be much more difficult, but even then the pastor must guard jealously the time spent in pulpit preparation and pastoral work.

Thirdly, there was the manner in which the first deacons were chosen. 'Therefore, brethren, seek out from among you seven men of good reputation, full of the Holy Spirit and wisdom, who we may appoint over this business' (Acts 6:3). The responsibility for electing those who should hold this important office was handed over to the members of the church. 'And the saying pleased the whole multitude. And they chose Stephen, a man full of faith and the Holy Spirit, and Philip, Prochorus, Nicanor, Timon, Parmenas, and Nicolas, a proselyte from Antioch, whom they set before the apostles, and when they had prayed, they laid hands on them' (Acts 6:5–6). Clearly this arrangement pleased the members since it enabled them to share in the decision-making process. They, the members, elected the candidates, but the apostle appointed them to their office.

Some pastors need to keep that in mind, and not overstep their pastoral authority by assuming the right to make all important decisions in the life of the local church. The members too have been called of God to share in the ministry of the church, and therefore have a share in the decision-making process.

The last thing to notice here is the character of the men chosen for the office of deacon. The apostles laid down the guidelines to help the members elect the right kind of men. They were to be 'men of good reputation, full of the Holy Spirit and wisdom'. This tells us that the practical social aspect of the church's work must not be minimised, and that it contains a spiritual dimension because it is a work done for God. If a man is to be a deacon, it is not sufficient that he is a good organiser and administrator, or that he is a sociable person, or understands money matters. He must also be a man who has been born again of God's Spirit, is prayerful, and has a deep desire to see the work of the church blessed of God.

Following the election of deacons the gospel spread even more rapidly, not only among the ordinary people of Jerusalem, but among the priesthood. 'Then the word of God spread, and the number of the disciples multiplied greatly in Jerusalem, and a great many of the priests were obedient to the faith' (Acts 6:7). One cannot help wondering if these two things are connected in some way. It is noticeable that the names of the seven deacons are all Greek. Can this mean that the rift between the Hellenists and the Hebrews was now healed, and because of that there was a better spirit in the church, and the work was further blessed of God?

Stephen the first Christian Martyr

Among the seven deacons the only two about whom we learn anything further are Stephen and Philip. Both became powerful evangelists. We shall have something to say about Philip later (chapter 7), but for now we concentrate on Stephen. His name is Greek (Stephanos) and means 'crown', which is very appropriate in his case, since he did indeed crown his life's work of witness with martyrdom, for which he received the 'crown of righteousness' (2 Timothy 4:8) at the hand of God.

'And Stephen, full of faith and power, did great wonders and signs among the people. Then there arose some from what is called the Synagogue of the Freedmen (Cyrenians, Alexandrians, and those from Cilicia and Asia), disputing with Stephen. And they were not able to resist the wisdom and the Spirit by which he spoke' (Acts 6:8–10). Stephen was clearly a man of natural gifts and ability, especially when it came to preaching and teaching the word of God. But he did not adopt this leadership role immediately—that only came later. He began with the much humbler role of 'serving tables', and it was only as the church expanded that his gifts of preaching and evangelising were recognised. That is a principle that applies to all God's people in Christian work. We must first prove ourselves faithful in the little things of life, and in the small opportunities that come to us for witness. Jesus taught this in his parable of the talents: 'His lord said to him, "Well done, good and faithful servant: you were faithful over a few things, I will make you ruler over many things. Enter into the joy of your lord"' (Matthew 25:21).

But more important than his natural gifts and ability was his spirituality. He was a man 'full of faith and the Holy Spirit'. Holiness is not something with which we are born, it is to be pursued in the Christian life, regardless of whether we have Stephen's ability. No one has a monopoly of the Holy Spirit, not even the Stephens of this life.

Evangelism not easy

Although a gifted evangelist, and able to do 'great signs and wonders' in the power of God, Stephen soon found that witnessing for Christ is not easy. His career as a preacher and evangelist was soon cut short when the Jews belonging to the Synagogue of the Freedmen opposed his message and had him arrested. 'And they stirred up the people, the elders, and the scribes; and they came upon him, seized him, and brought him to the council' (Acts 6:12).

We may be tempted to think that, if only we are faithful in preaching the truth of Christ in the gospel, our ministry or personal witness will be blessed, and we shall enjoy spiritual success. That is not always the case. We must be realistic and realise that we are dealing with a fallen world, and that the forces of darkness arraigned against us are immensely powerful. There are two things we must always keep in mind. First, God has promised to bless his word.

'For as the rain comes down, and the snow from heaven,
And do not return there,
But water the earth,
And make it bring forth and bud,
That it may give seed to the sower
And bread to the eater,
So shall my word be that goes forth from my mouth;
It shall not return to me void,
But it shall accomplish what I please,
And it shall prosper in the thing for which I sent it' (Isaiah 55:10–11).

But whilst we have this wonderful promise, we must not overlook that God says his word will accomplish what he pleases, not what pleases us, and will prosper—be successful—in the purpose he has in mind. That purpose may not be outward success in conversions or church growth, but may be hidden in the deepening of the spiritual life of the church, or the awakening of God-consciousness in the mind of the person we are witnessing to.

The other thing to keep in mind is that Satan is immensely powerful, and he does have his victories and successes in the ongoing Christian warfare, but only in the short term. He wins a battle here and there, but never the war itself. In Stephen's case he was behind the false witnesses and false charges that led ultimately to his martyrdom, and the outbreak of a wave of bitter persecution against the church (chapter 8). It was a victory, but only in the short term. In the long term the persecution led to the further growth of the church, with the believers scattering abroad. 'Therefore those who were scattered went everywhere preaching the gospel' (Acts 8:4). Satan always over-reaches himself sooner or later.

Reflecting Christ

In Acts 6:15 we are told something quite remarkable about Stephen. 'And all who sat in the council, looking steadfastly at him, saw his face as the face of an angel'. I am not sure what this expression means. Was it a supernatural radiance in the same way that the face of Moses shone with the glory and holiness of God when he came down from Mount Sinai? (Exodus 34:29). Or does it simply mean that his face expressed a sense of calm serenity and confidence in God? I don't know. But the expression certainly means that the members of the council were in no doubt that here was a man whose faith was real, and to whom Christ was everything. His features reflected that in some way.

In a certain degree we all reflect the light of the things we live by. If we live only at the low level of the cheap and superficial, putting self first and giving priority solely to the values of this life, then our lives will reflect that kind of outlook. If, on the other hand, we live in the light of God's truth and holiness, then our lives will reflect something of the glory of God in the Lord Jesus Christ. Our Lord made two very important statements about this. He said, 'I am the light of the world' (John 8:12), and 'You are the light of the world' (Matthew 5:14). In our own lives we reflect the light of Christ in the darkness, evil and hatred that characterises the world.

Stephen on Trial

We now move into chapter seven, and Stephen's trial before the council. This is a very long passage of sixty verses, but we have to look at it in some detail or we shall lose its significance—both for Stephen's defence, and for the history of the church. The false witnesses of Acts 6:13 charged him with wanting to change the law of Moses, and wanting to destroy the temple. Neither charge was true, and Stephen was at pains to show that he honoured both the law and the temple, but that in the on-going revelation of God in Christ they were now superseded. This naturally was a blow to everything the Jews held most sacred and, as we shall see, Stephen paid for that with his life.

He knew the Bible

Stephen based the whole of his defence on his knowledge of the scriptures. We saw earlier that when he was engaged in theological debate with those who opposed his message, 'they were not able to resist the wisdom and the Spirit by which he spoke' (Acts 6:10). Throughout the whole of this chapter he speaks eloquently of God's dealings with his people in the Old Testament. He was on firm ground doing this, since the Jewish leaders on the council were the very ones who claimed to be the authority on the scriptures. Paul used the same approach when dealing with the Jews in the synagogue at Thessalonica. 'Then Paul, as his custom was, went in to them, and for three Sabbaths reasoned with them from the Scriptures' (Acts 17:2).

There are two things here. First, as Christians we must give time to reading the Bible, God's word. Without its instruction and guidance we cannot grow in our Christian lives, or know how to act in the face of the different situations that meet us in daily life. It is, as the Psalmist says, 'a lamp to my feet, and a light to my path' (Psalm 119:105). The unique thing about the Bible is that, unlike any other book, it grows on you. The more you read it, the more you want to read it, and always the Holy Spirit breaks forth new light from the word.

Second, like Stephen, when we discuss the Christian faith with others, we should always base our arguments on the scriptures. That does not mean we have to mentally bludgeon people with isolated texts. We believe that the Bible is the revelation of the mind of God, and therefore whilst we still use our reason to try to convince people of its truth we will, like Paul, 'reason with them from the scriptures'.

The God of history

In his speech, Stephen gives a panoramic view of the history of the Jewish people, beginning with Abraham the father of the nation, and ending with Jesus Christ and his gospel. He believes that God is the God of history, working through the historical events of the nation to bring to fulfilment his grand design in the coming of Jesus the Messiah. The speech divides into six parts.

First, he deals with the call of Abraham Acts 7:1–8. 'Then the high priest said, "Are these things so?" and he said, "Brethren and fathers, listen: The God of glory appeared to our father Abraham when he was in Mesopotamia, before he dwelt in Haran, and said to him, 'Get out of your country and from your relatives, and come to a land that I will show you'".' Abraham was called by God to make a great sacrifice in leaving his country, his home, and his wider family to set out on a great pilgrimage of faith. He was leaving the certainties of the present for the uncertainties of the future, but he knew that God was with him, and that he knew the way. A large part of our Christian pilgrimage through life is like that. We obey God, and must learn to trust him even when we do not understand.

Next, Stephen turns his attention to Joseph and his place in the on-going purpose of God (Acts 7:9–16). 'And the patriarchs, becoming envious, sold Joseph into Egypt. But God was with him, and delivered him out of all his troubles, and gave him favour and wisdom in the presence of Pharaoh, king of Egypt; and he made him governor over Egypt and all his house'. A phrase used more than once in connection with Joseph in the Genesis story is, 'The Lord was with Joseph' Under God's direction he eventually became prime minister of Egypt and became the saviour of the people during the famine.

Joseph's life is best summed up in his words to his brothers who had sold him into slavery. 'But as for you, you meant evil against me; but God meant it for good, in order to bring it about as it is this day, to save many people alive' (Genesis 50:20). This teaches us that, in the overruling sovereignty of God, men may plan and scheme to work out their own evil designs, but nothing can ultimately prevent God's intention to bring to fruition the unity of all things in Christ.

The third picture given by Stephen is the deliverance of the Jewish people from slavery in Egypt (Acts 7:17–36). He recounts the early life of Moses, and then comes to the point where God speaks to him out of the burning bush. 'When Moses saw it, he marvelled at the sight; and as he drew near to observe, the voice of the Lord came to him "... I have surely seen the oppression of my people who are in Egypt; I have heard their groaning and have come down to deliver them. And now come, I will send you to Egypt" ... He brought them out, after he had shown wonders and signs in the land of Egypt, and in the Red Sea, and in the wilderness forty years'.

It is under Moses that the national history of Israel really begins. Under God he welded the different tribes into a nation with its own laws, commandments and institutions given him on Mount Sinai. The greatness of Moses lay in the fact that he gave up so much to serve God. He was brought up as a prince in the royal palace, and might well have become the next Pharaoh of Egypt, but he turned his back on all that to identify with God's people. 'By faith Moses, when he became of age, refused to be called the son of Pharaoh's daughter, choosing rather to suffer affliction with the people of God than to enjoy the passing pleasures of sin' (Hebrews 11:24–25). There is a worldly, cheap kind of Christianity, which makes no demands upon us and says in effect: 'being a Christian need not change your life-style in any way, you can do all the things you did before'. That is not true. When God calls us in Christ he expects us to turn away from the world's seductions, and to be prepared for service and sacrifice.

The fourth picture deals with Israel's rebellion (Acts 7:37–43). When Moses was forty days and forty nights on Mount Sinai the people turned to Aaron and said, 'Make us gods to go before us; as for this Moses who brought us out of the land of Egypt, we do not know what has become of him. And they made a calf in those days, offered sacrifices to the idol, and rejoiced in the works of their own hands'. This was the beginning of the idolatry that was to plague Israel throughout the remainder of its history, and for which she was eventually judged by God, and sent into exile. What is idolatry? It is anything that has priority in our lives over and above God himself. Home, family, work, career—all must take second place, and even evangelical Christians find that difficult at times. Unless we are vigilant, it can so easily happen that other things can gradually push God out from the centre to the perimeter of our lives.

The fifth point Stephen makes centres on the Tabernacle and the Temple, which were at the heart of Israel's history (Acts 7:44–50). 'Our fathers had the tabernacle of witness in the wilderness, as he appointed, instructing Moses to make it according to the pattern that he had seen. ... But Solomon built him a house. However, the Most High does not dwell in temples made with hands, as the prophet says: "Heaven is my throne, and earth is my footstool. What house will you build for me? says the Lord, or what is the place of my rest? Has my hand not made all these things?"'

Stephen has already dealt with the spirit of rebellion and idolatry that had characterised the history of Israel. But he is now treading on even more dangerous ground as he criticises the Jews for wanting to confine God to the temple in Jerusalem, whereas his worship belongs to all the nations of the world. Stephen would not see it himself, but the truth of what he was saying becomes evident in Acts as the church continues to grow, and moves out beyond the confines of Judaism and Jerusalem to the wider world. And that is still the objective of gospel witness today, to bring Christ to all the nations.

In the last section of Stephen's speech, Acts 7:51–53, we sense that he breaks off from what he was saying because he was suddenly filled with a spirit which is a mixture both of righteous anger and sadness towards the members of the council. 'You stiff necked and uncircumcised in heart and ears! You always resist the Holy Spirit; as your fathers did, so do you. Which of the prophets did your fathers not persecute? And they killed those who foretold the coming of the Just One, of whom you now have become the betrayers and murderers, who have received the law by the direction of angels and have not kept it'.

These were hard truths for the Jews to swallow. He was saying that the temple would no longer be the centre of worship, that they were resisting the leading of the Holy Spirit, that in persecuting the church they were rejecting God as their fathers had done in rejecting the prophets, and above all, they had broken and disobeyed God's law by crucifying the Lord Jesus who was the embodiment and fulfilment of the law.

Naturally all this infuriated the Jewish leaders. 'When they heard these things they were cut to the heart, and they gnashed at him with their teeth' (Acts 7:54). That was to be expected, because the truth can hurt and people do not like it. It is like that with the truth of the gospel; people can get very angry when faced with it. Paul calls it, 'the offence of the cross' (Galatians 5:11). I well recall some years ago shaking hands at the church door after the morning service when a visiting lady, charming and cultured, thanked me for the message but then added, 'However, I dislike intensely being told I am a sinner'. That is 'the offence of the cross'. But such an attitude must not deter us from preaching the gospel, and declaring all men sinners and in need of God's salvation in Christ.

The first Christian martyr

In speaking boldly as he did, Stephen was signing his own death warrant and so became the first Christian martyr. He died as he had lived, with the absolute certainty in his heart of that eternal world into which he was about to enter. 'But he, being full of the Holy Spirit, gazed into heaven and saw the glory of God, and Jesus standing at the right hand of God, and said, "Look! I see the heavens opened and the Son of Man standing at the right hand of God!" Then they cried out with a loud voice, stopped their ears, and ran at him with one accord; and they cast him out of the city and stoned him' (Acts 7:55–58).

This was a terribly cruel death, more like a mob lynching than a judicial trial. But what of the vision given to Stephen? He saw the glory of God. But what exactly does that mean? Did he see a light or radiance? We cannot say, but he certainly had a sense of the visible presence of God, and of Christ Jesus exalted to a place of honour and power at the right hand of God. But no one else present had that awareness of the presence of God and of the eternal world, because they were spiritually blind to such realities. As Paul says: '… the god of this age has blinded (those) who do not believe, lest the light of the gospel of the glory of Christ, who is the image of God, should shine on them' (2 Corinthians 4:4). We may not have the outward vision of Stephen, but with the eye of faith we too 'see' beyond this world, and this life, to the reality of heaven and the eternal world.

The Martyr Spirit

William MacDonald in his booklet, *True Discipleship*, points out that not all are called to lay down their lives for the gospel and to say with F.W.H. Myers:

'Come ill, come well, the cross, the crown,
The rainbow and the thunder;
I fling my soul and body down
For God to plough them under'.

But we can have the martyr spirit. It is from the word 'martyr' that we get our word 'witness', and in the way we live, and in our speaking for Christ, we can show the same intensity and zeal as those who gave their lives for him.

But whilst we, as believers, exalt and honour the blessed memory of those like Stephen who died for the gospel, there will be those who would argue that there are others, beside Christians, who are prepared to die for their religion or ideology. And we cannot gainsay that, when at the present time we are seeing young Muslims blowing themselves to pieces as suicide bombers. But there is a profound difference between Stephen's martyr death and theirs. And this is it.

'And they stoned Stephen as he was calling on God and saying, "Lord Jesus, receive my spirit". Then he knelt down and cried out with a loud voice, "Lord do not charge them with this sin". And when he had said this, he fell asleep' (Acts 7:59–60).

Like his Saviour, Stephen prayed for the forgiveness of those who were killing him. There is nothing of the blind ferocity and hatred we associate with the suicide bombers when they step aboard a bus, or enter a shopping precinct and blow themselves, and other innocent people, to pieces. That is the difference the Spirit of the Lord Jesus makes in a person's life. They are enabled to do what Jesus asks of them: 'But I say to you, love your enemies, bless those who curse you, do good to those who hate you, and pray for those who spitefully use you and persecute you' (Matthew 5:44).

One other thing to close this chapter. We are told in verse 58, 'And the witnesses laid down their clothes at the feet of a young man named Saul'. I find the mention of this fact very encouraging. Here is a young man, as fanatical as any of the Jewish council, participating in this foul murder, but who one day—through the power of God—would become the great apostle Paul. For my own part, I have no doubt whatever that the manner in which Stephen died was a factor in that conversion experience. The young

Saul saw the invincible faith of Stephen, and the spirit of love and forgiveness he showed to those who were carrying out the stoning, including Saul himself, and it was a picture that never left him.

Indeed, years later when speaking of his conversion experience, he refers to this incident (Acts 22:19–20). We learn two things from this experience of Saul. First, we ought not to despair of anyone's conversion. We may have prayed for someone for years, perhaps a member of our own family, and we feel that they will never be saved, and we are tempted to give up praying. Do not do it; just keep on praying, believing that God can do the seemingly impossible.

Second, we never know what impact our unconscious influences have upon other people. We may not be aware of it, but just like Stephen, the way we live and die, and the manner in which we face up to the circumstances of life in the power of God, have their effect upon the lives of others. In the death of Stephen and the conversion of Saul, we see very clearly how the blood of the martyrs is the seed of the church.

Expansion of the church

Read Acts chapter 8

In the chapters already considered we have seen that the church experienced tremendous growth in the early days of its existence, in spite of stiff opposition from the Jewish authorities. In this chapter the growth continues but is now of a different kind. The emphasis is not so much about numbers, as the geographical area covered by the church's witness. Christianity now begins to expand beyond the confines of Jerusalem in fulfilment of the command and promise given by Jesus: 'But you shall receive power when the Holy Spirit has come upon you; and you shall be witnesses to me in Jerusalem, and in all Judea and Samaria, and to the end of the earth' (Acts 1:8).

The effects of persecution

What is fascinating about the expansion of the church recorded in this chapter is the manner in which it was brought about. Following the martyrdom of Stephen, the church came under enormous pressure from the Jewish leaders. 'At that time a great persecution arose against the church which was at Jerusalem; and they were all scattered throughout the regions of Judea and Samaria, except the apostles' (Acts 8:1).

This hatred—directed at the preaching of the gospel—was intended to destroy the church's ministry, but in the providence of God it had the opposite effect, since those who were scattered took the gospel with them to the remote parts of the country and so expanded the church's influence. We read in verse 4 'Therefore those who were scattered went everywhere preaching the word'. This does not mean that they set themselves up as official preachers and teachers of the word of God, but that they communicated the gospel in ordinary conversation and by the way in which they lived. The believers did not choose to flee from Jerusalem of their own accord. They did so because they were in fear of their lives, and it must have seemed to them at the time to be a total disaster. But it turned out for the church's blessing. It is a wonderful instance of the truth contained in Psalm 76: 'Surely the wrath of man shall praise you' (verse 10). The Psalmist is saying that man's hostility and rebellion towards God is absorbed, in some way or other, into the divine purpose and turned to God's praise.

Or to put it another way it reminds us that God is in absolute control of earthly events, and when it pleases him to do so he can, and does, bring good out of evil. That is something we need to keep in mind when we are passing through some difficult experience in our own personal lives.

Saul of Tarsus

The first sentence in verse 1 of this chapter, 'Now Saul was consenting to his death', really belongs to the end of the previous chapter in connection with the martyrdom of Stephen. We have already suggested that the manner in which Stephen died impressed itself upon Saul and was a factor in his later conversion. But it did not happen right away. In the persecution that followed Stephen's death, Saul was a leading figure. 'As for Saul, he made havoc of the church, entering every house, and dragging off men and women, committing them to prison' (Acts 8:3).

Not all the Christians therefore were scattered, and this helps to explain why the apostles remained in Jerusalem. They probably felt, as leaders of the church, that they should remain in the city to help and comfort those who were unable to escape the persecution. But the remarkable thing was that they were not put in prison, or even put to death, as we might have expected. It can only have been that God was watching over these men in a special way. As for Saul, the manner of Stephen's death, far from softening his heart towards the believers in the first instance, only served to harden his heart and to cause him to make a frenzied attack upon the church. The zeal and brutality with which he did this says something about the psychology underlying his later conversion experience.

It seems to me that the memory of the gracious manner in which Stephen died, with a prayer on his lips, was a picture Saul was trying to obliterate from his mind by his increasing cruelty towards the Christians. We shall see in chapter 9 that, not content with persecuting them in Jerusalem, he even obtains special permission from the Sanhedrin to pursue believers in other parts of the country. Clearly his hostility towards Christ and his gospel grew stronger and deeper before his final surrender. And that is something that still happens in the conversion experience.

I have heard people say that when they were first convicted of their sinful condition by the Holy Spirit, instead of turning towards God, they only increased their resistance and even deliberately plunged deeper and deeper into sin as if to blot out their feelings of guilt. This work of conviction and breaking down a person's resistance is specifically the action of the Holy Spirit. Speaking of this the Lord Jesus said, 'And when he has come, he will convict the world of sin, and of righteousness, and of judgement' (John 16:8). In some instances this convicting experience will go on for weeks, or months, or even years, but eventually the Holy Spirit overcomes, and the person concerned is brought to repentance, and to faith in the Lord Jesus Christ. We do not know how long it actually lasted with Saul, but on the road to Damascus he too was broken down and brought to faith in Christ.

Philip in Samaria

Among those scattered by the outbreak of persecution was Philip, one of the seven deacons. Like Stephen he was a gifted evangelist and made his way down to the city of Samaria where he carried out a very successful ministry. 'Then Philip went down to the city of Samaria and preached Christ to them. And the multitudes with one accord heeded the things spoken by Philip, hearing and seeing the miracles which he did. For unclean spirits, crying with a loud voice, came out of many who were possessed; and many who were paralysed and lame were healed. And there was great joy in that city' (Acts 8:5–8).

What do we know about Philip? Not a great deal, but from the information given in Acts it is clear that he was a good and godly man. He had a natural gift for preaching God's word, and in Acts 21:8–9 he is described as Philip the evangelist, suggesting this was an official position he now held in the church. The same passage tells us that the apostle Paul enjoyed the hospitality of Philip's home, and this could mean that they were close friends. We also learn from these verses that Philip had four daughters who prophesied, which points to the godly influence of their father.

Philip's mission to Samaria was a further advance in the witness of the church, since he was preaching not only beyond the confines of Jerusalem but to a people of a different nationality. The Samaritans were half Jewish and half Gentile and represented a sort of natural bridgehead between Judaism and the wider world. Relations between Jews and Samaritans were anything but cordial, and the cause of their mutual dislike of each other went back many centuries to the time of Ezra and Nehemiah. When the Northern Kingdom of Israel fell to the Assyrians in 721 BC, a large part of the population was deported, and Assyrians settled in their place in Samaria, Israel's capital city. These newcomers intermarried with the Jews who had been left, and became known as Samaritans. Years later, when the Jews of the Southern kingdom of Judah returned from exile in Babylon and began rebuilding the temple (see Ezra, Nehemiah) the Samaritans wanted to help in the project, but the Jews refused. Thereafter the hostility between these two peoples became more intense, so that John, in telling the story of the woman at the well in Samaria (chapter 4), quotes her as saying to Jesus: 'how is it that you, being a Jew, ask a drink from me, a Samaritan woman? For Jews have no dealings with Samaritans'.

In the light of this past history therefore, Philip's evangelism in Samaria is of deep significance for the history of the church. It had always been the divine intention to bring the Gentiles into the kingdom of God. The books of Jonah and Ruth were written with that objective in mind. Jonah was commanded by God to preach to the pagan Ninevites, who in turn repented and many were brought to salvation. Likewise Ruth came to Israel from the pagan country of Moab, and was accepted among God's people because of her faith. Later, she married Boaz, and had a child named Obed who became the grandfather of King David thus making Ruth an ancestress of David's greater son the Lord Jesus Christ.

In Isaiah we have a wonderful prophecy concerning God's servant, the Messiah, in which the gospel as a light to the Gentiles is spelled out very clearly. 'I, the Lord, have called you in righteousness, and will hold your hand; I will keep you and give you as a covenant to the people, as a light to the Gentiles, to open blind eyes, to bring out prisoners from the prison, those who sit in darkness from the prison house' (Isaiah 42:6–7). The fulfilment of this prophecy can be found in Luke 2:29–32 and Luke 4:18–19.

We can now see that in Philip's ministry in Samaria we have a transition stage in the fulfilment of God's purpose for the Gentile world.

Simon the Sorcerer

Among those who were impressed with Philip's ministry in Samaria was a weird character called Simon, a sorcerer or magician who was held in high regard by the people. 'But there was a certain man called Simon, who previously practised sorcery in the city and astonished the people of Samaria, claiming that he was someone great, to whom they all gave heed from the least to the greatest, saying, "This man is the great power of God". And they heeded him because he had astonished them with his sorceries for a long time' (Acts 8:9–11).

The belief in sorcery or magic was rife in the ancient world, and its practitioners, like Simon, were to be found in every town and city. Paul encountered it in his ministry at Ephesus. 'And many who believed came confessing and telling their deeds. Also, many of those who had practised magic brought their books together and burned them in the sight of all. And they counted up the value of them, and it totalled fifty thousand pieces of silver' (Acts 19:18–20). The enormous amount of money mentioned is an indication of how popular the practice of magic was in those days.

If we are to understand the significance of what Simon was about, we must not, in the first place, dismiss all talk about sorcery and magic as a fraud on his part, and as sheer credulity on the part of the people. We read that the people were saying, 'This man is the great power of God'. We are not dealing here with the kind of magic associated with children's parties, with the magician doing card tricks and plucking coins out of people's ears. The magic power Simon demonstrated was both real and exceedingly dangerous. He was a vehicle of the powers of the occult and the forces of darkness. In short he was an agent of Satan.

In our society today this morbid interest in the occult is once again capturing the minds and hearts of people. In any large bookstore you will find countless books on black magic, astrology, spiritism, tarot cards, fortune telling etc. And as Christian believers we should be careful not to dismiss it all as superstitious nonsense and not worth worrying about. The growing popularity of Halloween among children, with its ghouls and witches is something every Christian parent needs to take very seriously. Why? Because all these things are associated, some more than others, with the powers of evil in the world. Even the seemingly 'harmless' interest in witches and wizards by children can develop into something more sinister if parents are not careful.

There is, however another aspect to all this. People who are seriously involved in the occult, like those of Samaria and Simon himself, have a firm belief in spiritual forces working in the world. That is why they described Simon as 'the great power of God'. They accepted, as do occultists today, that behind this material world there are cosmic powers which can be harnessed for their own purposes, or for the destruction of all that is wholesome, holy and true. In the mass media today there are forces at work which have, as their deliberate and calculated aim, the destruction of the church and the abolition of the Christian faith. Given half a chance they would close every church in the country.

But what all this also does, is to speak eloquently of the fact that man is not simply a higher form of animal life, but that he has a spiritual dimension to his being which sets him apart from the rest of creation. God made him in that way, and there is nothing he can do about it however strongly he denies it. 'Then God said, "Let us make man in our image, according to our likeness"' (Genesis 1:26). If man does not satisfy his spiritual dimension in the right way, by the worship of God his creator, then he will satisfy it in any way he can, including the occult. For satisfy it he must, because he is a spiritual being.

Believer's baptism

When Philip arrived on the scene at Samaria and began preaching the gospel, and performing signs and miracles in the power of God, many of the Samaritans turned from Simon and the occult and believed in the Lord Jesus Christ. Even Simon himself confessed Christ and was baptised. 'But when they believed Philip as he preached the things concerning the kingdom of God and the name of Jesus Christ, both men and women were baptised. Then Simon himself also believed; and when he was baptised he continued with Philip, and was amazed, seeing the miracles and signs which were done' (Acts 8:12–13).

The thing to notice here is the importance of baptism and its significance. In the early church baptism was by total immersion, and it represented union with Christ by dying to the world as the waters covered the candidate in the 'watery grave', and rising with Christ to new life as the candidate came up out of the water. It has the same significance in Baptist circles today. But as is clear from this passage and elsewhere in Acts, faith must always precede baptism. That is why it is described as 'believers' baptism. One gets baptised not in order to become a Christian, but because one already is a Christian. We are told distinctly that it was only after the Samaritans 'believed Philip as he preached the things concerning the kingdom of God' that they were baptised. The act of baptism, it is sometimes said, is the outward expression of an inner experience. Without that faith in Christ and the inner experience of sins forgiven, baptism becomes no more than an empty ritual. We shall see shortly that that was true of Simon's baptism.

The visit of Peter and John

When news of the great work Philip was doing in Samaria reached the Jerusalem church, the leaders there sent Peter and John to help in establishing the new church and to give the stamp of apostolic authority to Philip's ministry. 'Now when the apostles who were at Jerusalem heard that Samaria had received the word of God, they sent Peter and John to them, who, when they had come down, prayed for them that they might receive the Holy Spirit. For as yet he had fallen upon none of them. They had only been baptised in the name of the Lord Jesus. Then they laid hands on them, and they received the Holy Spirit' (Acts 8:14–17).

There are two points to notice here. First, this passage makes a nonsense of any suggestion that Peter had some special authority as the first Pope. He had no authority to send someone else, but was himself sent with John by the collective authority of the other apostles.

Second, and more important, what is the explanation concerning the Samaritan converts that they had 'only been baptised in the name of the Lord Jesus', and only now 'received the Holy Spirit' through the laying on of the apostles hands? Does it mean that their conversion and baptism was lacking in some way and needed some 'extra' blessing by the Holy Spirit to make it complete? Not at all. We are told distinctly that they believed in Christ and therefore they were regenerated by the Holy Spirit. Their conversion was real and complete, for the Lord Jesus had already made it clear that without the Holy Spirit a person cannot be born again (John 3:1–8).

It can only mean, therefore, that what the disciples did under the hand of God was to confer on the new converts the gifts of the Holy Spirit, speaking in tongues and performing miracles, which God had already given in the early days of the gospel. It seems to me that this can be the only explanation in the light of what we are told happened next.

A false confession

We now come back to the conversion and baptism of Simon the Sorcerer. 'And when Simon saw that through the laying on of the apostles' hands the Holy Spirit was given, he offered them money, saying, 'Give me this power also, that anyone on whom I lay hands may receive the Holy Spirit' (Acts 8:18–19). It is clear that Simon *saw* the effects of the Holy Spirit in the gifts of tongues and miracles and it explains why he wanted to purchase that power for himself. It also shows that his original claim to believe in Christ followed by baptism was a false confession. So what motivated him? It was the desire for power and self-aggrandisement. When he saw Philip performing signs and miracles, he recognised a power greater than his own and wanted it to increase his influence with the Samaritans. Later, when he again saw that same power being given by Peter and John in the laying on of hands, he tried to buy it.

All this raises some important points. Should Philip have seen through the falseness of Simon's profession of faith in Christ? I do not think we can blame Philip since virtually every pastor, myself included, has baptised folk on their profession of faith only to be bitterly disappointed when they have later fallen away. For all we can go on is what people profess with the mouth, only God knows the heart. But is this an argument for not baptising immediately on profession of faith, but should we wait to see it first being worked out in practice? There is also a warning here. Simon wanted to manipulate God's power for his own purposes and for that he was severely judged, as we shall see shortly. In a sense we can sometimes be guilty of the same thing. We try to influence or manipulate God into doing what we want him to do, and some of the strategies we use can be quite childish. We stop praying, give up reading the Bible, or refuse to attend God's house in an attempt to make him change his mind. But it is of no use. God cannot be manipulated, only obeyed.

Simon also tried to buy God's favour, but that did not work either. From this we get the word 'Simony', meaning the purchase of ecclesiastical office, which was quite common in the church of the Middle Ages. If you had the price you could become a bishop or cardinal. This attempt to purchase God's favour is not entirely dead among modern day Christians. Some attempt to buy salvation by their good works, or a monastic life-style, or through the sacrament etc. But it does not work. Salvation is the gift of God's free unmerited love in the Lord Jesus Christ. All we can do is accept it gratefully through faith.

Simon's judgement

The inclusion of this incident in the story of the early church serves as a warning above all that God will not tolerate treating the Holy Spirit with contempt. God's judgement was swift and harsh. 'But Peter said to him, "Your money perish with you, because you thought that the gift of God could be purchased with money! You have neither part nor portion in this matter, for your heart is not right in the sight of God. Repent therefore of this your wickedness, and pray God if perhaps the thought of your heart may be forgiven you. For I see that you are poisoned by bitterness and bound by iniquity". Then Simon answered and said, "Pray to the Lord for me, that none of the things which you have spoken may come upon me"' (Acts 8:20–24).

Notice first that not only does Peter say that Simon's money will perish, but he himself with it. It means that under the judgement of God he was on the way to eternal destruction unless he did something about it. And that is the position of all those who know nothing of true faith in Christ. They are under God's judgement and condemnation and the threat of eternal destruction looms over them. Like Simon their 'heart is not right in the sight of God'. Their only hope therefore is to do exactly what Peter advises Simon to do. 'Repent therefore'. That is the only way to avoid God's judgement. Repentance leading to faith in Jesus Christ.

Notice secondly that we are not told if Simon accepted Peter's advice. He simply asks that prayer be made for him to escape the punishment threatened. We get no feeling that there was any sense of deep contrition of Simon's part that he had grieved the Holy Spirit. As Paul puts it: 'For godly sorrow produces repentance leading to salvation' (2 Corinthians 7:10). Simon's sorrow was over the consequences of his sin, not sorrow for the sin itself. We hear no more of Simon in the book of Acts.

In John's gospel, our Lord's conversation with the woman of Samaria ended with a prophecy that there would be a great harvest of souls among the Samaritans (John 4:35–36). That prophecy was fulfilled in Philip's ministry and in what we are told in the last verse of this passage. 'So when they had testified and preached the word of the Lord, they returned to Jerusalem, preaching the gospel in many villages of the Samaritans' (Acts 8:25).

Philip moves on

In the final section of this chapter the scene suddenly changes and we find ourselves dealing with a totally different character from Simon the Sorcerer. It all begins with Philip receiving a strange message. 'Now an angel of the Lord spoke to Philip saying, "Arise and go toward the south along the road which goes down from Jerusalem to Gaza". This is desert. So he arose and went! (Acts 8:26–27).

Philip was given divine direction in a very positive way; an angel spoke to him. Later, in verse 29, 'Then the Spirit said to Philip...' Later still in verse 39, 'the Spirit of the Lord caught Philip away...' Speaking for myself, I have sometimes wished that I was given that kind of audible, unmistakable divine guidance and direction in God's work. Take for example moving from one pastorate to another. We are happy and settled in our present pastorate and God appears to be blessing the work, then suddenly out of the blue so to speak, we receive a call from another church to become their pastor. Immediately we are faced with a dilemma. Should we move on? Is our work in our present church done? Is it a call from God? Or are we attracted by better prospects? Any pastor who takes his ministry seriously will know what I am talking about.

The question of discerning God's guidance can be a difficult one, and there are no easy answers. But certain things can be said. We cannot sit around waiting for an audible voice from above to direct us. We must use the wisdom God gives us to make plans and decisions. We must also take account of the fact that God's revealed will is to be found in teaching and principles of his word in the New Testament. Philip did not have the guidance of the New Testament. Then again we must be perfectly honest in our motives for the direction we take. Finally we must present our plans and decisions to God in prayer.

And there is another aspect to this. If it is made unmistakably clear to us what God's guidance is, are we then prepared to follow it? It was a strange and difficult thing God commanded Philip to do. He had a very successful ministry going on in Samaria, and here was God telling him to go out into the desert. That must have seemed to him the last place for an evangelist. But he obeyed the divine direction. Are we prepared for that? To take God's leading wherever it may take us?

God prepares the way

Philip may well have wondered why God was taking him from such a positive field of evangelism in Samaria and leading him to a roadway in the desert. But God knows exactly what he is doing. We may be perplexed at times by his ways and methods, but God is never perplexed. In this instance he was preparing the way for a meeting between Philip and one particular man. 'And behold, a man of Ethiopia, a eunuch of great authority under Candace the queen of the Ethiopians, who had charge of all her treasury, and had come to Jerusalem to worship, was returning. And sitting in his chariot, he was reading Isaiah the prophet' (Acts 8:27–28).

The meeting with Philip led to the conversion of the Ethiopian who was baptised (Acts 8:36–37) and took his faith with him back to Ethiopia. We can now see the purpose God had in mind. This man held a powerful position in the Ethiopian government; he was treasurer to Candace the queen and would have exercised great influence for the gospel. It meant therefore a further expansion of the church. We should never think of evangelism as a hit-or-miss affair, but that God himself is in it preparing the way. We shall have something further to say in this regard when we come to the conversion of another Gentile, the centurion Cornelius.

A true seeker

God had also prepared the way for Philip in another sense. This man's heart had already been touched by the Spirit of God. He was a proselyte or God-fearer and had come from his own country in order to worship at the temple in Jerusalem. He was also a lover of God's word in the scriptures. 'Then the Spirit said to Philip, "Go near and overtake this chariot". So Philip ran to him, and heard him reading the prophet Isaiah, and said, "Do you understand what you are reading?"' (Acts 8:29–30). Here was a man reaching out to God, and seeking and searching for the truth. And God always loves those who seek after him. The Lord Jesus said, 'Seek, and you will find' (Matthew 7:7).

The Ethiopian was earnestly seeking answers to the spiritual questions that filled his mind, so that when Philip asked if he understood the scriptural passage he was reading he replied: ' "How can I, unless someone guides me?" And he asked Philip to come up and sit with him' (Acts 8:31). Here was a man with a teachable spirit. And that is something every true seeker requires if they want to know the truth of God's salvation. There are those, Christians I mean, who are averse to being taught out of God's word because they think they know it all already and have no need of teaching, especially of the deep kind that really digs into the scriptures. The apostle Paul had folk like that in mind when he wrote to Timothy: 'For the time will come when they will not endure sound doctrine, but according to their own desires, because they have itching ears, they will heap up for themselves teachers; and they will turn their ears away from the truth, and be turned aside to fables' (2 Timothy 4:3–4).

The passage the Ethiopian was reading was the fifty-third chapter of Isaiah which is a prophecy concerning the death of Christ, and he was anxious to know who the prophet was talking about. 'So the eunuch answered Philip and said, "I ask you, of whom does the prophet say this, of himself or of some other man?" Then Philip opened his mouth, and beginning at this scripture, preached Jesus to him' (Acts 8:34–35). It was a golden opportunity for Philip, and he was not going to miss it. He could see this man was looking for answers to his spiritual need.

How would we have handled that situation? Could we have handled it? Do we know the scriptures sufficiently to explain the way of salvation to an enquirer? Philip had only the Old Testament on which to base an explanation of Christ and his Cross. But we have the whole canon of scripture and the gospel laid out so clearly in the New Testament. Having heard and received the good news of salvation the Ethiopian requests baptism, following his profession of faith. 'Now as they went down the road, they came to some water. And the eunuch said, "See, here is water What hinders me from being baptised?" Then Philip said, "If you believe with all your heart, you may". And he answered and said, "I believe that Jesus Christ is the Son of God". So he commanded the chariot to stand still. And both Philip and the eunuch went down into the water, and he baptised him. Now when they came up out of the water, the Spirit of the Lord caught Philip away, so that the eunuch saw him no more; and he went on his way rejoicing' (Acts 8:36–39).

Here again, as in Samaria, Philip makes it clear that baptism must be preceded by a profession of faith in Christ. In future years the Ethiopian would look back to that meeting with Philip on a desert road as the greatest day of his life, for on that day he experienced a new-found joy and an end to all his seeking. His song would be:

'We would see Jesus—this is all we're needing;
Strength, joy, and willingness come with the sight;
We would see Jesus, dying, risen pleading;
Then welcome day! And farewell mortal night!

Philip moved on yet again, preaching the same glorious gospel. 'But Philip was found at Azotus. And passing through, he preached in all the cities till he came to Caesarea' (Acts 8:40).

The Damascus road experience

Read Acts chapter 9

This is a key chapter in the book of Acts, because it deals with the conversion of the man whom God would use to change the history and direction of the growing church. We have already seen how Christianity created a bridgehead between Jews and Gentiles in the evangelistic work of Philip in Samaria, and how this was taken a little further with the conversion of the Ethiopian eunuch. But at this stage, no real inroad had yet been made into the Gentile world. However all that was to change with the remarkable surrender of Saul of Tarsus to Christ as his Saviour and Lord. From now on the persecutor would himself become persecuted.

A man with a purpose

'Then Saul, still breathing threats and murder against the disciples of the Lord, went to the high priest and asked letters from him to the synagogues of Damascus, so that if he found any who were of the Way, whether men or women, he might bring them bound to Jerusalem' (Acts 9:1–2).

Saul was a man with a purpose, but it was a purpose of hate and vindictiveness. He believed himself to be on a religious mission to obliterate Christianity, and he pursued that mission with a ferocious and aggressive zeal. Such a burning zeal and enthusiasm for God is in a very real sense highly commendable, but in Saul's case it was, as he himself says later of his fellow-Jews, 'a zeal for God but not according to knowledge' (Romans 10:2). Saul was a true Israelite, and he loved God sincerely, but as yet he had no true knowledge or understanding of God's salvation through Christ. But that was about to change suddenly and dramatically before he reached his destination at Damascus.

Why was Damascus so important? Well, we know from ancient sources that there was a large Jewish colony in the city, and that it had about thirty or forty synagogues. Later, when describing his persecution of the Christians, Paul says: 'And I punished them often in every synagogue and compelled them to blaspheme; and being exceedingly enraged against them, I persecuted them even to foreign cities' (Acts 26:11).

An interesting point here is that the early believers were generally known as the people of the 'Way' (v.2). This name occurs at several places in Acts— 19:9, 23, 22:4, and 24:14. This was a good description, when you think of it, because it described their way of thinking and teaching, and especially their different way of life. Moreover, we must not overlook the fact that our Lord said of himself: 'I am the way' (John 14:6), meaning that he was the way to God, and to confirm that he added: 'No one comes to the Father except through me'. Later on in Acts we read: 'And the disciples were first called Christians in Antioch' (Acts 11:26). But this change of name did not take place until many years later.

The encounter with Christ

'As he journeyed he came near Damascus, and suddenly a light shone around him from heaven. Then he fell to the ground, and heard a voice saying to him, "Saul, Saul, why are you persecuting me?" And he said, "Who are you Lord?" Then the Lord said, "I am Jesus, whom you are persecuting. It is hard for you to kick against the goads". So he, trembling and astonished, said, "Lord, what do you want me to do?" Then the Lord said to him, "Arise and go into the city, and you will be told what you must do" (Acts 9:3–6).

Saul's conversion was one of the great spiritual events in the history of the world, and there are those for whom it is also one of the most controversial. Some liberal theologians dismiss the encounter with the risen Lord Jesus. They maintain that it was the result of the conflict going on in Saul's mind, arising out of his sense of guilt associated with the death of Stephen. It was mystical and visionary in character, they say, and not a real physical happening. For example, William Barclay even explains the light from heaven as an electrical storm which was characteristic of that particular region (Acts of the Apostles, Saint Andrew Press, p. 72).

The reason liberal thinkers attempt to rationalise the event in this way is because they cannot accept, in the first instance, the supernatural character of the conversion experience. Least of all do they accept that spiritual conversion, or being 'born again', results from a personal encounter with the Risen Christ; an encounter as real as Saul's and brought about by the operation of the Holy Spirit in the heart. Neither can they accept that the change it produces in the personality is so profound, that it is a once-for-all event that cannot be repeated. It is supernatural in the sense that man himself plays no part in it, since even his response to the claim of Christ is the result of God drawing man to himself. Paul, writing later puts it like this, 'For by grace you have been saved through faith, and that not of yourselves; it is the gift of God' (Ephesians 2:8).

Of course, the form of the experience will differ from one person to another. For example, the conversion of the Ethiopian was a quiet affair, whereas that of Saul was dramatic and full of incident. But the reality of it is exactly the same. Just as Saul was turned around from being a persecuting fanatic of the gospel to its most powerful advocate, so the ordinary Christian's feelings are changed by the power of the Holy Spirit from estrangement and hostility towards God to acceptance of the gift of salvation in Christ.

Spiritual Phenomena

What are we to make of the extraordinary spiritual phenomena that accompanied Saul's conversion—the light, the falling to the ground, the voice, the blindness, and the appearance of the risen Lord? And is there anything we can learn from these strange happenings that relates to our own conversion experience? What we can say is that the history of revival makes it perfectly clear that whenever there is an out-pouring of the Holy Spirit's power it seems always to be accompanied by some strange happenings. A Doctor Macphail in an address in 1909 at Aberdeen on the 1859 revival says: '...at times the entire assembly seemed as if it were one molten mass of humiliation before God in prostrations and fallings under an overwhelming sense of sin'. George Whitefield, after preaching three times in ten hours at the Cambuslang revival in 1742, said this: 'such a commotion surely was never heard of, especially at eleven at night. It far outdid anything I ever saw in America. For about an hour and a half there was such weeping, so many falling into deep distress and expressing it in various ways…their cries and agonies were exceedingly affecting'.

But what are we to make of it all? Is it simply emotional excitement, to be written off as sensual, psychological or even Satanic? In his 'Religious Affections' Jonathan Edwards says that 'the nature of man will of necessity be disturbed and excited at the sight of his own sin in the light of a Holy God'. In short, there is nothing neat and tidy about revival. Pentecost certainly was not neat and tidy. And when we look at the spiritual deadness of the Church today, we are tempted to say with Cynddylan Jones, a great Welsh preacher: 'Better the confusion and tumult of the city, than the order and tidiness of the cemetery'.

Saul's conversion then was anything but neat and tidy. It was extraordinarily powerful and full of exciting incident. William Barclay's assertion that the light from heaven was no more than an electrical storm is quite incredible. Was Saul so stupid that he did not know an electrical storm when he experienced one? When recounting his conversion later he says distinctly: 'at midday, O king, along the road I saw a light from heaven, brighter than the sun, shining around me and those who journeyed with me' (Acts 26:13). Clearly the light was supernatural, a manifestation of the Glory of God, like that given to the shepherds at the birth of Christ (Luke 2:9), or the light that shone in Peter's cell when he was miraculously released by the angel (Acts 12:7).

We may not experience the glory of God in physical light at our own conversion, but we certainly have the spiritual light of God's glory shining into our hearts. Indeed, Paul says this is exactly what happens when Christ comes into our life. 'For it is the God who commanded light to shine out of darkness, who has shone in our hearts to give the light of the knowledge of the glory of God in the face of Jesus Christ' (2 Corinthians 4:6).

'Then he fell to the ground and heard a voice saying to him, "Saul, Saul why are you persecuting me?"' We have already seen that in times of revival people fell to the ground under the overpowering sense of the presence of God, and the awareness of their own sin. It reflects an inner sense of brokenness, surrender and humiliation. That is what happens in a true conversion, we are broken inwardly by the convicting power of the Holy Spirit as we surrender our life to the Lordship of Christ. As to the voice—it was certainly audible, since not only did Saul hear it, but also the men with him (Acts 9:7).

Scores of Christians would gladly testify that, whilst they have not audibly heard the voice of God speaking to them, they nevertheless have definitely heard God speak to them in the depths of their soul. According to the scriptures God can speak to us in many different ways, through dreams and visions, through the human voice as with a preacher, through the written word of the Bible or a Christian book, or through a particular personal experience. The important thing is that we keep ourselves open and sensitive to the movement of the Holy Spirit in our lives so that we do not miss what God has to say to us.

Saul was not at first aware of who was speaking to him, so he asks the question: 'Who are you Lord?' and receives the reply, 'I am Jesus, whom you are persecuting'. Like many since, Saul was under the impression that he was persecuting some strange human sect, not that he was up against the very power of God himself. And what a comforting and uplifting thought that is, that Christ identifies with us in our sufferings and persecutions. Those authorities and governments in the world today, who are persecuting the church of God, little realise what they are up against, and how they can never hope to win in the end, for they are fighting God himself. Furthermore, they will pay for it dearly, either in this life or on the day of judgement. That is the implication of the phrase: 'It is hard for you to kick against the goads'. This is a proverbial saying, which referred to the ox-goad, a sharp piece of iron, which the stubborn ox kicked against only to its own hurt. Saul in his stubborn resistance to the gospel was kicking against God, but to no avail. God always wins in the end. That is a hard lesson to learn, and many have had to learn it the hard way.

With the encounter over, the arrogant young Saul is left a humbled and broken man with his sight gone. 'So he, trembling and astonished, said, "Lord, what do you want me to do?" then the Lord said to him, "Arise and go into the city and you will be told what you must do". (Acts 9:6). It is not Saul's purpose or what he wants to do that is important now, but what God wants to do, and the working of his purpose through Saul in the future.

So he was led by his travelling companions into Damascus—'And he was three days without sight, and neither ate nor drank' (Acts 9:9).

Doing the difficult thing

We now have another character coming into the picture. 'Now there was a certain disciple at Damascus named Ananias; and to him the Lord said in a vision, "Ananias." And he said, "Here I am, Lord"' (Acts 9:10). We dealt with another Ananias back in chapter 5, but this man is quite different. He was a true believer, and his faith was to be tested to the limit in what happened next. 'So the Lord said to him, "Arise and go to the street called Straight, and inquire at the house of Judas for one called Saul of Tarsus, for behold, he is praying. And in a vision he has seen a man named Ananias coming and putting his hand on him, so that he might receive his sight"' (Acts 9:11–12).

Here was God asking Ananias to do a very difficult thing—to give help and healing to a man whose purpose in coming to Damascus was to put himself and his fellow-believers in prison. He was not sure at first if he could do it; it was a real challenge to his faith. 'Then Ananias answered, "Lord, I have heard from many about this man, how much harm he has done to your saints in Jerusalem. And here he has authority from the chief priests to bind all who call on your name"' (Acts 9:13–14).

In the Christian life, God will sometimes ask us to do the most difficult and testing thing, either by directly calling us to a particular task or ministry, or indirectly by allowing us to face a difficult situation as a test of our faith. In 1793 William Carey—the pioneer of the Baptist Missionary Society—felt God calling him to Bengal in India. It was a difficult challenge. His wife was forty and expecting their fourth child, she had never travelled beyond the boundary of her own village, and had no desire to do so. Also, the small church of which he was the pastor begged him not to go, and his own father advised against it. But he obeyed and went. And we are glad he did so, for he became the forerunner of modern missions. His slogan was 'Attempt great things for God. Expect great things from God'. Faith needs to be tested from time to time.

Special men for special tasks

In spite of his reservations, Ananias was prepared to do what God was asking him, particularly when he was told what God had in mind for Saul. 'Go, for he is a chosen vessel of mine to bear my name before Gentiles, kings, and the children of Israel. For I will show him how many things he must suffer for my name's sake"' (Acts 9:15–16). All true conversions are wonderful and miraculous, but some are pivotal for the work of the kingdom of God. Saul's was like that; he was a 'chosen vessel', chosen for the specific work of taking the gospel to the Gentile world. Throughout the Bible and history God has always raised up his man for the hour, special men for special tasks.

Noah, Abraham, Joseph, Moses, Elijah and others in the Bible; and in history, Augustine, Savonarola, John Huss, Luther, Calvin, Wesley and others; these were all God's men for the hour. And God can do the same with us, perhaps to a lesser degree, but it is the same grace given sufficient for the task in hand.

Ananias and Brother Saul

'And Ananias went his way and entered the house; and laying his hands on him he said, "Brother Saul, the Lord Jesus, who appeared to you on the road as you came, has sent me that you may receive your sight and be filled with the Holy Spirit". Immediately there fell from his eyes something like scales, and he received his sight at once, and he arose and was baptised. So when he had received food, he was strengthened. Then Saul spent some days with the disciples in Damascus' (Acts 9:17–19).

Three points to notice here. First, Ananias believed in the reality of Saul's conversion. What a delightful greeting he gave him—'Brother Saul'. The man who had been his enemy was now a brother in Christ. Only the power of God through the Holy Spirit can bring about a change like that.

Second, Ananias did not hold Saul's past against him. Not everyone finds it easy to do that, and Saul must have been extremely grateful. There were those in Damascus who still viewed him with deep suspicion. 'Then all who heard were amazed, and said, "Is this not he who destroyed those who called on this name in Jerusalem, and has come here for that purpose, so that he might bring them bound to the chief priests?"' (Acts 9:21). Even the apostles at Jerusalem found it difficult to accept the new Saul until Barnabas spoke up for him. 'And when Saul had come to Jerusalem, he tried to join the disciples, but they were all afraid of him, and did not believe that he was a disciple. But Barnabas took him and brought him to the apostles.

And he declared to them how he had seen the Lord on the road, and that he had spoken to him, and how he had preached boldly at Damascus in the name of Jesus' (Acts 9:26–27).

From the Christian perspective, and especially within the fellowship of the church, we must be prepared to accept a man as he is, and not concentrate on what he was before he came to Christ. Time itself will prove whether his past has been wiped out, but in the meantime let us accept him, or her, as a brother or sister in Christ.

Third, the part Ananias played in the conversion experience of Saul illustrates what a great privilege it is to be used of God in bringing someone to know Christ as their Lord and Saviour. Ananias was God's instrument, not only to restore Saul's physical sight, but also to give him spiritual sight into the truth of salvation. Saul was 'filled with the Holy Spirit' (Acts 9:17). From the human standpoint we can say that Ananias was the man who gave Paul to the church, and to the Gentile world.

There is no joy so great as the joy of being used of God to win a soul for eternity. In that marvellous book 'The Soul Winner', Spurgeon says, 'Sceptics and modern-thought men have little to do with converts: those who labour for conversions believe in conversions: those who behold the processes of regeneration see a miracle wrought, and are certain that "this is the finger of God". It is the most blessed exercise for a soul, it is the divinest ennobling of the heart, to spend yourself in seeking to bring another to the dear Redeemer's feet. If it ended there, you might thank God that ever he called you to a service so comforting, so strengthening, so elevating, so confirming, as that of converting others from their evil ways'.

Saul's ministry begins

From almost the first moment of his conversion Saul began what was to be his life's work thereafter, the ministry of preaching and evangelisation. Back in verse 20 we read: 'Immediately he preached the Christ in the synagogues, that he is the Son of God'. But his was to be no easy, comfortable ministry. The Lord had said to Ananias: 'For I will show him how many things he must suffer for my name's sake' (Acts 9:16). That suffering began right from the outset. It was infuriating to the followers of

Judaism that one of their most able young scholars, trained in the tradition of the Pharisees (Acts 26:5) should have deserted them to become a follower of the Way. They were determined to assassinate him. 'Now after many days were past, the Jews plotted to kill him … Then the disciples took him by night and let him down through the wall in a large basket' (Acts 9:23–25).

Undaunted, Saul made his way to Jerusalem and continued his ministry of preaching and evangelising. But again an attempt was made on his life. 'And he spoke boldly in the name of the Lord Jesus and disputed against the Hellenists, but they attempted to kill him. When the brethren found out, they brought him down to Caesarea and sent him out to Tarsus' (Acts 9:29–30). Clearly, more than any of the other apostles he was to become the special target of both Greek-speaking and Hebrew-speaking Jews.

Edification of the Church

'Then the churches throughout all Judea, Galilee, and Samaria had peace and were edified. And walking in the fear of the Lord and in the comfort of the Holy Spirit, they were multiplied' (Acts 9:31). The first wave of persecution was now over and the churches in the regions mentioned were able, for a time, to enjoy a period of peace. This was a profitable time for the church, for the believers were edified. The word 'edified' means essentially 'teaching' by which Christians are strengthened and built up in their faith. Up to this point the concentration in the church had been on evangelisation and reaching out into the community to bring others to Christ. And we have seen this was happening on a large scale. But now there was the need for the local fellowships to consolidate, and to deepen the spiritual foundations of the members.

That same balance is required in the local church today. There has to be evangelism and reaching out to the community with the Good News of the gospel, but at the same time God's people in the church have to be edified and taught the great doctrines of scripture so that they are strengthened in their understanding of the faith. There have to be two kinds of growth, numerically and spiritually, in numbers and in depth. Otherwise a church becomes unbalanced. If all the emphasis is on evangelisation the church may grow in size but its members will have only a superficial grasp of the gospel. Likewise, if a church is inward looking and concentrates only on depth of teaching, its people can become cold and hard and super-spiritual in their own thinking.

It seems to me those early believers got the balance just about right. The people were 'edified', and their number 'multiplied'.

Peter centre-stage

The greater part of this ninth chapter has focussed on Saul's conversion and activity. But we shall hear no more about him until chapter 13, the events of which are several years into the future. Instead, for the remainder of this chapter, verses 32–43, the emphasis is once again on Peter's apostolic ministry.

'Now it came to pass, as Peter went through all parts of the country, that he also came down to the saints who dwelt in Lydda. There he found a certain man named Aeneas, who had been bedridden eight years and was paralysed. And Peter said to him, "Aeneas, Jesus the Christ heals you. Arise and make your bed". Then he arose immediately. So all who dwelt at Lydda and Sharon saw him and turned to the Lord'. (Acts 9:32–35).

We have already dealt with the healing ministry in the early church (Acts 5:12–16). What is of interest here is the use of the term 'saints' to describe the early Christians. It is mentioned again in verse 41, and Ananias had used it in verse 13 of the believers in Damascus. It is also the word Paul uses to address believers at the beginning of several of his epistles. But what exactly is meant by the word saint? Today, in the minds of many people it seems to have a totally different meaning from that in the New Testament.

In the Roman Catholic tradition a person becomes a 'saint' when he or she is canonised by the church. This happens years, even centuries, after their death and involves a complicated process to prove their holiness and sanctity, including their ability to have performed miracles. All this of course is totally foreign to the New Testament, and has given people today the distorted idea that a saint is a figure in a stained glass window, with a halo and medieval dress.

So what is the New Testament understanding of a saint? First, the word in Greek is 'hagios', which carries the meaning of 'holy' and 'separate' and 'different'. The New Testament Christian was a saint because he or she lived a holy life, which made them different or separate from the people of the world. Writing to the Corinthian Christians, Paul begins his letter: 'To the church of God which is at Corinth, to those who are sanctified in Christ Jesus called to be saints...' (1 Corinthians 1:2). Who were these people? Were they super-spiritual, mystical, otherworldly individuals? Not at all, they were just ordinary people who lived and worked in the great seaport of Corinth, and among whom would be some who were slaves. But they had one thing in common. They had all been called of God's Spirit to be faithful in Christ Jesus and to strive, by his grace, to live a holy life different from that of the world around them. They were 'called to be saints'.

Now that may come as a shock to some Christians. For if you were to ask the average church member, 'Are you a saint?' they would immediately deny it and say something like 'O no, I do not claim to be a saint, I am simply trying, with God's help, to live a life that is pleasing to him'. And that is because they have the wrong idea of sainthood in the New Testament understanding of the word. The important question is, do we know Christ as our Lord and Saviour? If we do, then we are saints of God, called to live a life of holiness that makes us different from the world around us.

Dorcas, a lovely Christian

We dealt with the question of miracles back in chapter 4, but the miracle recorded in this next passage was something quite different—the raising to life of a dead person! 'At Joppa there was a certain disciple named Tabitha, which is translated Dorcas. This woman was full of good works and charitable deeds which she did. But it happened in those days that she became sick and died. When they had washed her, they laid her in an upper room. And since Lydda was near Joppa, and the disciples had heard that Peter was there, they sent two men to him, imploring him not to delay in coming to them' (Acts 9:36–38).

One wonders why the Christians at Joppa sent for Peter. Was it because they felt the need of the comfort and spiritual help he could give them, in the loss of Dorcas? For it seems evident that she was held in high regard by the other believers in the fellowship. She was a woman with a gracious personality, who was active and practical in her Christian faith, and deeply loved by everyone. We all know something of the loss to the local church when a member like that is taken from us. Dorcas represents all those ordinary believers we know nothing about, but without whose vital faith and hard work, life in the local church would be much poorer. The folk at Lydda may have sent for Peter because they hoped, or expected, that he might overcome the power of death and raise Dorcas to life again. We are not told anything which suggests that, but they most certainly would have heard all about the miracles of healing which Peter had performed in Jerusalem. Whatever the reason in sending for Peter, he went to them in their hour of need, and in that respect proved himself to be a true pastor of God's people. It is sometimes said that the greatest ability in a pastor is his availability.

Raising the dead

'But Peter put them all out, and knelt down and prayed. And turning to the body he said, "Tabitha, arise". And she opened her eyes, and when she saw Peter she sat up. Then he gave her his hand and lifted her up; and when he had called the saints and widows, he presented her alive. And it became known throughout all Joppa, and many believed on the Lord. So it was that he stayed many days in Joppa with Simon, a tanner' (Acts 9:40–43).

I can understand Peter putting everyone out of the room. He was about to undertake a tremendous act of faith in raising a dead person to life, and he wanted no distraction in seeking God's power through prayer. This was the kind of praying that can be hard work, and calls for absolute concentration and focussing on God. So often our minds wander in prayer, and our attention gets broken by our thoughts. Real praying is hard, concentrated effort, like Jacob wrestling with the angel. In this instance the prayer accomplished a special miracle for the glory of God and the benefit of others, and not only for Dorcas herself. For it became known 'throughout Joppa, and many believed on the Lord'.

In the New Testament there are five instances of individuals miraculously raised from the dead: the young man in Nain, Jairus's daughter, Lazarus, Dorcas, and Eutychus. But in no single instance are we told about the death experiences of these individuals. For example, in the case of Dorcas we might wish to ask: What happened to her soul when she was lying dead? Did it leave her body, and return again? And if so, where did it go? If her soul went to heaven she surely would not have wanted to come back to her body only to go through the process of sickness and death yet again? It is useless to speculate about these things however, since it would seem that the Holy Spirit has deliberately kept these matters from us.

However, there are other things that can be said quite positively. When Peter said with the power and authority of Christ, 'Tabitha, arise', she heard his voice and was restored. And when Jesus himself said to Jairus's daughter, 'little girl, I say to you arise', she too heard his voice and was restored. Speaking of the resurrection of the believer at the coming of Christ, John says we, too, shall hear his voice. 'Most assuredly, I say to you, the hour is coming, and now is, when the dead will hear the voice of the Son of God, and those who hear will live' (John 5:25).

Resurrection of the body

The raising of Dorcas, and the others mentioned, points forward to the resurrection morning. 'For the Lord himself will descend from heaven with a shout, with the voice of an archangel, and with the trumpet of God. And the dead in Christ will rise first' (1 Thessalonians 4:16). But with this difference, Dorcas, Lazarus and others were brought back to a restoration of the old body to enjoy life everlasting. 'For this corruptible must put on incorruption, and this mortal must put on immortality' (1 Corinthians 15:53).

What will it be like, this new spiritual body of ours? The answer is it will be like the risen glorified body of Christ. 'For our citizenship is in heaven, from which we also eagerly wait for the Saviour, the Lord Jesus Christ, who will transform our lowly body that it may be conformed to his glorious body' (Philippians 3:20–21). It will be a body no longer the victim of disease and pain. We will not have to nurse it, and care for it, and patch it up with spare parts to keep it going like a piece of well-worn machinery. Instead, it will be a spiritual body perfectly suited for the spiritual environment of our new home in heaven.

Admission of the Gentiles

Read Acts chapters 10 and 11

When we dealt with chapter nine we said it was a key chapter in Acts because it recorded the conversion of Saul of Tarsus who was to become Paul, the great apostle to the Gentiles. But this chapter too is a turning point in the church's history, because whereas tentative moves had been made towards the Gentile world by Philip in Samaria, and in the conversion of the Ethiopian, what we now have is the official admission of the Gentiles into the church. This was a revolutionary step, not only for the Jewish church but also in Peter's own experience of the gospel. God was about to break down in his mind the prejudice towards Gentiles built up over centuries, and to release him from the straightjacket of Jewish thinking.

Cornelius, a devout man

'There was a certain man in Caesarea called Cornelius, a centurion of what was called the Italian Regiment, a devout man and one who feared God with all his household, who gave alms generously to the people, and prayed to God always' (Acts 10:1–2). Centurions are mentioned elsewhere in the Gospels and in Acts, but Cornelius appears to have been a rare specimen since—although he was a professional soldier in the Roman army—he was also a devout God-fearer. How he came by this knowledge of the true God we cannot say, but he was certainly sincere according to the light of faith that he had. He brought up his family in the knowledge of God, he prayed regularly and he gave generously to those in need.

Taken at its face value that would be a fair description of thousands of people who belong to the church in our country today. They would regard themselves as Christians because they believe in God, are devout and sincere, attend worship regularly, are morally upright, and give generously to worthy causes. And all that is highly commendable. But we cannot overlook the fact that, like Cornelius, they still need to hear and accept the saving gospel of the Lord Jesus Christ. It was for that very reason that God spoke to him in a vision, and told him to send for Peter.

'About the ninth hour of the day he saw clearly in a vision an angel of God coming in and saying to him, "Cornelius!" And when he observed him, he was afraid, and said, "What is it, Lord?" So he said to him, "Your prayers and your alms have come up for a memorial before God. Now send men to Joppa, and send for Simon whose surname is Peter. He is lodging with Simon, a tanner, whose house is by the sea. He will tell you what you must do"' (Acts 10:3–6).

This is clearly telling us that, however deeply religious and earnest a person might be, if they are not born again by the Holy Spirit through repentance and faith in Christ, they have not truly entered into God's kingdom. We recall the instance of the scribe who came to Jesus and questioned him about the greatest commandment. He was sincere and loved God's word and Jesus said to him by way of encouragement, 'You are not far from the kingdom of God' (Mark 12:34). Jesus wanted him to take the final step of faith. Since although he was 'not far' from the Kingdom of God he was still not in it. That is exactly the position of those dear people we are now describing. In their devoutness and sincerity they are 'not far' from the kingdom of God, but without Christ they are still not in it. 'Nor is there salvation in any other, for there is no other name under heaven given among men by which we must be saved' (Acts 4:12).

Like the Ethiopian mentioned in chapter eight, Cornelius too was a man seeking the truth of God. He had found some of the answers he was looking for, but he clearly was not fully satisfied and was reaching out for deeper spiritual understanding. And God did not disappoint him, but set in motion the train of events that were to lead to his salvation. God's promise is: 'You will seek me and find me, when you search for me with all your heart' (Jeremiah 29:13).

God uses men

Although God revealed himself to Cornelius in an angelic visitation, it was not the angel who was used to bring him into the joy of salvation, but the human agent, Peter. The angel simply passed on the message: 'Now send men to Joppa, and send for Simon whose surname is Peter' (Acts 10:5). There are two important points here.

First, this shows us how important preaching is in the total ministry of the church, and how it is the primary means instituted by God for making known the truth of salvation. I believe it was Thomas Watson the old puritan who said, 'God had only one son, and he made him a preacher'. And as we study the gospels we find that although our Lord spent time healing the sick and performing miracles for people's comfort and blessing, the greater part of his ministry was given to preaching the Good News of the kingdom of God. When Peter eventually arrives at the house of Cornelius he does not simply engage in social conversation with the people gathered there, he preaches the gospel to them (Acts 10:34f).

In his letter to the Romans Paul stresses the centrality of the preached word. 'How then shall they call on him in whom they have not believed? And how shall they believe in him of whom they have not heard? And how shall they hear without a preacher? And how shall they preach unless they are sent? As it is written: "How beautiful are the feet of those who preach the gospel of peace, who bring glad tidings of good things!"... So then faith comes by hearing, and hearing by the Word of God' (Romans 10:14–17).

Second, we see in this incident how God chooses to work through men rather than through movements, through individuals rather than through organisations. Nor do they have to be extraordinary individuals. Peter himself was ordinary enough when Christ first called him, but it was on a rock-like faith such as his that the church would be built. Perhaps that is our mistake—in our churches we keep looking for better methods, better machinery, better schemes to further the kingdom, but God is looking for better men and women, those who are wholly committed to the gospel.

Cornelius acted

Following the visit by the angel, and the divine instruction to send to Joppa for Peter, Cornelius immediately did something about it. He did not waste a moment's time reflecting on whether he should take the matter further. He was in earnest about his soul, and we get a strong feeling that he got things moving straight away. 'And when the angel who spoke to him had departed, Cornelius called two of his household servants and a devout soldier from among those who waited on him continually. So when he explained all these things to them, he sent them to Joppa' (Acts 10:7–8).

We spoke earlier of those people who believe in God, are devout and sincere and attend worship regularly, but who have never taken that final step of personal faith in Christ that would bring them into God's kingdom. They seek, but do not seem to find. For where salvation is concerned, there has to come a point at which the seeking ends and something decisive is actually done about it. In this respect no man was ever more sincere and devout in the exercise of his religion than John Wesley. He had already been a clergyman in the Church of England for nine years, but was still seeking the assurance of salvation in the depths of his own soul, and was continually questioning others who claimed to have it. And then, on Wednesday 24 May 1738, he resolved not to depend any longer on his own sanctity and pursuit of righteousness, but to throw himself wholly on God's mercy by trusting in Christ alone for salvation. Here is how he describes in his own words what happened.

'In the evening I went very unwillingly to a society in Aldersgate Street, where one was reading Luther's preface to the Epistle to the Romans. About a quarter before nine, while he was describing the change God works in the heart through faith in Christ, I felt my heart strangely warmed. I felt I did trust in Christ, Christ alone for salvation: and an assurance was given me that he had taken away my sins, even mine, and saved me from the law of sin and death' (*Wesley's Journal,* 1903 condensed edition, vol. 1, p. 54). It was only when Wesley resolved to act positively by committing his life to Christ for salvation that he experienced inner peace. No one, however devout, can simply drift imperceptibly into salvation. There has to be a definite, conscious desire to embrace Christ as Saviour and Lord.

Peter's vision

As we move into the second half of chapter 10 the scene changes from Cornelius's house in Caesarea to the house of Simon the tanner in Joppa, where Peter is staying. He had gone on to the rooftop to pray when he suddenly received a vision. '... He fell into a trance and saw heaven opened and an object like a great sheet bound at the four corners, descending to him and let down to the earth. In it were all kinds of four-footed animals of the earth, wild beasts, creeping things, and birds of the air. And a voice came to him, "Rise, Peter; kill and eat". But Peter said, "Not so, Lord! For I have never eaten anything common or unclean". And a voice spoke to him again the second time, "What God has cleansed you must not call common". This was done three times. And the object was taken up into heaven again' (Acts 10: 10–16).

What we have here is a repeat of what God did in the conversion of the Ethiopian eunuch through the ministry of Philip. We said then that evangelism is never a hit-and-miss affair, and that God was involved in it by preparing the way for the meeting between Philip and the eunuch. The same thing now happens with Peter and Cornelius. Through the visit of the angel, God had already prepared the heart of Cornelius to receive the gospel from the mouth of Peter. But thirty miles away in Joppa, God—at the same time—was preparing the heart and mind of Peter for the meeting that would eventually take place between the two men. By means of the vision God wanted to break down in Peter's mind the deep-seated Jewish prejudice towards Gentiles which had been built up over centuries. According to Jewish law there were certain animals which were considered unclean, and therefore could not be eaten (Leviticus 11) When God told him in the vision to "kill and eat", Peter flatly refused. "Not so Lord! For I have never eaten anything common or unclean". But the voice rebuked him. "What God has cleansed you must not call common".

Peter was slow at first to grasp the meaning of the vision, and the fact that it was given three times tells us two very important things. First, it shows how deep Peter's prejudice was, and second, it shows God's insistence that prejudice and bigotry have no place in the gospel's scheme of things. He wanted Peter to have a world-wide outlook embracing all mankind within the offer of salvation, Jew and Gentile alike. Just as there is no distinction between clean and unclean foods, so there is no distinction in God's mind between people concerning the gospel. Peter began to get a clearer understanding of what God was telling him when he spoke to him yet again. 'While Peter thought about the vision, the Spirit said to him, "Behold, three men are seeking you. Arise therefore, go down and go with them, doubting nothing; for I have sent them"' (Acts 10:19–20). And when Peter finally arrived at the house of Cornelius, the message, as we shall see, got right through to his heart and mind and his prejudice was conquered.

Prejudice and bigotry are always to be deplored, especially in the Christian believer. To be prejudicial is to pre-judge without full knowledge of the facts, and it can so distort our thinking that it can make us deliberately blind to what is true and lovely, even when we know it to be so. It can take different forms. There is religious prejudice, social prejudice, racial prejudice, national prejudice, and so on. It can also become an expression of our personal dislike and jealousy and pride, and can be a tool that Satan uses with great effect in the hearts of God's people to hinder the gospel. In the area of evangelism, which is where Peter's prejudice was most deeply rooted, it can make us hard and uncaring of the spiritual needs of others, and self-satisfied and complacent with our own spiritual condition.

In this regard it has to be said that some evangelical churches require as radical a change in outlook as God brought about in Peter. Some churches are far too parochial and inward-looking, directing all their thought and energy to their own spiritual needs and hardly ever touching the world outside their doors. We must of course, as was said earlier, keep a right balance between responsibility to our own church and responsibility to the wider community. But we must, by all means, resist the temptation to withdraw within ourselves because we find evangelism to be so difficult today. The violence of the age, the hardness of people's hearts, and the open glamorisation and commercialisation of sin all militate against speaking out for Christ, and induce us to concentrate on ourselves alone. That is what Peter would have done in relation to the Gentiles if God had not insisted otherwise.

The meeting

When Peter finally arrived at the house of Cornelius he found a considerable number of people waiting to receive him. 'And the following day they entered Caesarea. Now Cornelius was waiting for them, and had called together his relatives and close friends. As Peter was coming in, Cornelius met him and fell down at his feet and worshipped him. But Peter lifted him up, saying, "Stand up; I myself am also a man"' (Acts 10:24–26).

The first point of interest here is the readiness with which Cornelius, his family and friends, wait to receive the message Peter will give them. This is brought out again when Cornelius explains to Peter why he had sent for him, and ends with the words: '...Now therefore, we are all present before God, to hear all the things commanded you by God' (Acts 10:33). What a congregation! Eager, expectant, willing to be taught and ready to receive whatever God would say to them through the preacher.

Does this say anything to us about the spirit—and the frame of mind—with which we attend worship on the Lord's Day? Do we come with eagerness and expectancy to hear what God has to say to us? I am reminded here of Paul's words to the Thessalonians. 'For this reason we also thank God without ceasing, because when you received the word of God which you heard from us, you welcomed it not as the word of men, but as it is in truth, the word of God, which also effectively works in you who believe' (1 Thessalonians 2:13). It is possible to be in a congregation and hear the gospel preached, and to hear it only as the word of a man—the preacher. When that happens a person may find it interesting, intellectually stimulating, and even perhaps comforting. But because they do not hear it as the word of God it will do nothing to feed their soul, or to enlighten their minds in the truth of salvation, or the understanding of God's purposes in Christ.

When we listen to the preacher in God's house we should not say to ourselves: "I wonder what he is going to say this morning," but, "I wonder what God will say to me personally out of his word this morning".

The second point of interest in this meeting between Peter and Cornelius is the reaction of both men. Cornelius fell down at Peter's feet in reverence and adoration because he was God's servant. But we get a strong feeling that Peter was embarrassed by this. 'But Peter lifted him up, saying, "Stand up; I myself am also a man"' (Acts 10:26). We like his humility. How strange therefore that the Pope, who claims to be Peter's successor, is perfectly willing for people to kneel before him and kiss his hand in homage. Years later when writing his epistles Peter says: 'God resists the proud, but gives grace to the humble. Therefore humble yourselves under the mighty hand of God that he may exalt you in due time' (1 Peter 5:5–6).

For most of us a humble spirit does not come easily. There is something deep in our human nature that loves the adulation and praise of our fellow men. That 'something' is our ego, our self-consciousness. We all have an ego and there is nothing wrong with that except when it turns into egocentricity, and unhealthy concentration on self-importance. In today's society we are encouraged through advertising and consumerism to adopt a philosophy that elevates the ego, and panders to the self. But it can only lead to a discontented spirit and the ugly itching covetousness we see so much of today.

I repeat, a humble spirit does not come naturally for most of us. We have to work to cultivate it. And we can not do it alone. That is why Peter says: 'humble yourselves under the mighty hand of God, that he may exalt you in due time'. If we are not first willing to humble ourselves under God, we certainly will not be humble towards anyone else. The Lord Jesus said: 'Take my yoke upon you and learn from me, for I am gentle and lowly in heart, and you will find rest for your souls' (Matthew 11:29).

God has no favourites

As a result of his meeting with Cornelius and his friends, Peter's prejudice was totally rooted out, and he saw with crystal clarity that there is no favouritism with God. 'Then Peter opened his mouth and said: 'In truth I perceive that God shows no partiality, but in every nation whoever fears him and works righteousness is accepted by him' (Acts 10:34–35). He continues this theme of God's willingness to save all men through Christ right down to verse 43 ending with the words: 'To him all the prophets witness that, through his name, whoever believes in him will receive remission of sins' (Acts 10:43).

The great truth that had burst upon Peter's mind, that God is not partial and has no favourites among men or nations, was later accepted officially by the church, as we shall see in chapter 11. It is also echoed in many other parts of the New Testament. James says: 'My brethren, do not hold the faith of our Lord Jesus Christ, the Lord of glory, with partiality'. He then gives an illustration of what he means. 'For if there should come into your assembly a man with gold rings, in fine apparel, and there should also come in a poor man in filthy clothes and you pay attention to the one wearing the fine clothes and say to him, "You sit here in a good place", and say to the poor man, "You stand there", or "Sit here at my footstool", have you not shown partiality among yourselves, and become judges with evil thoughts?"' (James 2:1–4).

Favouritism or partiality of this kind has no place in the Christian life as is clear from the way in which God has used some of the lowliest and poorest people to further the Gospel. John Bunyan was a tinker without any formal schooling, yet God used him to write one of the most influential books the world has ever known. William Booth was a pawn-broker's assistant at one time, but under the hand of God he created the organisation for social and spiritual good that is now world-wide—the Salvation Army. And where would we stand in the matter of our salvation if it depended on God showing preference because of our goodness, or intelligence, or wealth or social standing? As it is he treats us all alike: 'for all have sinned and fall short of the glory of God' (Romans 3:23).

The anointing of the Spirit

Peter had not even finished his message when something profound happened. 'While Peter was still speaking these words, the Holy Spirit fell upon all those who heard the word. And those of the circumcision who believed were astonished, as many as came with Peter, because the gift of the Holy Spirit had been poured out on the Gentiles also. For they heard them speak with tongues and magnify God' (Acts 10:44–46).

Here was another Pentecost happening, this time in connection with the Gentiles, and even the Jews accompanying Peter could not argue against it. They were 'astonished'. To us it seems natural enough that where the Word of God is preached as Peter had done, and the Holy Spirit honours that word, men should then be saved whoever they are. But that is because we ourselves have been privileged to receive that salvation. For those circumcised Jews it was a real shock to the system that God should care as much about Gentiles as he did about them. It was all so incredibly new and exciting that in no time at all the news reached the Jerusalem church.

As we move into chapter 11 it is evident that there ought to be no division at this point since it forms the sequel to Peter's experience in the house of Cornelius. 'Now the apostles and brethren who were in Judea heard that the Gentiles had also received the word of God. And when Peter came up to Jerusalem, those of the circumcision contended with him, saying "You went in to uncircumcised men and ate with them!" But Peter explained it to them in order from the beginning' (Acts 11:1–4). In response to this criticism Peter simply related the facts of what had happened in the house of Cornelius (verses 4–17), and since facts are such stubborn things the protest quickly died down and this new and exciting development in the church was accepted. 'When they heard these things they became silent; and they glorified God, saying, "Then God has also granted to the Gentiles repentance to life!"' (Acts 11:18).

Two things emerge from this passage. First, it demonstrates clearly that Peter had no special primacy or authority in the church as claimed by the Roman Catholics. He was held accountable for his actions like everyone else, and even had to defend himself against the charges wrongly made against him. Second, by simply recounting how the Holy Spirit had come upon Cornelius and his household Peter was providing his fellow-Jews with evidence they simply could not refute. It was as though he said to them: 'You may not like the idea of Gentiles receiving the gift of the Holy Spirit, but that in fact is what happened'. Where the gospel is concerned the fact of personal experience is still the best evidence to an unbelieving world. When people see the truth of Christianity demonstrated in our own lives, that is much more likely to silence their opposition than any intellectual argument we might present them with.

A new direction

From this point onwards, the history of the church in Acts takes a new direction and is chiefly concerned with the spread of the gospel in the Gentile world beginning at Antioch, one of the most important cities in the Roman empire. 'Now those who were scattered after the persecution that arose over Stephen travelled as far as Phoenicia, Cyprus, and Antioch, preaching the word to no one but the Jews only. But some of them were men from Cyprus and Cyrene, who, when they had come to Antioch, spoke to the Hellenists, preaching the Lord Jesus. And the hand of the Lord was with them, and a great number believed and turned to the Lord' (Acts 11:19–21).

The preaching of the gospel had great success in Antioch, so much so that the Jerusalem church sent Barnabas to give them encouragement and direction. They could not have sent anyone better, as we discovered from our study of the character of Barnabas back in chapter 4:36–37. 'When he came and had seen the grace of God, he was glad, and encouraged them all that with purpose of heart they should continue with the Lord. For he was a good man, full of the Holy Spirit and of faith. And a great many people were added to the Lord' (Acts 11:23–24). It was clear to Barnabas that this new direction the church was taking was perfectly in line with God's will, and was progressing so fast that he would never cope with it alone. At this point he brings Saul into the picture, because he was aware that God had already sent him to be the apostle to the Gentiles. 'Then Barnabas departed for Tarsus to seek Saul. And when he had found him, he brought him to Antioch. So it was that for a whole year they assembled with the church and taught a great many people. And the disciples were first called Christians in Antioch' (Acts 11:25–26).

The new name 'Christians' fitted well with the new direction of the church and had threefold significance. First, it shows that the preaching of the church and its ministry was centred on the person of Christ. Second, it identified the believers as a significant number and force in the community. Third, it served to signify that the Gentile converts were not simply an offshoot of Judaism, but belonged to an entirely new and different movement.

Church order

The final section in this chapter is of particular interest because it introduces us to two further offices in the church, prophets and elders, in addition to apostles and deacons. 'And in these days prophets came from Jerusalem to Antioch. Then one of them, named Agabus, stood up and showed by the Spirit that there was going to be a great famine throughout all the world, which also happened in the days of Claudius Caesar' (Acts 11:27–28). Agabus is mentioned again in Acts 21:10–11, when he prophesies what will happen to Paul if he insists on going to Jerusalem. The office of prophet occurs also in Acts 13:1 and 15:32. The prophet travelled around the various churches and carried out a ministry of prediction (foretelling), and proclamation (forthtelling). They were men endowed with the special gift of wisdom by the Holy Spirit, and their main task was to give guidance to local churches.

In response to the prophecy of Agabus of the coming famine in Judea, the Gentile church in Antioch showed its unity with, and concern for, their Jewish brethren in the mother church at Jerusalem by sending relief. 'Then the disciples, each according to his ability, determined to send relief to the brethren dwelling in Judea. This they also did and sent it to the elders by the hands of Barnabas and Saul' (Acts 11:29–30). Unlike the prophets, the elders remained in one place and were responsible for discipline and government in the local church. They are mentioned frequently: Acts 14:23, 1 Timothy 4:14; Titus 1:5; and they are sometimes called presbyters. The elders were of two kinds: those chiefly concerned with church government were 'ruling elders', and those mainly concerned with preaching were 'teaching elders' (1 Timothy 5:17) or pastors.

From all this we get a picture of the church gradually becoming more organised and united as it continued to grow and prosper under the hand of God.

Peter's imprisonment

Read Acts chapter 12

Virtually the whole of this chapter is concerned with Peter's miraculous escape from prison. But what adds to its interest is the fact that this is the last we shall hear of Peter's activity in the early church in Acts. From chapter 13 onwards everything is centred on Paul and his missionary journeys as he spearheads the new direction the church takes into the Gentile world.

The Herods and persecution

The chapter opens with a fresh wave of persecution breaking out against the mother-church at Jerusalem. 'Now about that time Herod the king stretched out his hand to harass some from the church. Then he killed James the brother of John with the sword' (Acts 12:1–2). People tend to get confused with the different Herods mentioned in the Gospels and Acts, so let us clarify who the main ones were. First, there was Herod the Great. He reigned at the time of the birth of Jesus, and was responsible for the massacre of the children of Bethlehem (Matthew 2). Then there was Herod Antipas who was responsible for beheading John the Baptist at the request of Herodias and her daughter (Mark 6). And in the present chapter we have Herod Agrippa the grandson of Herod the Great.

Although Agrippa was educated in Rome and spent a considerable time there being on good terms with the emperors, he nevertheless had strong Jewish feelings, and—according to Josephus the Jewish historian—he was 'exactly careful in the observance of the laws of his country, not allowing a day to pass without its appointed sacrifice'. This adherence to Judaism explains his persecution of the church, and his desire to please the Jews by imprisoning Peter. 'And because he saw that it pleased the Jews, he proceeded further to seize Peter also. Now it was during the Days of Unleavened Bread. So when he had arrested him, he put him in prison, and delivered him to four squads of soldiers to keep him, intending to bring him before the people after Passover' (Acts 12:3–4).

Herod had already put James to death and he fully intended executing Peter as well. But since it was Passover, when no executions were allowed, he had to defer carrying out the sentence until after the festival. Both James and Peter therefore were victims of Herod's desire to please the Jews. But we must keep in mind that it was not simply Herod and the Jews that the early Christians were up against. Behind the persecution and imprisonment of Peter was all the malignant power of the evil one. Herod was simply a tool in the hands of Satan, just as those governments and rulers are in parts of the world today where there is strong opposition to the gospel of Christ. In the church we need to be acutely aware that the enemy faced by those early believers is still prowling the world today.

A W Tozer reminds us that, from the Christian perspective, we are to see the world as a battleground and not a playground; we are here to fight and not to frolic. And of course he is absolutely right.

Prayer versus prison

'Peter was therefore kept in prison, but constant prayer was offered to God for him by the church' (Acts 12:5). Martin Luther said he would rather have an army against him than a hundred men and women praying. We know exactly what he meant, but Herod would not have understood it. He thought he was up against Peter and the other misguided people who belonged to the church. But in reality he was up against all the mighty powers of heaven being harnessed by the prayers of God's people.

In the spiritual warfare we are engaged in the greatest weapon in our armoury is the power of prayer. The church in this instance was again faced with a crisis situation. First Stephen was put to death, then James, and now there was the real possibility that Peter would be taken from them as well. With the leaders being gradually removed, what could they do? They had no one in authority to plead their cause, and they were far removed from having influence in high places. But they believed strongly in the power of prayer, and they harnessed it for the battle in hand.

But this was not a prayer hurriedly flung up to heaven. It was a period of intercession, which seems to have lasted for the whole of the time Peter was in prison. We are told distinctly, 'constant prayer was offered to God for him by the church'. We know it was night-time when Peter was eventually delivered (Acts 12:6), and in verse 12, when he arrived at the house of Mary, we learn that 'many were gathered together praying'. It might well have been the early hours of the morning by this time, so the gathered Christians may have been praying through the greater part of the night.

Intercessory prayer is a great privilege, for it is a means God himself has provided whereby he acts on our behalf. There are scores of examples in the Bible of the effectiveness of intercessory prayer, and that should encourage us to engage in it. Samuel rated it so highly that he believed it to be a sin if he failed to use it in his ministry to Israel. 'Moreover, as for me, far be it from me that I should sin against the Lord in ceasing to pray for you' (1 Samuel 12:23). And God instructed his servant Job to pray for the friends who had treated him so badly. 'My servant Job shall pray for you. For I will accept him, lest I deal with you according to your folly; because you have not spoken to Me what is right as My servant Job has' (Job 42:8).

One of the exciting things about intercessory prayer, to my mind, is its secrecy. We may have a member of our family, or a friend, we are longing to see coming to faith in Christ. But all our attempts to talk about salvation are strongly resisted, and it is made perfectly clear that they would rather we did not talk about it. What they cannot do is stop us praying, and they are not even aware of it.

Peace amid crisis

In verse 6 we have one of the most remarkable statements in the whole narrative of Peter's imprisonment. 'And when Herod was about to bring him out, that night Peter was sleeping, bound with two chains between two soldiers, and the guards before the door were keeping the prison'.

Is that not amazing? Here is Peter in a prison cell, chained at either hand to a soldier, aware that James—his brother in Christ—has already been executed, and knowing that he is to undergo the same fate the next morning, and what is he doing? He is sleeping fast like a child, as if he were in a comfortable bed at home! It is a wonderful example of the words of Isaiah: 'You will keep him in perfect peace, whose mind is stayed on you, because he trusts in you' (Isaiah 26:3). Or this from the Psalmist: 'He gives his beloved sleep' (Psalm 127:2). It also reminds us of the Saviour asleep in the boat in the middle of a storm (Matthew 8:23–27).

This picture of Peter sleeping on the eve of his execution, and sleeping so soundly the angel had to strike him, is surely teaching us that those who trust in God absolutely can know an inner peace, even in the most severe crisis. Ours is a frenetic and neurotic age when so many people appear agitated and disturbed, and even fearful under the pressures of modern life, and they would give anything for so much as a handful of real peace. John Henry Jowett, one time minister of Westminster Chapel, wrote, 'how can God give us peace when our life is hurrying at a precipitate rate? I have stood in the National Gallery and seen people gallop round and glance at twelve of Turner's great paintings in the space of a few minutes. Surely we might say to them: "Be still, and know Turner". How much more then should we say to ourselves: "Be still and know that I am God"' (Psalm 46:10).

If we want to quieten the inner conflict and turmoil that can characterise our life, then we must come to know peace *with* God, before we can experience the peace *of* God in our heart. As Paul puts it: 'Therefore having been justified by faith, we have peace with God through our Lord Jesus Christ' (Romans 5:1). He means that when we are reconciled to God and at peace with him through the sacrifice of Christ, we know our sins are forgiven, heaven is our home, and our conscience is at rest. It is only then that the peace of God can reign in our hearts. And it is a peace, which Christ contrasts sharply with the ephemeral peace of the world when he promised, 'Peace I leave with you, my peace I give to you, not as the world gives do I give to you. Let not your heart be troubled, neither let it be afraid' (John 14:27).

The deliverance

Peter's escape from prison is one of the most thrilling and exciting episodes in the New Testament, especially since God himself planned it all. 'Now behold, an angel of the Lord stood by him, and a light shone in the prison; and he struck Peter on the side and raised him up, saying, "Arise quickly!" And his chains fell off his hands' (Acts 12:7). Now let us stop there for a minute and consider what really happened, because it is amazing the extraordinary lengths liberal commentators will go to in order to avoid accepting a miraculous account like this. William Barclay writes: 'in this story we do not necessarily need to see a miracle. It may well be the story of a thrilling rescue and escape' (*Acts,* Saint Andrew Press, p101). He is implying that Peter's deliverance is similar to the Colditz story of British POW's who escaped from the notorious prisoner of war camp in the Second World War. How Peter's friends were supposed to 'rescue' him when he was guarded by sixteen soldiers, and chained to a guard by both hands, Barclay does not say. Or take this comment: 'To be sure, there is always the possibility that this story, like the other similar ones in the Acts, has been embroidered by later hands, and that the story as it now stands is the produce of fact around which the filaments of fiction have been affectionately woven' (*Acts, Interpreter's Bible.* Abingdon Press, 1954, p. 155).

This liberal approach has to be rejected for two fundamental reasons. First, it denies the power of prayer such as the church was engaged in during the imprisonment, and second, it denies the element of the supernatural and miraculous in God's dealings with mankind. For we are told specifically that 'an angel of the Lord stood by him, and a light shone in the prison'. It reminds us of the supernatural light that shone around Saul on the Damascus road. Furthermore, if we reject the miraculous in Peter's deliverance then we must do the same with accounts of other deliverance's in the Bible—the deliverance from Egypt by the miracles God did through Moses; the deliverance of Jonah from the great fish; the deliverance of the three men from the fiery furnace; the deliverance of the Jews from Exile and so on. Follow this route and we end up rejecting the veracity of the Bible's message altogether.

So what should our position be when it comes to God's power to deliver from the critical situations that face us in this life? We should adopt the approach of the three men about to be cast into the fiery furnace in their answer to king Nebuchadnezzar. 'Our God whom we serve is able to deliver us from the burning fiery furnace, and he will deliver us from your hand, O king. But if not, let it be known to you, O king, that we do not serve your gods, nor will we worship the gold image which you have set up' (Daniel 3:17–18). There you have the two sides of faith. On the one hand we need not doubt for one minute that God 'is able to deliver us', because he has the power to do so. As Wesley puts it in one of his hymns: 'Give me the faith which can remove and sink the mountain to a plain'. That is the confidence of faith. But then comes the other statement. 'But if not, let it be known to you, O king, that we do not serve your gods'. That is the courage of faith. We believe God has the power to deliver, but if he chooses not to do so—for whatever reason—then we accept that as well, without it diminishing our faith in any way. That is what God asks of us, and I believe it was Peter's frame of mind in his prison cell, and why he was fast asleep in such a critical situation. It was all in God's hands.

One other thing arising out of this verse. If we should doubt at any time God's power to deliver, then we should remind ourselves of the most glorious deliverance of all, which he accomplished in delivering us from the power and penalty of sin through the Cross of Christ. Wesley must surely have had this incident in mind when he wrote these lines:

'Long my imprisoned spirit lay
Fast bound by sin and nature's night;
Thine eye diffused a quickening ray—
I woke; the dungeon flamed with light;
My chains fell off, my heart was free.
I rose, went forth, and followed thee'.

What a glorious deliverance it is when we enter into the fullness of salvation in Christ. The light of the glory of God shines into our heart, the chains of sin that bind us fall away, and we rise and enter into the joy of perfect freedom.

Our limitations

'Then the angel said to him, "Gird yourself and tie on your sandals"; and so he did. And he said to him, "Put on your garment and follow me". So he went out and followed him, and did not know that what was done by the angel was real, but thought he was seeing a vision. When they were past the first and second guard posts, they came to the iron gate that leads to the city, which opened to them of its own accord; and they went out down one street, and immediately the angel departed from him' (Acts 12:8–10).

The part Peter played in the drama of his escape was very limited in comparison with all that the angel did. He dressed himself and followed the angel, and that was about all. God did the rest. That illustrates our human limitations. There are certain things in this life that we cannot do in, and of, ourselves. The power of God is needed to help us out, however clever and civilised we consider ourselves to be. But modern man is slow to take this lesson on board. In his arrogance and in his pride in his advancing knowledge and technology he thinks he can do just about anything, and that he has no need of God's direction and intervention. 'What do I need God for' he says in effect. 'I have my own powers and abilities, and I can shape my own destiny and achieve my own salvation in this life. God is obsolete'. Modern man's creed is encapsulated in those lines of Swinburne:

'But God, if a God there be, is the
Substance of men which is Man.
Glory to Man in the highest! For
Man is the master of things'
(*Hymn to Man*)

Or this by William Ernest Henley:

'It matters not how strait the gate,
How charged with punishments the scroll,
I am the master of my fate;
I am the captain of my soul'
(*Invictus*)

But where has this arrogant spirit got us? I am writing this when in a recent speech the Prime Minister warned us that we are living in a dangerous and unstable world. Terrorism is no longer a mere threat but a dreadful reality, and it is now commonplace to see our police at airports and important buildings carrying sub-machine guns. All this speaks volumes concerning man's inability, with all his boasting, to govern and control the world for the betterment of society and for the good of all. And that, it must be said, is with the civilising influences of millennia behind us. The truth is that outside of God man is a very limited creature indeed, because he is the victim of his own fallen nature.

But there is a lesson here for believers too. The miraculous element looms large in this story. But it is significant that God did not do miraculously for Peter what Peter could do for himself. Only God's power could shine the light of heaven into the dark cell, break the chains, lead Peter safely past the guard posts, and open the iron gate that led to freedom. The other things Peter had to do for himself—put on his clothes and sandals, and get up and follow the angel. In any situation calling for deliverance, God has given us a measure of ability and sanctified common sense, and he expects us to use these gifts. What we can do, we must do, and leave the rest to God. And this applies, in a sense, in the area of our salvation. Only God's power can initiate the deliverance from sin through the convicting work of the Holy Spirit in the heart. And until God begins the process we are as helpless to break with sin as Peter was to break the chains of his imprisonment. But the responsibility to respond in obedience and faith to that movement of God's Spirit is ours, just as Peter had to respond in obedience to the command of the angel to follow him to freedom.

Assurance and deliverance

'And when Peter had come to himself, he said, "Now I know for certain that the Lord has sent his angel, and has delivered me from the hand of Herod and from all the expectation of the Jewish people"' (Acts 12:11). Up to this point Peter was like a man in a dream, hardly comprehending what was happening to him. Back in verse 9 we are told that when the angel first appeared, Peter felt that the whole experience was a vision, it was so unexpected and unreal, especially since he had woken from a deep sleep. But the moment the angel left him, he 'came to himself', and knew that his deliverance was a reality, and he praised God. 'Now I know for certain that the Lord has sent his angel and has delivered me...'

At the spiritual level the parallel to Peter's experience is the believer's inner assurance and certainty that his salvation and deliverance from the penalty and power of sin is real and for all eternity. He is able to say with Peter, 'Now I know for certain ... that the Lord has delivered me'. Or, as

Paul puts it: 'I know whom I have believed and am persuaded that he is able to keep what I have committed to him until that Day' (2 Timothy 1:12). Or this: '… being confident of this very thing, that he who has begun a good work in you will complete it until the day of Jesus Christ' (Philippians 1:6).

But having said that it is true to say that many, if not most of us, do in fact struggle at times between confidence and doubt, hope and fear, trust and despair. And as long as we live in this sinful world this struggle will continue, since it is a part of the spiritual warfare we are engaged in as God's children. The important thing, especially where the assurance of salvation is concerned, is that we do not allow Satan to exploit these times of uncertainty, and undermine our faith in God's keeping power. For God *will* keep us, that is his promise. We must turn to passages like this: 'My sheep hear my voice, and I know them, and they follow me. And I give them eternal life, and they shall never perish; neither shall anyone snatch them out of my hand' (John 10:27–28). When we remind ourselves of a promise like that, our feeble wavering faith is turned to confidence and certainty.

God exceeds our expectations

When the angel had left Peter the next question facing him was, where do I go from here? Then after a few moments reflection he decided to make for the house of Mary. 'So, when he had considered this, he came to the house of Mary, the mother of John whose surname was Mark, where many were gathered together praying' (Acts 12:12). Why this house? Probably because Peter knew that it was a place where the believers were accustomed to meet, just as other disciples met in similar house groups in other parts of the city. After all, there were no church buildings at that time, and the Christians had to use their homes as meeting places. Who knows? We may slowly be drifting back to that early pattern of church life and organisation in our country if the decline in spiritual life continues. But whatever happens, there will always be God's remnant meeting for worship and praise, whether in individual homes, church buildings, or elsewhere.

For it is not *where* we meet that is most important, but *why* we meet together. In this instance the believers were meeting together to pray for Peter's situation. And when *we* meet together, the object must be to glorify God and to encourage one another by our prayers and praise and worship.

The writer to the Hebrews urges us to 'consider one another in order to stir up love and good works, not forsaking the assembling of ourselves together, as is the manner of some, but exhorting one another, and so much the more as you see the Day approaching' (Hebrews 10: 24–25).

When Peter arrived at Mary's house, what happened? 'And as Peter knocked at the door of the gate, a girl named Rhoda came to answer. When she recognised Peter's voice, because of her gladness she did not open the gate, but ran in and announced that Peter stood before the gate. But they said to her, "You are beside yourself!" Yet she kept insisting that it was so. So they said, "It is his angel". Now Peter continued knocking, and when they opened the door and saw him, they were astonished. But motioning to them with his hand to keep silent, he declared to them how the Lord had brought him out of the prison. And he said, "Go, tell these things to James and to the brethren". And he departed and went to another place' (Acts 12:13–17).

Some commentators draw the conclusion that because the Christians in the house did not accept Rhoda's statement that Peter was at the door, they therefore did not believe that God could answer their prayer. But I do not go along with that, and regard it as a somewhat unjust criticism. The truth is we do not know that they were praying for Peter's deliverance. James had already been put to death, and they may have anticipated that the same would happen to Peter. Therefore they may well have been praying that God would give him the grace to face up to his execution with courage and not weaken in his faith. So when they saw him at the door, they were astounded and overjoyed. God had not only answered their prayers, but had done far more than they expected. This should not surprise us, for we have a mighty God who often exceeds our expectations.

Divine retribution

But even that was not the end of the story. In the final verses of this chapter we see what a violent and evil tyrant Herod really was. 'Then, as soon as it was day, there was no small stir among the soldiers about what had become of Peter' (Acts 12:18). The words: 'no small stir' indicates that Herod and his men were baffled and agitated by Peter's disappearance and realised this was no ordinary escape. That was why they had Peter guarded so closely with sixteen soldiers, and chained on either hand. In the light of all the supernatural things that had happened in Jerusalem, Herod was taking no chances that something equally strange might happen with Peter. But although the supernatural *had* occurred in Peter's case, the significant thing is that it did not affect in the slightest Herod's attitude towards God or the church. He was as contemptuous as ever, and in an outburst of ferocity he blamed the guards and had them put to death (Acts 12:19).

But Herod was to pay a terrible price for his contempt of God, as the final verses make clear. He had fallen out with the people of Tyre and Sidon, and in due course a public session was arranged at which he gave a great oration. 'So on a set day Herod, arrayed in royal apparel, sat on his throne and gave an oration to them. And the people kept shouting, "The voice of a god and not a man!" Then immediately an angel of the Lord struck him, because he did not give glory to God, and he was eaten by worms and died' (Acts 12:21–23). Josephus the Jewish historian gives a vivid account of this scene in book 19 of his Antiquities. He describes how Herod was dressed in a robe of silver, which glinted in the sun so that the people cried out that he was a god. Suddenly he was struck down with dreadful pain, and after suffering from a dreadful disease in the bowels for five days, he died in terribly agony at the age of fifty-one.

What do we gather from all this? It shows that Herod was a typical example of the person our Lord had in mind when he speaks of the unpardonable sin, or the sin against the Holy Spirit (Matthew 12). It refers to the man or woman whose heart is so hardened, and who is so obdurate in their hatred and rejection of God, that they put themselves beyond redemption. There are many examples in scripture: Pharaoh, Ahab, Jezebel, Belshazzar, and Judas. Herod, by his callousness, his violence against the church, and his pride and blasphemy in receiving the worship that belongs to God alone, brought upon himself the divine retribution. The whole incident is a grave warning to everyone that God is not mocked.

With the death of Herod, and the threat of persecution removed for the time being, we read in the final verse, 'But the word of God grew and multiplied'.

The first missionary journey

Read Acts chapter 13

Before we begin our exposition of the chapter, a word of explanation is necessary. Chapter twelve ends with the words: 'And Barnabas and Saul returned from Jerusalem when they had fulfilled their ministry, and they also took with them John whose surname was Mark' (Acts 12:25). This takes us back to the closing verses of chapter 11 where we are told that Barnabas and Saul were sent by the brethren at Antioch with a gift for the members of the church at Jerusalem who were suffering hardship because of the famine. The episode of Peter's imprisonment therefore, is a kind of interlude between these two references. Barnabas and Saul have now returned to Antioch bringing with them John Mark, whose home was in Jerusalem (Acts 12:12), and who would accompany them on the first missionary journey with which our present chapter opens.

The church at Antioch

'Now in the church which was at Antioch there were certain prophets and teachers: Barnabas, Simeon who was called Niger, Lucius of Cyrene, Manaen who had been brought up with Herod the tetrarch, and Saul. As they ministered to the Lord and fasted, the Holy Spirit said, "Now separate to me Barnabas and Saul for the work to which I have called them". Then, having fasted and prayed, and laid hands on them, they sent them away' (Acts 13:1–3).

We need not say anything about prophets and teachers since we dealt with their role when looking at church order at the end of chapter 11. But fasting is twice mentioned, and that calls for some comment. The principle of fasting has always had its place in the life of the church, but it was never intended by God to become an end in itself, and for that reason it is not commanded in either the Old or New Testaments. The only fast commanded by God was on the Day of Atonement when the whole nation repented of its sins (Leviticus 16:29). But people did fast in Biblical times, and the practice has continued all through the history of the church. The reformers, Luther, Calvin and Knox fasted. So did Whitefield, Wesley and other leaders of the eighteenth century evangelical awakening. David Brainard, apostle to the Indians, and pastor Hsi of China also fasted. These were all mighty men of God so that fasting must have some significance in the spiritual life.

One of the criticisms made of Jesus was that he and his disciples did not practice fasting, (except for the forty days in the wilderness) whereas the disciples of John the Baptist and the Pharisees did (Mark 2:18). From the reply of Jesus we gather that fasting had become almost an essential principle of the Christian life and more or less an end in itself, instead of a means to an end. Fasting has its place as a Christian discipline. But the warning here, and it applies to other things in the Christian life, is against elevating a secondary matter into a primary and essential principle for salvation and the life of holiness.

Barnabas and Saul set apart

At this point the name order is 'Barnabas and Saul', but from verse 9 in this chapter not only is Saul's name changed to Paul, but the order thereafter is 'Paul and Barnabas'. But we saw back in chapter 4, when Barnabas is first introduced, that he would not have minded that one bit. After all, it was he who introduced Paul to the church at Antioch since he knew he was the man God had called to be the apostle to the Gentiles. When the disciples of John the Baptist expressed a jealous regard for him because people were leaving him to follow Jesus, he replied: 'He must increase, but I must decrease' (John 3:30). That would have been the mind-set of Barnabas in his relation to Paul, and it shows us what a big man he really was.

But both men were equally called of God by the Holy Spirit, '"Now separate to me Barnabas and Saul for the work to which I have called them". Then, having fasted and prayed and laid hands on them, they sent them away' (Acts 13:2–3). This setting apart by the church underlies the practice in today's church of ordaining men to the pastorate, or commissioning them for overseas mission. But in the case of Barnabas and Saul it was God himself who called them, but men who separated them. This teaches us that if a man is not called of God in the first instance, then no ceremony of ordaining or commissioning will impart to him that authority which signifies it is from God.

Another aspect here is that whilst Barnabas and Saul were special men separated for a special task, there is also a call to separation that applies to all Christians. In Christ we are called out of darkness into light; to be separate from the world for a life of service and holiness. We said something about this when looking at the meaning of the word 'saint' back in chapter 9:32. The separation the New Testament urges on us is not the monastic principle of physical separation from the world. It is being in the world but not of it. We do not share its values and standard, or agree with its emphasis on the material as opposed to the spiritual. In the apostle's words: 'do not be conformed to this world, but be transformed by the renewing of your mind, that you may prove what is that good and acceptable and perfect will of God' (Romans 12:2).

First stop Cyprus

'So being sent out by the Holy Spirit, they went down to Seleucia, and from there they sailed for Cyprus. And when they arrived at Salamis, they preached the word of God in the synagogues of the Jews. They also had John as their assistant' (Acts 13:4–5).

The choice of Cyprus as the starting point of their missionary work may well have had something to do with the fact that Barnabas came from there (Acts 4:36). It suggests that he was concerned to take the good news of the gospel to his own people first. That would have been perfectly natural, since we ourselves have a similar desire when it comes to the salvation of members of our own family and our friends. Jesus too began his earthly ministry in his hometown. 'So he came to Nazareth, where he had been brought up' (Luke 4:16). It can sometimes be very difficult to witness for the gospel in one's own family, because they know us better than strangers know us, and may have a slight prejudice when we start talking about our new life in Christ.

Indeed, Jesus himself encountered that kind of prejudice when he preached at Nazareth. 'And many hearing him were astonished saying … "Is this not the carpenter, the Son of Mary, and brother of James, Joses, Judas and Simon? And are not his sisters here with us?" So they were offended at him'(Mark 6: 2–3). Further in this same passage we read: 'Now he could do no mighty work there. ... And he marvelled because of their unbelief' (Mark 6:5–6). So witnessing to our family and friends can be difficult because they know us better than strangers do, and may even have seen a different side to our character in the past. Nevertheless, in our home and among our friends is still a good place to begin with the gospel because, if we can survive that, we need have no fear of speaking to others.

John Mark

'They also had John as their assistant' (Acts 13:5). This is the John Mark whose mother was Mary, the owner of the house where the disciples had been praying for Peter when in prison (Acts 12:12). He is mentioned several times in the epistles, but what do we know about him?

'John' was his Hebrew name, but Mark (Marcus) was a Roman name. The reason for his adopted name is not clear, but it was not uncommon among first-century Jews. From Colossians 4: 10 we learn that he was a cousin of Barnabas, he had a godly background with a Christian mother, and two godly men like Barnabas and Paul as role models. Tradition holds that the young man who followed Jesus on the night of his arrest, and fled naked when the soldiers seized him, was none other than Mark himself (Mark 14:51–52). If so, it shows that he wanted to follow Jesus to the end, whereas the disciples had already fled from the scene.

When Paul and Barnabas reached Perga on this first missionary journey, Mark left them and returned to Jerusalem (Acts 13:13). Why he did this we have no idea. Was it because he could not face up to the hardships and demands of the journey? We do not know. Other reasons suggested are homesickness, illness, and even that he was offended at Paul's taking over the leadership from his cousin Barnabas. What is clear is that Paul did not like it one bit, and when Barnabas suggested taking Mark with them on the next journey he flatly refused, and the two brothers fell out for a while (Acts 15:36–41).

After this upset we hear no more of Mark in Acts, but mention of him comes up again in the epistles. In Colossians 4:10–11 he is back in the company of Paul who was in prison in Rome, so clearly all is forgiven. And in 2 Timothy 4:11 Paul commends him as being helpful to him in his ministry.

At the end of his first epistle Peter refers very affectionately to Mark as 'my son'. This reference is important because it shows that a very close relationship existed between the old apostle and the young John Mark, and the younger man was converted under Peter's ministry making him a son in the faith in the way Paul refers to Timothy. But more importantly, this relationship underlies the Gospel which Mark would later write. Papias, who was the bishop of Hierapolis about AD 140, gives an account of the origin of Mark's gospel which is so important that we quote it in full:

'Mark, who was Peter's interpreter, wrote down accurately, though not in order, all that he recollected of what Christ had said or done. For he was not a hearer of the Lord or a follower of his. He followed Peter, as I have said, at a later date, and Peter adapted his instruction to practical needs, without any attempt to give the Lord's words systematically. So that Mark was not wrong in writing down some things in this way from memory, for his one concern was neither to omit not falsify anything that he had heard.'

We learn from this that Mark's gospel is the record of what Peter, an eyewitness, preached and taught about the Lord Jesus Christ. Mark therefore was a man who may have fallen or failed at one point in his life, but he recovered and was greatly used of God. Someone has said that a Christian is not a man who does not fall, but one who, when he falls, gets up by the grace of God and carries on.

Sergius Paulus

'Now when they had gone through the island of Paphos, they found a certain sorcerer, a false prophet, a Jew whose name was Bar-Jesus, who was with the proconsul, Sergius Paulus, an intelligent man. This man called for Barnabas and Saul and sought to hear the word of God' (Acts 13:6–7). Sergius Paulus, a high Roman official, is described as an 'intelligent' man meaning that he was a thinking man and an enquirer after truth. The presence of Elymas Bar-Jesus (Son of Jesus or Joshua) as a member of his staff suggests that. Elymas was a Jew and a false prophet. He would have had a knowledge of the Old Testament therefore, but would have distorted and perverted the scriptures to promote his own false teaching.

Sergius Paulus enjoyed a good position and life-style, but at the same time he seems to have been seeking something more satisfying, and was reaching out for a greater spiritual understanding of life. But the nearest he got to that was the false spirituality offered him by Elymas the sorcerer. Back in chapter 8 we met up with Simon, another sorcerer. We said then that such people represent the dark evil forces at work in the world, but that they also show that man has a spiritual dimension to his being, and that he is driven to satisfy it in whatever way he can. Sergius Paulus was seeking such spiritual satisfaction, but he was looking in the wrong direction.

Openness to God's word

A turning point in the life of Sergius Paulus came about with the arrival of Paul and Barnabas at Paphos. He heard of their preaching and was sufficiently interested to want to hear them. 'This man called for Barnabas and Saul and sought to hear the word of God'. Like Cornelius the Roman centurion, Sergius Paulus—although a pagan—was genuinely seeking answers to the great issues of life, and that is why God made it possible for him to hear the good news of salvation from his servants. For the person who is dissatisfied with the intellectual and material answers of life and is reaching out for a deeper understanding, God will open up the way. In some way or other—a sermon, a tract, a book, or the Christian witness of a friend or colleague—he will come into contact with the truth of God's word. When that happens, the next step lies with that person. The Lord Jesus said: 'he who seeks finds' (Matthew 7:8).

The clash of powers

Every soul won for the kingdom of God is at the centre of a great battle between the spiritual powers. That was true of Sergius Paulus. On the one hand the power of the Holy Spirit was working through Paul as he explained the way of salvation, and on the other hand the principalities and powers of darkness were working through Elymas. 'But Elymas the sorcerer (for so his name is translated) withstood them, seeking to turn the proconsul away from the faith. Then Saul, who also is called Paul, filled with the Holy Spirit, looked intently at him and said, "O full of all deceit and all fraud, you son of the devil, you enemy of all righteousness, will you not cease perverting the straight ways of the Lord?"' (Acts 13:8–10).

What was at stake in this struggle was the immortal soul of the proconsul. And so it is with every person who is convicted in their heart by the Holy Spirit. In the depths of their soul they hear the Spirit saying, 'God gave his Son to die for you and take away your sins. He wants you as his child if only you will believe'. And at the same time they hear Satan saying, 'Do not believe all this talk about salvation, you are no better or worse than anyone else. Just put it out of your mind'. And so the battle continues. But Satan lost the battle for the soul of Sergius Paulus. Paul had seen through Elymas the moment he first met him, and now in the power of the Spirit he deals with him very effectively. '"And now, indeed, the hand of the Lord is upon you, and you shall be blind, not seeing the sun for a time". And immediately a dark mist fell on him, and he went around seeking someone to lead him by the hand. Then the proconsul believed, when he saw what had been done, being astonished at the teaching of the Lord' (Acts 13:11–12).

When it says that the proconsul 'believed', it must mean that he came to faith in the gospel of Christ for he saw the power of God in what happened to Elymas and accepted the teaching of Paul and Barnabas relating to salvation. These two things must always go together—the teaching of the gospel, and the practice of the gospel as an evidence of its truth.

Paul preaches at Antioch

'Now when Paul and his party set sail from Paphos, they came to Perga in Pamphylia, and John, departing from them, returned to Jerusalem. But when they departed from Perga, they came to Antioch in Pisidia, and went into the synagogue on the Sabbath day and sat down. And after the reading of the Law and the Prophets, the rulers of the synagogue sent to them, saying, "Men and brethren, if you have any word of exhortation for the people say on". Then Paul stood up, and motioning with his hand said, "Men of Israel, and you, who fear God, listen"' (Acts 13:13–16).

This passage is of great interest because it gives an insight into the order of worship in the synagogue, and records Paul's first sermon in considerable detail. The Antioch mentioned here is not the same as the Syrian Antioch from which Paul and Barnabas set out on their missionary journey. In the order of service, prayers would first be offered by the ruler of the synagogue, then came the reading of the Law and the Prophets with interpretation for those not speaking Hebrew. After this came the sermon when it was customary for the ruler to invite any distinguished person present to preach. This was Paul's chance and he was quick to take advantage of it. The same thing happened when Jesus attended the synagogue at Nazareth and preached from Isaiah 61:1–2 (Luke 4).

The sermon

Paul's sermon begins at verse 17 and extends to verse 41. It is interesting to compare the message with Peter's sermon (Acts 2) and Stephen's speech before the Sanhedrin (Acts 7), for many of the basic elements are the same. In the early church there was a consistency in the message preached, so that people were left in no doubt as to what the gospel really was. Today, sadly, there is a great deal of confusion in people's minds because what they hear from some pulpits is not the authentic note of the gospel, but a mish-mash of scripture mixed with a lot that is no more than human opinion.

In looking at Paul's sermon, rather than dealing with it in detail, we shall simply give an outline of its contents. It falls naturally into six parts.

Part one, verses 17–22. God is the God of history. Paul shows this by outlining the history of the chosen people from the deliverance from Egypt to the reign of David. We must be careful in our preaching to give a true perspective of God's rule. He is sovereign of the universe, governing and controlling all things by the word of his power. But at the same time we must show that he is also presently involved in the personal history of men and nations. He is the life-principle underlying our very existence and we can have a personal relationship with him.

Part two, verses 23–26. Jesus is the consummation of history and of God's eternal purpose. History is not meaningless; there is an end in view. The idea that history is a cycle endlessly repeating itself has no place in the Bible's teaching. Instead, God is seen to have a purpose in mind which he fulfilled in the coming of Christ into our world, and which will be brought to its final consummation when Christ returns to this earth. In verse 23 Paul says: '…according to the promise, God raised up for Israel a Saviour—Jesus'.

Part three, verses 27–29. But men rejected Christ as the fulfilment of God's purpose. 'And though they found no cause for death in him, they asked Pilate that he should be put to death' (Acts 13:28). In their spiritual blindness and wickedness men rejected God's love extended to them in Christ but put him to death on the Cross. The Cross shows us therefore both the depth of God's love for mankind, and the depth of man's sin and wickedness.

Part four, verses 30–37. The resurrection of Jesus shows that in spite of man's rejection, the purpose of God in Christ cannot be defeated. 'But God raised him from the dead. He was seen for many days by those who came up with him from Galilee to Jerusalem, who are his witnesses to the people' (Acts 13: 30–31) The resurrection is the heart of the gospel and it was the cornerstone of the preaching in the early church.

Part five, verses 38–39. The Good News of the gospel is that the forgiveness of sins is open to all. 'Therefore let it be known to you, brethren, that through this man is preached to you forgiveness of sins' (Acts 13:38). Paul also uses the word 'justified', meaning that through faith in Christ's sacrifice for sin, we are declared righteous and cleansed from sin in God's sight.

Part six, verses 40–41. Finally, Paul gives a warning of God's judgement on those who refuse to repent of their sins and reject the offer of forgiveness. He quotes a passage from the prophet Habakkuk 1:5. 'Behold, you despisers, marvel and perish! For I work a work in your days. A work which you will by no means believe, though one were to declare it to you' (Acts 13:41). The warning is that to reject the gospel of Christ is to perish in one's sins, and to lose out on the gift of eternal life.

These are among the main building blocks in evangelical preaching in every age, and we must not neglect them in our preaching today.

Blessing and reproach

The last section in this chapter, verses 42–52, deals with the mixed reception given to Paul's message in the synagogue. 'So when the Jews went out of the synagogue, the Gentiles begged that these words might be preached to them the next Sabbath. Now when the congregation had broken up, many of the Jews and devout proselytes followed Paul and

Barnabas, who, speaking to them, persuaded them to continue in the grace of God. On the next Sabbath almost the whole city came together to hear the word of God. But when the Jews saw the multitudes, they were filled with envy; and contradicting and blaspheming, they opposed the things spoken by Paul' (Acts 13:42–45).

The picture is one of success and failure. On the one hand there were those, especially the Gentiles, who were deeply impressed with the word of God and were keen to hear more. There were also those who responded to the word of God with a positive act of believing faith. 'Now when the Gentiles heard this, they were glad and glorified the word of the Lord. And as many as had been appointed to eternal life believed' (Acts 13:48). But sadly, there was a third group made up of the Jews who rated the message with contempt and blasphemy, and were so incensed that they had Paul and Barnabas thrown out of the city. 'But the Jews stirred up the devout and prominent women and the chief men of the city, raised up persecution against Paul and Barnabas, and expelled them from their region' (Acts 13:50).

So what are we to learn from all this? Well, it clearly shows that we must be realistic in our ministry of the word and not expect the gospel to succeed with everyone. All three categories mentioned in this passage are to be found in modern day congregations. There are those impressed with the message of the Bible and who will sit under it week by week, and are keen to discuss it and ask questions, but never come to the act of believing faith in Christ. Paul refers to such people as, 'always learning and never able to come to the knowledge of the truth' (2 Timothy 3:7). It is so easy to lose patience with these people and to get fed up with them always asking questions and 'halting between two opinions' without it leading anywhere. But we must not give up on them.

Then, praise God, we also have in our congregations those who do respond to the preached word in believing faith. That is what makes the work of preaching worthwhile. For there is no joy or satisfaction so great as to know that God has used you to bring a soul to salvation in Christ Jesus. Indeed, the Lord himself said that it is the only thing on earth that brings joy in heaven. 'Likewise, I say to you, there is joy in the presence of the angels of God over one sinner who repents' (Luke 15:10).

Then there are those in our congregations whose hearts are as hard as flint where the gospel is concerned. They may not show it in outward hostility, though sometimes that does happen. But they can come Sunday by Sunday and never give the slightest indication in any way that the word of God is affecting them. Of course all this is made perfectly clear in the parable of The Sower (Mark 4:1–9). But the main thrust of the parable is that there has to be a sower, and the seed of the word of God must be sown. Paul's charge to Timothy still holds good: 'Preach the word! Be ready in season and out of season. Convince, rebuke, exhort, with all longsuffering and teaching' (2 Timothy 4:2). That is our task. The results we must leave in God's hands.

Paul and Barnabas were clearly not dejected or depressed with the mixed reception their preaching had received. For we read in conclusion: 'and the disciples were filled with joy and with the Holy Spirit'. There was a work to be done, and they got on with it.

The journey continues

Read Acts chapter 14

In this chapter Paul and Barnabas continue their missionary journey passing through the cities of Iconium, Lystra, and Derbe. From Derbe they strike out for home, retracing their steps through Lystra, Iconium, and Antioch in Pisidia, encouraging and strengthening those who had earlier received the gospel. By the end of this chapter they have arrived back at the church in Antioch from where they had set out approximately three years earlier.

When studying the missionary journeys of Paul and his companions we should always keep in mind what dangerous undertakings they really were. We shall see in this chapter that they were attacked by their fellow Jews, and on one occasion Paul was actually stoned and left for dead. In addition, travel in those ancient times was a hazardous business because of the constant danger of attack from the bandits who infested remote areas. In 2 Corinthians we have a graphic account of such dangers given by Paul himself.

'Are they ministers of Christ?—I speak as a fool—I am more: in labours more abundant, in stripes above measure, in prisons more frequently, deaths often. From the Jews five times I received forty stripes minus one. Three times I was beaten with rods; once I was stoned; three times I was shipwrecked; a night and a day I have been in the deep; in journeys often, in perils of waters, in perils of robbers, in perils of my own countrymen, in perils of the Gentiles, in peril in the city, in peril in the wilderness, in perils in the sea, in perils among false brethren; in weariness and toil, sleeplessness often, in hunger and thirst, in fasting often, in cold and nakedness ... In Damascus the governor, under Aretas the king, was guarding the city of the Damascenes with a garrison desiring to arrest me; but I was let down in a basket through a window in the wall, and escaped from his hands' (2 Corinthians 11:23–27, 32–33).

Compared with all this, what we have to put up with today by way of indifference or hostility to the gospel is trivial, and the heroism and unshakeable faith of these men should inspire us to spread the good news of salvation through Christ in every way we can.

On to Iconium

'Now it happened in Iconium that they went together to the synagogue of the Jews, and so spoke that a great multitude both of the Jews and of the Greeks believed' (Acts 14:1). Here Paul and Barnabas repeat what they had done earlier in other places where they had preached. They made straight for the local synagogue. This seems to have been a definite strategy in Paul's missionary work. Almost always in arriving in a new locality he would make for the local synagogue in the hope of being given the opportunity to preach to his fellow-Jews. God had appointed him an apostle to the Gentiles, but he always had a compassionate heart for the salvation of his own people. We recall his moving words in Romans 9, 'I have great sorrow and continual grief in my heart. For I could wish that I myself were accursed from Christ for my brethren, my countrymen according to the flesh' (verses 2–3). Jeremiah likewise wept over the spiritual state of his people (Jeremiah 9:1). And let us not forget that sad picture of the Lord Jesus weeping over Jerusalem (Luke 19:41–44).

Do we ever weep over the spiritual state of our nation? Does it bring tears to our eyes when we see how far removed we are from the laws and commandments of God? Are we appalled by the high level of crime and violence in society, the deceit and fraud in business and commercial life, the lack of spirituality among so many of our leaders, the trashiness of so many TV programmes, and the practical atheism of the general population? And do we have a desire to do something about it? For if we, who know God and have experienced salvation in Christ, do not weep over our nation, it is certain no one else will.

Trouble ahead

At first it seemed all was going to go well at Iconium, since we are told that a 'great multitude both of Jews and of the Greeks believed'. But trouble was not long in coming. It never is when the gospel is making headway and people are blessed by it. Satan cannot afford to let that happen, and he is always seeking to undermine and hinder God's work. In this instance the troublemakers were once again the unbelieving Jews. 'But the unbelieving Jews stirred up the Gentiles and poisoned their minds against the brethren' (Acts 14:2). The phrases 'stirred up', and 'poisoned the minds' indicate clearly that the Jews were deliberately intent on doing as much harm to Paul and Barnabas as they could.

Whether consciously or otherwise they were being manipulated as the tools and instruments of Satan to do his evil work in stirring up mob-violence. 'But the multitude of the city was divided: part sided with the Jews, and part with the apostles. And when a violent attempt was made by both the Gentiles and Jews, with their rulers, to abuse and stone them, they became aware of it and fled to Lystra and Derbe, cities of Lycaonia and the surrounding region. And they were preaching the gospel there' (Acts 14:4–7).

The opposition of the Jews was particularly evil because they not only rejected the gospel themselves, but they 'poisoned the minds' of others who might otherwise have believed. It reminds us of the criticism Jesus made of the scribes and Pharisees. 'But woe to you scribes, and Pharisees, hypocrites! For you shut up the kingdom of heaven against men; for you neither go in yourselves, nor do you allow those who are entering to go in' (Matthew 23:13). This poisoning of people's minds is going on today in a very direct and concentrated manner through the mass media, and in the teaching of secular humanism in our schools and colleges.

Our children especially are having their minds poisoned by much of what they see on the TV screen and the Internet. Christians too can have their minds poisoned through the subtle brain-washing that goes on all the time by what we watch on TV, and what we read in the newspapers and magazines. We need to be on our guard against this attempt to wash our minds clean of all that is Christlike and wholesome in our thinking and in our approach to life. Paul puts it like this. 'Beware lest anyone cheat you through philosophy and empty deceit, according to the tradition of men, according to the basic principles of this world, and not according to Christ' (Colossians 2:8).

Faith through the word
In this section, Acts 14:8–20, Paul and Barnabas arrive at Lystra where they

have a very strange experience, being regarded by the people as gods come down to earth. It all began with the healing of a lame man. 'And in Lystra a certain man without strength in his feet was sitting, a cripple from his mother's womb, who had never walked. This man heard Paul speaking. Paul, observing him intently and seeing that he had faith to be healed, said with a loud voice, "Stand up straight on your feet!" And he leaped and walked' (Acts 14:8–10).

What is of special interest here is not so much the miracle itself, since Paul and Barnabas had performed miracles and signs earlier at Iconium. What is significant in this instance is that Paul could see that the man had faith to be healed. The question is how or what did Paul see? Was there something in the man's manner or in the look on his face perhaps? Clearly, Paul—under the influence of the Holy Spirit—might well have discerned the man's thoughts and feelings. As Calvin says, 'the cripple's faith was revealed to Paul by the secret inspiration of the Spirit' (*Acts*, St Andrew Press, 1966, vol. 2, p. 5).

But there could be another explanation. The man had been listening to Paul preaching God's word. And as Paul himself says in Romans 10: 'faith comes by hearing, and hearing by the word of God' (verse 17). Under Spirit-filled preaching, faith is created in the heart and mind of the hearer, whether it is faith leading to salvation, or faith for the healing of the body. It is one and the same faith.

Mistaken for gods

The miracle that brought healing to the man had an electrifying effect upon the people. 'Now when the people saw what Paul had done, they raised their voices, saying in the Lycaonian language, "The gods have come down to us in the likeness of men!" And Barnabas they called Zeus, and Paul, Hermes, because he was the chief speaker. Then the priest of Zeus, whose temple was in front of their city, brought oxen and garlands to the gates, intending to sacrifice with the multitudes' (Acts 14:11–13).

Barnabas may have been called Zeus, the chief of the gods, because he was a more imposing figure than Paul. On the other hand, Paul was called Hermes, the god of speech, because he was the main preacher. Both however were horrified by this outburst of adulation, and tried to put a stop to it. 'But when the apostles Barnabas and Paul heard this, they tore their clothes and ran in among the multitude, crying out and saying, "Men why are you doing these things?"' (Acts 14:14–15). Paul then spoke very seriously to them to try and correct their thinking. It was not exactly a sermon, more of a short speech, but he did have three basic points he wanted to impress on them.

First, men's praise and worship must be given only to the true and living God who brought all creation into being. 'We also are men with the same nature as you, and preach to you that you should turn from these useless things to the living God, who made the heaven, the earth, the sea, and all things that are in them' (Acts 14:15). Many are content to believe that the universe is a result of impersonal mechanical forces, and that there is no need for worship and praise to a personal creator. But that is not the teaching of scripture, as Paul makes clear. Behind the workings of this wonderful universe, with its changing seasons and its complex structures in animal and plant life, there is a living, personal Providence who governs, and guides and watches over all things. Furthermore, because I myself am a part of creation, it means that this mighty creator God has a personal interest in me. He is alert to my needs, he hears my prayers, and he assures me in different ways that my welfare is his concern.

Second, God has been very patient with mankind throughout the ages. '...Who in bygone generations allowed all nations to walk in their own ways' (Acts 14:16). Over the centuries the Gentile pagan nations had worshipped their own gods and idols, and relied upon their own wisdom and understanding. They showed no desire to worship the true and living God, but continued in their darkness and ignorance. But God was very patient with them, and did not wipe them off the face of the earth as he had once done at the time of the Flood. At that time God promised that he would not destroy the world again in the same way, and with patience he bore with man's waywardness, and ultimately he sent his Son into the world to die for man's sins, and to show the full extent of his love and forgiveness.

But let us keep in mind that no one should presume on God's patience where sin and rejection is concerned. The Bible clearly teaches that deliberate, wilful rejection of God can lead to the withdrawal of his Spirit, not because he is unwilling to save, but because man refuses to be saved. We see this limitation of God's patience in our Lord's instruction: 'Do not give what is holy to the dogs; nor cast your pearls before swine' (Matthew 7:6).

Third, God has never at any time left himself without a witness in the world. 'Nevertheless he did not leave himself without witness in that he did good, gave us rain from heaven and fruitful seasons, filling our hearts with food and gladness. And with these sayings they could scarcely restrain the multitudes from sacrificing to them' (Acts 14:17–18).

What Paul is saying is that men have no excuse for not knowing God, for he has revealed himself in different ways, not least in the creation. Our planet earth is orderly and dependable, because it is governed by eco-systems which are constantly adapting to sustain the many life-forms in plants, animals and insects. Every thing has its own place and function in the scheme of things, giving coherence to the whole. And if it is asked who or what keeps this incredible juggling going, whereby everything is finely tuned and sensitively balanced, the answer the Bible gives is the Almighty Creator God.

In his letter to the Romans, Paul makes the same point about God's witness in creation. 'For since the creation of the world his invisible attributes are clearly seen, being understood by the things that are made, even his eternal power and Godhead, so that they are without excuse' (Romans 1:20). Furthermore, God's witness, the Bible teaches, extends beyond the creation and may be seen in the world's history, which is not meaningless, but has direction and purpose, because God is guiding and directing the affairs of men and nations. And one day history will come to its climax with the return of Christ to this earthly scene to judge the living and the dead, and to sum up all things in ushering in the new heaven and the new earth, 'the home of the righteous'.

One other thing needs to be said about God's witness. He makes it known in the preservation of a remnant among his own people in every age and generation. However God-denying things might appear to be in any period in history, there will always be those who are faithful to the word of God. In our own nation, at the present time, we are living in a day of small things spiritually. Nevertheless there is a faithful remnant holding to the truth of the gospel, and they are to be found in our towns and cities, in shops and factories, in schools and colleges, living for Christ and resisting the flood of evil and unbelief.

Satan never gives up

'Then the Jews from Antioch and Iconium came there [Lystra]; and having persuaded the multitudes, they stoned Paul and dragged him out of the city, supposing him to be dead' (Acts 14:19). This verse spells out very clearly that Satan, the great adversary of our souls, never gives up easily in his attempts to destroy our faith. We said earlier that the unbelieving Jews were tools and instruments manipulated by Satan to do his evil work. We now see that in the determination and tenacity they showed in pursuing Paul and Barnabas to Lystra, where they stirred up the mob to stone Paul. It is this Satanic energy in the manipulation of men that is behind all the filth and immorality of our time, and especially in attacks upon the church of God.

At the end of our Lord's temptations in the wilderness we read—'Now when the devil had ended every temptation, he departed from him until an opportune time' (Luke 4:13). So Satan did not give up even where our Lord was concerned, and through the attacks of the Pharisees and Sadducees to undermine the ministry of Jesus, he returned again and again. And on the very last night of his life, Christ—in the agony of the garden of Gethsemene—had to struggle with the evil one yet again. We are to learn from all this that the devil's malice is endless, and we must not drop our spiritual guard, for he is always looking for that 'opportune time' to strike again.

The manipulation of Satan may also be seen in the fickleness of the crowd and the emptiness of human popularity. They had stoned Paul and dragged him out of the city for dead, and yet—only a short time before—his popularity with the crowd was running so high that he and Barnabas were regarded as gods, and the adulation given them knew no bounds. So much for human popularity and praise. It reminds us of the crowd who one day were hailing Jesus with shouts of 'hosanna', and shortly afterwards were crying out 'crucify him'. When George Whtefield at the age of twenty-two began preaching in London, his fame spread so rapidly that he was in danger of being destroyed by it. He says in his journal:

'The tide of popularity began to run very high. In a short time I could no longer walk on foot as usual, but was constrained to go in a coach from place to place to avoid the hosannas of the multitude. They grew quite extravagant in their applause, and had it not been for my compassionate High Priest, popularity would have destroyed me. I used to plead with him to take me by the hand and lead me unhurt through this fiery furnace. He heard my request and gave me to see the vanity of all commendations but his own' (quoted by Arnold Dalimore, *'George Whitefield'* Banner of Truth, vol 1, p. 133).

Someone has said that there are three estimates of our lives. What others think of us, what we think of ourselves, and what God thinks of us. And only the last counts for anything.

Paul's courage

When we are told that the mob dragged Paul out of the city 'supposing him to be dead', some commentators interpret that as meaning he was actually dead. We then read, 'However, when the disciples gathered around him, he rose up and went into the city. And the next day he departed with Barnabas to Derbe' (Acts 14:20). It is then thought that he was resuscitated by a special miracle. But another explanation might be that when the other disciples 'gathered around him' they were praying for his recovery, and God answered their prayers.

But whatever the explanation, we cannot fail to be moved by the profound courage of this man in going back into the city where the mob had stoned him. John Wesley, who knew all about facing mobs from his own preaching in the open air, used to say; 'Always look a mob in the face'. And that is what he did. The following extract from his journal for Thursday 12 September 1745 bears that out.

'I came to Leeds, preached at five, and at eight met the society; after which the mob pelted us with dirt and stones a great part of the way home. The congregation was much larger the next evening; and so was the mob at our return, and likewise in higher spirits, being ready to knock out all our brains...' (*Journal,* vol 1, p. 208).

We are bound to ask: Where did these men get their incredible courage? It certainly had nothing to do with their physique. Both Paul and Wesley were physically small men. Of Paul it is said: '... his letters are weighty and powerful ...but his bodily person is weak' (2 Corinthians 10:10). And a further description from a second century document (*Acts of Paul and Thecia*) states: 'a man of little stature, thin haired, and crooked in the legs'. Likewise Wesley was no heavyweight either, since he only stood five feet two inches in height. But what both men had plenty of, in common with many of God's servants in history, was the boldness of the Holy Spirit (Acts 4:13).

Back to base

During their missionary journeys Paul and Barnabas had made many converts through the preaching of the gospel, and they now decided to retrace their steps in order to encourage and strengthen these converts in their newfound faith. 'And when they had preached the gospel to that city and made many disciples, they returned to Lystra, Iconium, and Antioch, strengthening the souls of the disciples, exhorting them to continue in the faith, and saying, "we must through many tribulations enter the kingdom of God"' (Acts 14:21–22).

Paul and Barnabas realised that whilst evangelism and the winning of souls to Christ is tremendously important, it must not end there. New converts have to be taught the great truths of scripture and be given a spiritual framework for their new-found faith. It was not enough that they should *be* Christians, but also that they should know *why* they are, and be able to articulate their faith when questioned about it by others. As Peter says, 'be ready to give a defence to everyone who asks you a reason for the hope that is in you, with meekness and fear' (1 Peter 3:15).

Appointment of elders

A further measure taken for the strengthening of the churches was the appointment of elders. 'So when they had appointed elders in every church, and prayed with fasting, they commended them to the Lord in whom they had believed' (Acts 14:23). If the new believers were to grow in their faith it was essential that effective leadership should be provided. But who were these leaders, since these new churches had only recently been formed from a totally pagan background? We have no answer to that, but we must accept that they were men who stood out from among the rest as having the necessary gifts for leadership in the church. We are also told that fasting and prayer accompanied the appointment of elders, so that Paul and Barnabas could do more than commend these infant churches and their spiritually immature leaders to the care and keeping of Almighty God.

All this points us to an important principle in the work of overseas missions today, namely, that every effort is made to reduce dependence upon western missionaries by appointing leaders from among the indigenous people as soon as possible. A good example of this is the enormous advance made by the church in China following the expulsion of western missionaries by the Communists. God watched over this infant church and provided from among their own people the leadership that was required.

So the first missionary journey came to a close as Paul and Barnabas made their way home, arriving finally at Antioch from where they had set out some years before. 'Now when they had come and gathered the church together, they reported all that God had done with them, and that he had opened the door of faith to the Gentiles. So they stayed there a long time with the disciples' (Acts 14:27–28). The church at Antioch consisted of both Jews and Gentiles, so that the report would have been received with mixed feelings. The statement that God 'had opened the door of faith to the Gentiles', would at least, have created great surprise among the Jewish element. But it was perfectly evident that 'faith' and not 'circumcision' was henceforth the key factor in the church's ministry, and that this was God's decision and not man's. In the next chapter of Acts, the question of circumcision will be finally dealt with, once and for all, by the first Council held at Jerusalem.

The Jerusalem Council

Read Acts chapter 15

W e indicated at the end of the previous chapter that the entry of Gentiles into the church was bound to lead to controversy over the matter of circumcision. That matter now comes to a head in this fifteenth chapter with the arrival of certain Jews at the church in Antioch.

'And certain men came down from Judea and taught the brethren, "Unless you are circumcised according to the custom of Moses you cannot be saved". Therefore, when Paul and Barnabas had no small dissension and dispute with them, they determined that Paul and Barnabas and certain others of them should go up to Jerusalem, to the apostles and elders about this question … And when they had come to Jerusalem they were received by the church and the apostles and the elders; and they reported all things that God had done with them. But some of the sect of the Pharisees who believed rose up, saying, "It is necessary to circumcise them, and to command them to keep the Law of Moses"' (Acts 15:1, 2, 4–5).

The problem stated

No real Christian likes controversies and conflicts in the church because they can do untold harm to the gospel in the eyes of the world. But sometimes the cause of disagreement is so fundamental that the truth itself is at stake, and must be defended even at the cost of disunity. That was the position as Paul and Barnabas saw it, and they were prepared to take the matter all the way to the Jerusalem Council to get a final decision. The problem quite simply was this. As more and more Gentiles came into the church the believing Jews were insisting that they should observe the Law of Moses including the rite of circumcision. In fact they were saying that a man had first to become a Jew in order to become a Christian.

This was something Paul and Barnabas simply could not tolerate, since they had seen at first hand how the power of the Holy Spirit had worked in the hearts of Gentiles bringing them to faith and salvation in Christ. It was a question of vital importance therefore, and the decision they would come to would affect the whole future of the church. If Gentiles had to submit to the Law and the rite of circumcision, it would mean that they had to earn their salvation instead of receiving it as the free gift of the grace of God.

When to disagree

Commenting on this passage Martin Luther says; 'We must not yield or give up this article (salvation by grace), though heaven and earth, and whatever will not endure, perish.' Calvin was of the same mind. 'Peace is certainly a pleasing word; but cursed is the peace that is obtained at so great a cost that there is lost to us the doctrine of Christ, by which alone we grow together into a godly and holy unity'.

Because we live in a fallen world, disagreements are bound to arise at times even among believers, and it is not always clear whom to unite with, and from whom to separate. For some the problem is not as acute as it was for Paul and Barnabas. Within the present day ecumenical movement no price is too high to pay for unity, not even Biblical truth and doctrinal purity. A W Tozer says: 'Maybe what we need in religious circles today is not more union but some wise and courageous division. Everyone desires peace but it could be that revival will follow the sword' (Essay, *Divisions are not always bad*).

Meeting the Council

Paul and Barnabas were well received by the Council at Jerusalem, and after the preliminary discussion Peter was the first one to get up and speak. 'Now the apostles and elders came together to consider this matter. And when there had been much dispute, Peter rose up and said to them; "Men and brethren you know that a good while ago God chose among us, that by my mouth the Gentiles should hear the word of the gospel and believe"'(Acts 15:6–7). Peter was here referring to the conversion of the Gentile Cornelius and his household, which had taken place about ten years before (Acts 10).

He was in a strong position in referring back to this incident because he was able to show that God, in giving the Gentiles the gift of the Holy Spirit, was treating them no differently from themselves. 'So God, who knows the heart, acknowledged them by giving them the Holy Spirit, just as he did to us, and made no distinction between us and them, purifying their hearts by faith' (Acts 15:8–9).

The other point Peter makes is that the law, with all the artificial rules put upon it by the scribes and Pharisees, would enslave men instead of setting them free. 'Now therefore why do you test God by putting a yoke on the neck of the disciples which neither our fathers nor we were able to bear?' (Acts 15:10). Ritualism and the strict observance of rules and regulations can save no one, only faith in Christ. As Paul urges the Galatians: 'Stand fast therefore in the liberty by which Christ has made us free, and do not be entangled again with a yoke of bondage' (Galatians 5:1).

Paul and Barnabas were the next to speak, but we are only told that they related to the Council the work God had done among the Gentiles on their missionary journey (Acts 15:12). The members of the Council listened in silence, and then James made his contribution.

Who was James?

Before coming to what James had to say, we need to identify him, and say something about his role in the Council, since he summed up the whole discussion and made the final decision. He is generally spoken of as the bishop or leader of the Jerusalem church, and is identified as the brother of Jesus. Speaking of a visit he made to Jerusalem to discuss matters with the apostles, Paul says: 'I saw none of the other apostles—only James the Lord's brother' (Galatians 1:19).

We know quite a lot about James, both from the scriptures and from secular sources. Josephus, the Jewish historian, says that he was martyred for the faith. 'Ananus [High Priest] … thinking that he had a good opportunity because Festus [Roman Governor] was dead … held a judicial Council and brought to it the brother of Jesus—who was called Christ—James was his name, and some other on the charge of violating the Law. He gave them over to be stoned to death' (*Antiquities,* Book 20:9.i). Eusebius, in his *Ecclesiastical History,* 2:23, gives a further description. 'James, he whom all from the time of our Lord to our own day call the Just … was holy from his mother's womb; wine and strong drink he drank not … no razor touched his head … And alone he would enter the temple, so that his knees were callous like a camel's in consequence of his continual kneeling in prayer to God and beseeching pardon for the people'.

One other insight into James' character comes from his own epistle. He takes no special pride in the fact that he was our Lord's earthly brother, but in the first verse simply describes himself as, 'a bondservant of God and of the Lord Jesus Christ'. So here we have a man who was just and holy, a man of prayer and of a humble disposition.

One other thing needs to be said about James, which is quite revealing. During the earthly ministry of Jesus, James and his brothers were very sceptical of his Messianic claims and highly critical of him. 'Now the Jews Feast of Tabernacles was at hand. His brothers therefore said to him, "Depart from here and go into Judea, that your disciples also may see the works that you are doing. For no one does anything secret while he himself seeks to be known openly. If you do these things, show yourself to the world". For even his brothers did not believe in him' (John 7:2–5).

We learn from this that one can get very close to God in Christ, without ever coming to complete and total surrender of one's life to him in faith. One can belong to a Christian family, attend church services, even move in Christian circles, and yet never know Christ personally as Lord and Saviour. But James and his brothers came to faith in Christ eventually, for we are told in Acts 1 that he and his brothers were with their mother Mary and the disciples in the upper room engaged in prayer while waiting for the coming of the Holy Spirit.

Furthermore, Paul tells us that after his resurrection Jesus made a special appearance to James. 'After that he was seen by James, then by all the apostles' (1 Corinthians 15:7). If we have a loved one who is outside the family of God, the experience of James encourages us not to give up praying. God has his own time-scale in these matters. It was only after the resurrection of Jesus that James came to faith. But when that happened his life really blossomed, and he became the leader of the Jerusalem church.

The final decision

It was James who summed up the deliberations of the Council and made the final decision. 'And after they had become silent, James answered, saying, "Men and brethren, listen to me"' (Acts 15:13). His speech is then given in full and consists of two parts. In the first part (verses 16–18) he comes down firmly on the side of those who believed that the Gentiles should be admitted into the church through faith in Christ, and he gives a biblical quotation from the book of Amos 9 to back up his argument.

In the second part (verses 18–21) he gives some helpful advice to ease relations between Jew and Gentile. He laid down four rules for the Gentile Christians to follow. First, they should abstain from food sacrificed to idols. Paul deals with this problem in great detail in 1 Corinthians 8. Second, they should abstain from sexual immorality, for the Christian is called to a life of purity and holiness. Third and fourth they were to abstain from eating the meat of strangled animals and the blood. Behind this was the Jewish teaching (Genesis 9) that the life was in the blood and was therefore sacred. In the sacrificial system of the Old Testament the meat of the animal was intended for food, but the life-blood of the sacrifice symbolised in a substitutionary manner the guilty life of the sinner.

The Council accepted the conclusion of James, and having embodied it in an official letter, its delivery to the churches was entrusted to Paul and Barnabas accompanied by Judas and Silas, leaders of the church (Acts 15:22–29). They were well received by the church at Antioch (Acts 15:30–35), and when the letter was read the members were greatly encouraged by the positive decision of the Council. So ended this first doctrinal discussion in the church.

When brethren fall out

The concluding verses of this chapter (Acts 15:36–41) record an unhappy episode involving Paul and Barnabas, these two godly men who had gone through so much together. 'Then after some days Paul said to Barnabas, "Let us now go back and visit our brethren in every city where we have preached the word of the Lord, and see how they are doing".' Barnabas had no problem with this suggestion since, like Paul, he would have been interested to see if the new converts had made spiritual progress following their last visit. But the sticking point was John Mark.

'Now Barnabas was determined to take with them John called Mark. But Paul insisted that they should not take with them the one who had departed from them in Pamphylia, and had not gone with them to the work. Then the contention became so sharp that they parted from one another' (Acts 15:37–39).

This was no mild disagreement, but had a certain deep bitterness to it. So deep in fact that we never read of Paul and Barnabas working together again. Although it does seem from 1 Corinthians 9:6 that the bitterness was eventually forgotten. It is pointless to try and apportion blame for the quarrel, since both seem to have been equally intransigent, an irresistible force against an immovable object—'Barnabas was *determined*', 'But Paul *insisted*'. Perhaps it was a case of a man's virtue becoming his greatest weakness—Paul's strength of character becoming harshness and severity, and the mildness of Barnabas becoming soft and flabby in consideration of Mark being his nephew.

But there are certain things we can learn even from a passage like this. To begin with, the very fact that this incident is recorded by Luke is a testimony to the veracity of the Bible. It might be thought that it would have been better not to have mentioned it at all, since it shows God's servants in such a poor light. But the Bible is God's word, and deals only with the truth even when, as in this case, it leaves us with a sense of disappointment. Let us keep in mind that the Bible portrays the lives of God's people, with both their triumphs and failings, as an encouragement and a warning. We should ask for God's grace to help us to emulate their strengths, and not to copy their failings. Paul tells us that 'whatever things were written before, were written for our learning, that we through the patience and comfort of the scriptures might have hope' (Romans 15:4).

This incident also teaches us to beware of the little things that can spoil our Christian characters and fracture relationships between believers. Here were two men who had faced some really big obstacles together—the hardships of travel, persecution from fellow Jews, and the violence of mobs. And in all this they were as one. But now, when faced with a relatively simple matter, such as whether John Mark should accompany them, they fall out with each other. I find that quite incredible, and yet it is true to life. It is the little things that we allow at times to irk and annoy us, and which the devil is quick to exploit if we give him half a chance.

Finally, we learn from this incident how God in his sovereignty, overrules for good, and will not allow our inconsistencies and foibles to prevent the on-going work of his kingdom. For after the quarrel the proposed single missionary journey became two, and the two workers became four. 'Then the contention became so sharp that they parted from one another. And so Barnabas took Mark and sailed to Cyprus; but Paul chose Silas and departed, being commended by the brethren to the grace of God. And he went through Syria and Cilicia, strengthening the churches' (Acts 15:39–41).

The entry into Europe

Read Acts chapter 16

The second missionary journey of Paul which begins in this chapter extends to Acts chapter 18:22. On their first journey, Paul and Barnabas began at Cyprus and ended at Derbe and Lystra, from where they retraced their steps for home. This time however, accompanied by Silas, Paul travels in the opposite direction beginning at Derbe and Lystra. But what makes this chapter so deeply significant is that Paul travels from east to west, crossing the Aegean Sea and taking the gospel from the continent of Asia to the continent of Europe.

A son in the faith

'Then he came to Derbe and Lystra. And behold, a certain disciple was there, named Timothy, the son of a certain Jewish woman who believed, but his father was Greek. He was well spoken of by the brethren who were at Lystra and Iconium. Paul wanted to have him go with him. And he took him and circumcised him because of the Jews who were in that region, for they all knew that his father was Greek' (Acts 16:1–3).

Timothy was the son of a mixed marriage, and in all probability he was converted under Paul's ministry when he visited Lystra on his first missionary journey some years before. The apostle had a warm affectionate regard for the younger man, and in his first letter addresses him with the words: 'To Timothy, a true son in the faith' (1 Timothy 1:2). As an unbeliever his father would have had no part in Timothy's spiritual upbringing, but both his grandmother and mother were Christians and had a determining influence upon him. Paul writes: '… when I call to remembrance the genuine faith that is in you, which dwelt first in your grandmother Lois and your mother Eunice, and I am persuaded is in you also' (2 Timothy 1:5).

From the Christian standpoint it is difficult enough bringing up children in the increasingly secular atmosphere of today, but where there is no support from the father the burden is even greater. But God gives grace even in that kind of situation, as is evident from the way in which Timothy's grandmother and mother handled it in the pagan world of New Testament times. For here was a young man who went on to become a missionary, a church leader, and a pastor.

One other thing to be said about Timothy is that he seems to have had a very low self-image. The picture we get is of a rather diffident, hesitant, timid personality. Paul writes to him: 'therefore I remind you to stir up the gift of God which is in you through the laying on of my hands. For God has not given us a spirit of fear, but of power and of love and of a sound mind' (2 Timothy 1:6–7). And again in his Corinthian letter Paul seems to be mindful of Timothy's sensitive character when he says; 'And if Timothy comes, see that he may be with you without fear; for he does the work of the Lord, as I also do' (1 Corinthians 16:10).

But in spite of his personality problems, and his lack of those dynamic qualities we usually associate with leadership, Timothy was greatly used of God. For he had the one thing that really matters, a great love for Christ and the gospel of salvation that he was called upon to preach.

As Paul and his companions continued their journey they informed the churches of the decision reached by the Jerusalem Council concerning the matter of circumcision. 'And as they went through the cities, they delivered to them the decrees to keep, which were determined by the apostles and elders at Jerusalem. So the churches were strengthened in the faith, and increased in number daily' (Acts 16:4–5). On the face of it, therefore, it seems as if Paul was going back on that decision when he circumcised Timothy before taking him on the journey. But Timothy was a special case because he was half Jew and half Gentile. His circumcision had nothing to do with his salvation, but was purely a matter of expediency to avoid unnecessary trouble among the Jews. Had Paul not circumcised Timothy, it might well have hindered his work among the Jewish population.

The lesson to be derived from this incident is perfectly straightforward. In the Christian life, and in the work of the gospel, we must be wise enough to know when to stand on principle, and when to compromise. We recall our Lord's criticism of the scribes and Pharisees. 'Blind guides, who strain at a gnat and swallow a camel!' (Matthew 23:24). Here were men who were ignoring the great principles of God's law while making a stubborn stand on the trivial and unimportant. The same failure today has ruined churches. May God save us from that.

The Macedonian call

'Now when they had gone through Phrygia and the region of Galatia, they were forbidden by the Holy Spirit to preach the word in Asia. After they had come to Mysia, they tried to go into Bithynia, but the spirit did not permit them. So passing by Mysia, they came down to Troas' (Acts 16:6–8). It seems that it was Paul's intention to preach the gospel to certain cities in Asia, but every door was shut to him. He was 'forbidden by the Holy Spirit'. The manner in which this restraint was put on him we are not told. It may have been that certain impressions on his mind, together with particular circumstances, convinced him inwardly that he was not to go in that direction. However it happened, it teaches us that we need at all times to be sensitive to the moving and guiding of the Holy Spirit in the work of the gospel. And that can only happen when we are living close to God.

Paul eventually arrived at Troas, which was on the coast and opposite Macedonia, a Roman province embracing the northern part of modern Greece. It was here that he made one of the most momentous decisions of his life. 'And a vision appeared to Paul in the night. A man from Macedonia stood and pleaded with him, saying, "Come over to Macedonia and help us." Now after he had seen the vision, immediately we sought to go to Macedonia, concluding that the Lord had called us to preach the gospel to them' (Acts 16:9–10).

We have here an exciting development in the spread of Christianity, with its view of Europe being won for Christ and—beyond that—the whole world. That vision is slowly being realised today, but not without its difficulties. Whereas Europe was especially blessed to be the first continent to receive the gospel, in our own day it is the only continent where the gospel is not advancing. The call to evangelise Europe, therefore, is once again as real and urgent as it was in Paul's time.

But why is Europe so spiritually impoverished? Well, let us go back for the moment to the Macedonian incident. The Greece of that day represented the highest aspirations of the human spirit in culture, philosophy and learning. And yet at its heart there was a need, expressed in the plea 'come over and help us', which could not be satisfied by human wisdom and culture alone. Paul was so right when he later wrote, 'Where is the wise? Where is the scribe? Where is the disputer of this age? Has not God made foolish the wisdom of this world? For since, in the wisdom of God, the world through wisdom did not know God, it pleased God through the foolishness of the message preached to save those who believe' (1 Corinthians 1:20–21).

Today Europe is back in the same position. As part of western civilisation and culture we have reached the very heights in the advancement of learning, science, and technology. But where has it got us? In our overweening pride and conceit we have jettisoned God and Christian values, and Europe has become a spiritual desert. Two world wars, and the political and economic fragmentation of Europe at the present time, is stark evidence of that.

Some writers have concluded that the man who appeared to Paul in his vision was none other than Luke, the author of Acts. They base this theory on the use of the pronoun 'we' in verse 10—'we sought to go to Macedonia'. Luke is indeed informing us that he joined Paul's party at this point, but there is no suggestion whatever that he was the 'man of Macedonia'. There are several other passages in Acts where the use of 'we' probably means that Luke was present at that time.

Arrival at Philippi

'Therefore, sailing from Troas, we ran a straight course to Samothrace, and the next day came to Neapolis, and from there to Philippi, which is the foremost city of that part of Macedonia, a colony. And we were staying in that city for some days' (Acts 16:11–12).

From Luke's remark that they stayed in that city 'for some days', we gather that Paul's visit to Philippi was a brief one. And yet he accomplished a good deal in that short time, including the laying of the foundation of the Philippian church which may well have begun as a house-group in the home of Lydia (Acts 16:40). That apart, the church itself grew strong and virile, being well grounded in the Christian faith.

Over the years, Paul developed a deep affection for the Philippian Christians addressing them as 'my joy and crown' (Philippians 4:1). It was the only church from which Paul was willing to accept material help, which in itself is a striking testimony to the love they had for him. Philippi was a Roman colony so that Paul, as a Roman citizen, would have been perfectly at home there. Indeed, we shall see later that he uses his Roman citizenship to good effect when he is imprisoned by the Philippian authorities (Acts 16:37–38).

A riverside prayer meeting

'And on the Sabbath day we went out of the city to the riverside, where prayer was customarily made; and we sat down and spoke to the women who met there' (Acts 16:13). Paul and his companions made for the riverside because they expected to find people there engaged in worship and prayer. But how did this custom begin? It seems to have started during the exile of the Jews in Babylon, when they no longer had the temple as a centre of worship. Instead they would gather together at the riverside for prayer, and to learn about the Law. When the exile was over they continued this practice by building synagogues as centres for prayer and worship. But it was required by Jewish law that there had to be a minimum of ten adult males in the community before a synagogue could be built. Philippi—as a Roman colony—had a tiny Jewish population so there was no synagogue, and the women were left to meet for prayer and worship at the riverside. Where were the men?

This group of devout women made up Paul's first congregation in Europe. What do we learn from that? Well, in the first place it presents us with a picture of many of our churches today, where the women are the majority in the congregation and membership. And what a debt we owe them! Often it is they, and not the men, who take the initiative, and provide the dynamic when it comes to organising the local church and promoting the work of God. In some churches women have taken on the leadership roles, either because the men will not do it, or because they are not there to do it. In both church and home today we are suffering from a crisis of leadership because men have abdicated their responsibility in this regard, and that is a denial of scriptural teaching.

Another insight arising out of this passage concerns the use of resources in God's work. Churches and individuals can be very negative in this, and in the meantime little, if anything, gets done. One hears the complaint, 'If only we had a bigger building, better facilities, more young people'. Or from the individual, 'if only I had the time, or were a better speaker, or was not so nervous'. In this negative way we delude ourselves about what we *would* do if we had all the resources we wanted. But the women at the riverside did not wait for a synagogue to be built; they simply got on with the business of Sabbath worship. I am sure God is more interested in what we *are* doing in the present with the resources we already have, however small and meagre. After all, if there is no synagogue there is always the riverside!

Europe's first convert

'Now a certain woman named Lydia heard us. She was a seller of purple from the city of Thyatira, who worshipped God. The Lord opened her heart to heed the things spoken by Paul. And when she and her household were baptised, she begged us, saying, "If you have judged me to be faithful to the Lord, come to my house and stay". So she persuaded us' (Acts 16:14–15).

Lydia seems to have been an intelligent, dynamic personality who had made her mark in the business world. Thyatira, where she came from, was the centre of the purple woollen industry from which the finest clothes were made for royalty and the nobility. She appears to have done well in business, and was a woman of some considerable means with a large house and servants. We gather that from being told that she and her 'household' were baptised, and that her house was big enough to provide hospitality for Paul and his companions.

Lydia was a woman who believed in the need for prayer, and she was a worshipper of the true God. But she knew nothing of God's salvation until Paul preached to her and the other women about the Lord Jesus Christ. It was only then that she came to saving faith, and later was able to say, "If you have judged me to be faithful to the Lord". She reminds us of Cornelius, who we looked at earlier in chapter 10. He, too, believed in prayer and worshipped God, but he still needed to have Peter come and preach the gospel to him.

There are thousands of folk in the churches up and down our country today who are like Lydia. They are earnest and sincere in their worship, they believe in God and in prayer, and they live good moral lives. But they know nothing whatever of personal salvation through faith in Christ. Mainly, I suspect, because they have never heard the saving gospel preached from the pulpit. Ask them if they have been born again of the Holy Spirit and they will look at you very suspiciously and may even take offence. That is because they have been led to believe that being a Christian means you attend church and believe in God. They have no understanding at all of being inwardly convicted of sin by the Holy Spirit, and putting their faith in the sacrifice of Christ as the only one to cleanse them of sin. 'For there is no other name under heaven given among men by which we must be saved' (Acts 4:12).

But how did Lydia come to that certainty of faith, it might be asked. Was it a case of making a mental decision to believe in the Lord Jesus? No, it was not that. Had it been that, she might well have made another mental decision the next day not to believe in Christ. What we are told is 'The Lord opened her own heart, to heed the things spoken by Paul'. Lydia did not open her own heart, neither was it Paul's doing. It was God, through the power of the Holy Spirit, who inwardly convicted Lydia of her sin and her need of a Saviour by honouring the word preached by Paul. And that is one reason why believers need to bring their unbelieving friends and acquaintances under the faithful preaching of the gospel. God will do his own work in opening their hearts to bring them to a believing faith in Christ.

One other thing we see here. After coming to faith Lydia did two positive things. First, she was baptised, along with the members of her household. Baptism is not in itself what makes a person a believer, but it is the outward expression and witness to the faith that one is a believer. Second, she put her new-found faith into practice by offering the hospitality of her home to Paul and his friends. There is quite a lot of emphasis in the New Testament about Christians being generous in the matter of hospitality. One reason is that we not only express God's grace in doing this, but also our homes can become centres for prayer and evangelism. It is highly probable that the church at Philippi, that developed later, began originally as a house-group in Lydia's home where the believers met for prayer and fellowship. When

Paul and Silas left prison we read in verse 40, 'So they went out of the prison and entered the house of Lydia; and when they had seen the brethren, they encouraged them and departed'.

Confrontation of powers

'Now it happened, as we went to prayer, that a certain slave girl possessed with a spirit of divination met us, who brought her masters much profit by fortune-telling. This girl followed Paul and us, and cried out, saying, "These men are servants of the Most High God, who proclaim to us the way of salvation." And this she did for many days. But Paul, greatly annoyed, turned and said to the spirit, "I command you in the name of Jesus Christ to come out of her". And he came out that very hour' (Acts 16:16–18).

We dealt in some detail with the subject of demon possession back in chapter 5, and again in chapter 8 when dealing with Simon the Sorcerer. We have nothing to add to that except to say that it is significant that it should surface again at this particular time. For the truth is that up to this point the powers of evil have had a free hand on the continent of Europe. But now the gospel is making inroads into Satan's territory, and he does not like it. Hence the confrontation between the power of darkness, represented in this demon possessed girl and her masters on the one hand, and the power of truth and righteousness, represented by Paul and his fellow-missionaries on the other.

In this particular confrontation the powers of darkness clearly lost out for, by the power of God, Paul cast out the spirit and the girl was healed. What is remarkable in this incident is the testimony of the girl herself to the power of God. 'These men are the servants of the Most High God who proclaim to us the way of salvation' (Acts 16:17). It is similar to those other testimonies by demonic agencies to the holiness of Christ given in the gospels. For example, the Gaderene demoniac cried out; 'What have I to do with you, Jesus, Son of the Most High God? I implore you by God that you do not torment me' (Mark 5:7). It is amazing that whereas men will try their best to deny the deity of the Lord Jesus, Satan and his emissaries do not.

But the girl's healing was not the end of the matter. Now that she was of no use to them, her masters took it out on Paul and Silas. 'But when her masters saw that their hope of profit was gone, they seized Paul and Silas and dragged them into the marketplace to the authorities' (Acts 16:19). They accused them of being troublemakers through their teaching of the gospel, and they were put in prison. 'And when they had laid many stripes on them, they threw them into prison, commanding the jailer to keep them securely. Having received such a charge, he put them into the inner prison and fastened their feet in the stocks' (Acts 16:23–24).

We can see that behind all this, the motive of greed and covetousness was at work in the hearts of these men. They had exploited the girl's affliction for the purpose of making money. And in that sense they were as much possessed by the power of evil as she had been. The spirit of greed and covetousness is a terrible affliction, and our Lord, and the New Testament as a whole, have a lot to say about it.

Not that money and material possessions are in themselves intrinsically evil, but the love of them can mean that God has to compete with them in our lives in order to get his way with us. Jesus warns of that danger, 'For where your treasure is, there your heart will be also' (Matthew 6:21). And Paul; similarly says, 'For the love of money is a root of all kinds of evil' (1 Timothy 6:10). That is certainly true where the life of our nation is concerned. At the heart of our society there is an ugly itching covetousness which is a prime factor in much of the discontent and unhappiness so many seem to be experiencing. And it can happen to Christians too. If we are not careful, little by little the love of money and material possessions can so grip our hearts that something drops out of our spiritual lives, and worldliness sets in. We need to pray that it might not happen to us.

A prison experience

In this final section of the chapter we find Paul and Silas in a wretched situation. They have been put in prison, and because the jailer has been given a special charge about their safety, he put them in the darkest part of the dungeon with their feet in the stocks. Nor should we forget that before their imprisonment they had both been lacerated with a severe whipping. Their pain and discomfort must have been almost unbearable. But the amazing thing is that we are not told that they were crying out in pain or voicing any resentment. Instead, they were praying and singing. 'But at midnight Paul and Silas were praying and singing hymns to God, and the prisoners were listening to them' (Acts 16:25). As one commentator puts it; 'Those old prison walls, which were accustomed to echo groans and sighs, resounded now with the unearthly strains of joy and praise' (Griffiths Thomas *Acts of the Apostles*, p. 271).

The fact was that Paul and Silas, although they were not aware of it at this point, were about to witness a double miracle. They would be miraculously set free, and their jailer would be miraculously saved. And it can be like that with us. We can find ourselves in a really tight spot with no idea of what may happen next. But if our trust is firmly in God through our prayers and praises, God can enter into that situation and everything can miraculously be changed for the better.

'Suddenly there was a great earthquake, so that the foundations of the prison were shaken; and immediately all the doors were opened and everyone's chains were loosed'. (Acts 16:26). It really is amazing the way in which liberal commentators seek to rationalise an incident like this, rather then accept that God's power was at work in a miraculous way. William Barclay dismisses the entire account in a single sentence: 'This was a district where earthquakes were by no means uncommon' (*Acts* St Andrews Press, p.136). That may be so, but it in no way contradicts the conclusion that the hand of God was in it. It is the timing of the earthquake that is important. If we believe that God is the God of creation, then he can easily use natural phenomena for his own purposes.

Furthermore, we must not overlook the fact that Paul and Silas had been praying and singing praises. Is it unreasonable to believe that God heard and answered their prayers? If it is, then we might as well give up praying altogether, since it is all a waste of time! The criticism is also made that it is highly improbable that the other prisoners would not have escaped, or that the jailer would not have attempted to prevent them doing so, 'And the keeper of the prison, awaking from sleep and seeing the prison doors open, supposing the prisoners had fled, drew his sword and was about to kill himself. But Paul called with a loud voice, saying, "Do yourself no harm, for we are all here"' (Acts 16:27–28).

But again we must not ignore the effect that the prayers and praises of Paul and Silas had upon them. We are told distinctly that 'the prisoners were listening to them' (Acts 16:25). The other prisoners would have been aware that Paul and Silas were worshippers of the true God, and what with the earthquake and the loosening of their shackles, they would have been overawed by the whole experience.

The jailer's conversion

'Then he called for a light, ran in, and fell down trembling before Paul and Silas. And he brought them out and said, "Sirs, what must I do to be saved?" So they said, "Believe on the Lord Jesus Christ, and you will be saved, you and your household." Then they spoke the word of the Lord to him and to all who were in his house' (Acts 16:29–32).

'What must I do to be saved?' Undoubtedly the most important question anyone could ask in his or her lifetime. And the answer is equally important. 'Believe on the Lord Jesus Christ and you will be saved'. But what exactly was in the jailer's mind when he asked that question? G. Campbell Morgan's answer is as follows: 'there was no evangelical faith in this. He did not mean, "What must I do to be eternally saved? He had not got nearly as far as that. It was fear, panic, and his own solution of this difficulty was suicide' (*Acts of the Apostles*—quoted in the Bethany Parallel Commentary, p. 804).

I do not agree. The jailer was awe-struck, and 'fell down trembling before Paul and Silas', but not because he feared or panicked for his life before the Roman authorities. He had been assured by Paul that the prisoners were all safe. He had no difficulty in that respect therefore the jailer may not have understood the full import of what he was asking. But he knew that Paul and Silas were God's servants and that they preached the way of salvation (Acts 16:17); that the earthquake gave them and the other prisoners an opportunity to escape which they did not take advantage of; and that they had a regard for his own life and safety. In short, he knew they were different, and he wanted whatever it was that made that difference and gave them the joy, and serenity, and confidence they had shown in the face of their sufferings.

Paul's reply, 'Believe on the Lord Jesus Christ and you will be saved', may seem on the face of it to be too brief and simple and in need of amplification, for it does not explain *how* believing in Christ brings salvation. Paul was well aware of that, since we are told that 'they spoke the word of the Lord to him and to all who were in his house'. That is, they explained further the way of salvation. But belief, or faith in the person of the Lord Jesus Christ, is still the initial step in salvation, and no amount of explanation or amplification can make up for that if it is missing.

It is evident that the jailer's conversion was real and genuine from the two things that followed. First, he put his new-found faith into practice. 'And he took them the same hour of the night and washed their stripes ... Now when he had brought them into his house, he set food before them; and he rejoiced, having believed in God with all his household' (Acts 16:33–34). Second, he and his household, who had come to faith in Christ, were baptised.

A time to speak

Up to this point Paul and Silas had put up with a good deal of ill treatment for the sake of the gospel, and without a word spoken in their self-defence. But with all that had happened the time had now come to speak. 'And when it was day the magistrates sent the officers, saying, "Let those men go". So the keeper of the prison reported these words to Paul, saying, "The magistrates have sent to let you go. Now therefore depart, and go in peace." But Paul said to them, "they have beaten us openly, uncondemned Romans, and have thrown us into prison. And now do they put us out secretly? No indeed! Let them come themselves and get us out"' (Acts 16:35–37).

The scriptures tell us that 'to everything there is a season ... A time to keep silence, and a time to speak' (Ecclesiastes 3:1,7). But we all need wisdom to be able to discern the one from the other. Paul felt it was right for him to speak up on this occasion. Was he simply standing on his dignity when demanding his rights as a Roman citizen? I do not think so. The rule of law is meant to be obeyed. And injustice had been done, and the magistrates themselves needed to be made aware of that. In the Christian life we must not confuse meekness with weakness, and it is part of our duty and witness to speak out against injustice in all its forms.

Paul may also have had in mind that by showing his respect for the rule of law he would make life easier for the believers he and Silas were leaving behind. 'So they went out of the prison and entered into the house of Lydia; and when they had seen the brethren, they encouraged them and departed' (Acts 16:40).

Preaching at Thessalonica and Athens

Read Acts chapter 17

In this chapter we learn something of the coming of Christianity to two very important centres in the ancient world. There was Athens, which had long since passed her glory, but was still regarded as the world's mecca of culture and learning; and there was Thessalonica, the capital of the province of Macedonia and a flourishing seaport. Its population of some 200,000 was mainly Gentile, but it also had a Jewish colony. This city was to be the scene of great success in Paul and Silas' work of evangelisation, and out of it there came a flourishing church to which Paul addressed two of his letters a couple of years later.

Today in modern Salonika tourists are shown a mosque which it is said is on the very spot where the synagogue stood in which Paul preached the gospel.

Preaching in the synagogue

'Now when they had passed through Amphipolis and Appollonia, they came to Thessalonica, where there was a synagogue of the Jews. Then Paul, as his custom was, went in to them and for three Sabbaths reasoned with them from the Scriptures, explaining and demonstrating that the Christ had to suffer and rise again from the dead, and saying, "This Jesus whom I preach to you is the Christ"' (Acts 17:1–3). There are three strands we can identify in Paul's preaching. It was rational, biblical, and evangelical.

For three Sabbaths 'he reasoned with them from the scriptures'. If that means anything at all, it suggests that he entered into a debate or dialogue with those in the synagogue, taking the eternal truths of the gospel and presenting them in a propositional form. He did not simply harangue them, or recite proof texts, or give a series of platitudes. Nor did he appeal only to their emotions and feelings, although their hearts would have been touched at some point. Instead, he appealed to their minds and wills, and undergirded his exposition of gospel truth with the principles of sound reasoning.

This approach to preaching is equally important today, because there is a form of preaching in evangelical circles which lays great emphasis upon experience and feelings, but without much thought. That is simply emotionalism. But one of the great purposes of preaching is to inform the mind and to illuminate people's understanding of the gospel. We dare not by-pass the mind therefore. At the same time we must not go to the other extreme and turn our preaching into an arid, intellectual exercise devoid of all love and feeling. There is a balance to be struck, since we are to minister to the whole person, and God must be worshipped with all the faculties with which he has blessed us. 'You shall love the Lord your God with all your heart, with all your soul, with all your strength, and with all your mind' (Luke 10:27).

Paul's preaching was not only rational it was also biblical. He did not rely on his powers of reasoning alone to persuade his hearers of the truth of the gospel. He reasoned with them 'from the scriptures'. Had he depended on reason alone he would have been a rationalist bringing every question of faith and conduct to the bar of human judgement. And that was certainly not his style, although it has to be said that there are those in our pulpits who come very close to that. They deny many of the great doctrines of scripture, such as the resurrection, and the substitutionary atonement; they reject the miracles, and in general shape their message to make it acceptable to man's reasoning in matters concerning religion.

Paul however recognised the limitations of the human mind. It can take us so far in our understanding of the purposes of God and, as we have shown, we should never despise the part that the human intellect plays in our Christian lives. But that part is circumscribed where God is concerned. In the book of Job, Zophar both asks and answers a very important question about understanding God. 'Can you search out the deep things of God? Can you find out the limits of the Almighty? They are higher than the heaven—what can you do? They are deeper than Sheol—what can you know? Their measure is longer than the earth and broader than the sea … For an empty-headed man will be wise when a wild donkey's colt is born a man' (Job 11:7–12).

What Zopher is saying is that man has about as much hope of understanding the infinity and complexity of God's character by his own powers of reasoning alone, as a donkey has of becoming a man. Man's only hope therefore is for God to make himself known to man. And that is what he has done in the revelation of the Bible. Our preaching and reasoning therefore must be firmly rooted in scripture. This also raises the question of the authority with which we preach. When a preacher deals with such big issues as the nature and destiny of man, heaven and hell, salvation and judgement, he needs more than the authority of his own reasoning to give substance and credibility to his message.

Indeed it is this lack of authority in so much preaching that accounts in a large part for the drift from our churches today. People are dissatisfied when all they hear are the opinions of the man in the pulpit. They are bound to ask themselves in what way is the message different from what they read in the newspapers, or what they hear politicians are saying. Whereas when the Bible is preached people are aware that it is not simply the word of the preacher. Jesus and the apostles rested their authority on the scriptures, and in this respect the disciple is not above his master.

Paul's preaching in the synagogue was also evangelical. By that we mean that it was centred entirely on the person of Christ, his atonement and resurrection. '... explaining and demonstrating that the Christ had to suffer and rise again from the dead, and saying, 'This Jesus whom I preach to you is the Christ' (Acts 17:3). That was always Paul's emphasis wherever he preached, as he makes clear to the Corinthians. 'For I determined not to know anything among you except Jesus Christ and him crucified' (1 Corinthians 2:2).

And that must be our emphasis. To preach Christ crucified does not mean we shall always be dealing with those texts and passages in the Bible which mention the Cross. But it does mean that all our preaching will have an evangelistic thrust to it, pointing men and women to Christ as the only remedy for man's sin. To quote John Stott, 'In his death Jesus did something objective, final, absolute and decisive; something which enabled him to cry on the cross, "It is finished", something which was described by the author of the epistle to the Hebrews as 'one sacrifice for sins for ever'; something which turns Christian good advice into glorious good news; which transforms the characteristic mood of Christianity from the imperative (do) into the indicative (done); which makes evangelism not an invitation to do something, but a declaration of what God has already done in Christ' (quoted by Timothy Dudley-Smith in *Authentic Christianity*, IVP, p. 54).

The response in the synagogue

'And some of them were persuaded; and a great multitude of the devout Greeks, and not a few of the leading women, joined Paul and Silas' (Acts 17:4). It seems contradictory to be told that some were persuaded, and also that 'a great multitude' came to faith in Christ. But the reference to 'some' points only to the Jews in the synagogue, whereas the 'great multitude' was made up of the Gentiles. These were proselytes to Judaism worshipping in the synagogue, who—when they heard the gospel—turned to Christ. As for the 'leading women' mentioned, they would have come from the leading families in the city.

What we have here is the wide spectrum from which early Christians gathered its converts. People from all walks of life were brought to Christ. It reminds us of the same wide appeal made by George Whitefield during the eighteenth century evangelical revival. He not only preached to the coal miners of Bristol, in the open air, but also in the drawing rooms of some of England's nobility. The gospel of Christ is timeless in the sense that it does not belong to any particular culture, nor is it directed to any group of people, but is meant for everyone. 'For all have sinned and fall short of the glory of God' (Romans 3:23), therefore all are in need of the salvation to be found only in Christ.

But the response to Paul's preaching was not all positive, there was also a negative re-action such as we have seen in the earlier part of his ministry. The unbelieving Jews stirred up the mob. 'But the Jews who were not persuaded, becoming envious, took some of the evil men from the marketplace and gathering a mob, set all the city in an uproar and attacked the house of Jason, and sought to bring them out to the people. But when they did not find them, they dragged Jason and some brethren to the rulers of the city, crying out, "These who have turned the world upside down have come here too"' (Acts 17:5–6).

In their anger and ignorance the unbelieving Jews never spoke a truer word. For that is exactly what the gospel does, it revolutionises a person's life, turning it upside down and changing that person's scale of priorities. The things once considered most important to that person, such as possessions, pleasure and personal ambition move downwards, and other things like prayer, worship and the Bible are given first place.

Searching the word

How long Paul and Silas remained in Thessalonica we cannot say, but in all probability it was considerably longer than the three weeks (Sabbaths) mentioned, since in his epistles Paul suggests that he settled down to follow his trade when he was there (1 Thessalonians 2:9, 2 Thessalonians 3:7–8). But even when they finally left, that was not the end of their problems. In the section in verses 10–15 the unbelieving Jews followed them to Berea, and once again stirred up the crowd. But this was not before the apostles had gained considerable success in their ministry among both Jews and Gentiles.

'Then the brethren immediately sent Paul and Silas away by night to Berea. When they arrived, they went into the synagogue of the Jews. These were more fair-minded than those in Thessalonica, in that they received the word with all readiness, and searched the scriptures daily to find out whether these things were so. Therefore many of them believed and also not a few of the Greeks, prominent women as well as men' (Acts 17:10–12). There are several insights to be touched upon here.

First, the Jews at Berea were 'more fair-minded' (NIV 'of more noble character') than those of Thessalonica. They listened to Paul and 'received the word with all readiness'. In short they had a teachable spirit, and no preacher can ask for more than that. We all know something of the other kind—people with an unteachable spirit and a closed mind. It is impossible to enter into an intelligent discussion or to reason with such people. Sad to say such a mental attitude is not entirely absent among believers, and shows itself in an unwillingness to accept pastoral authority, or to being taught out of God's word. They think they know it all and have nothing further to learn. But that is the very opposite of the meaning of Christian discipleship. The word disciple (Greek mathetes) literally means pupil or learner. We are all learners in the Christian life, and God will always have more light to break forth from his word.

Second, the Berean Jews 'searched the scriptures daily to find out whether these things were so'. Earlier, when we considered Paul's preaching at Thessalonica, we stressed the importance of appealing to people's reason. The response of the Bereans was a good illustration of that very thing. They were not credulous or unthinking in listening to Paul, but brought their minds to bear on the scriptures in order to discover if what he preached agreed with the word of God.

This showed great spiritual discernment on their part, something that is greatly needed in congregations today, for there are preachers who are not above what Paul condemns as 'handling the word of God deceitfully' (2 Corinthians 4:2); or as J B Phillips translates: 'no dishonest manipulation of the word of God'. What Paul means is, we should not make the scriptures say what we want them to say, or adapt our message in any way to suit trends in modern thinking. And the only way for members of the congregation to safeguard against that kind of false teaching is by knowing their Bible, and searching the word of God for themselves.

Third, when they satisfied themselves that this new message of the gospel was in agreement with the teaching and prophecies of the Old Testament, the Berean Jews embraced it in faith. 'Therefore many of them believed, and also not a few Greeks, prominent women as well as men' (Acts 17:12). The profession of these new converts therefore was not superficial, and likely to evaporate when Paul and Silas would leave them, but it was rooted solidly in the word of God. Having accomplished all that he could do in Berea, Paul was persuaded by his friends to leave the city in view of the hostility stirred up by the unbelieving Jews, and headed for Athens. 'So those who conducted Paul brought him to Athens; and receiving a command for Silas and Timothy to come to him with all speed, they departed' (Acts 17:15).

Before following Paul to Athens, I feel we ought to say something about Silas. We looked at Timothy earlier.

Man in the shadows

I describe Silas as a man in the shadows simply because, in the missionary work of the church, his role in Acts is overshadowed by that of Paul. Yet, in a strange way, that is his greatest virtue. He was himself a very gifted man, and yet he was quite content to take the second place, both to Paul and Peter. In his first epistle Peter says, 'By Silvanus our faithful brother as I consider him, I have written to you briefly…' (1 Peter 5:12). When Peter says he had written with the help of Silas, it could mean that Silas had taken down the content of the letter from Peter and gave it its final literary shape. Scholars tell us that the Greek of this epistle is polished and cultivated, not the kind of language Peter, a fisherman, would have used. Silas, on the other hand, was a highly gifted man and a Roman citizen like Paul.

In Acts 15:22 Silas is described as a leader and an emissary of the church, and in chapter 15:32 he is described further as a prophet who 'exhorted and strengthened the brethren.' The description of prophet is not used in the sense of being a foreteller of future events, but a 'forth-teller' of the gospel of Christ. In other words he was a preacher. Paul bears that out in his second letter to the Corinthians; 'For the Son of God, Jesus Christ, who was preached among you by us—by me, Silvanus, and Timothy—was not Yes and No, but in him was Yes' (chapter 1:19). With such gifts and qualities Silas could easily have been an 'up front' man, but he was perfectly willing to remain in the background and the shadows as long as the gospel was preached and God was glorified.

An idolatrous city

'Now while Paul waited for them at Athens, his spirit was provoked within him when he saw that the city was given over to idols' (Acts 17:16).

Athens at this time had long since passed her political importance and military greatness, but was nevertheless revered world-wide as a centre of philosophy and learning, of culture, art, and architectural magnificence represented by her many temples. But as Paul walked through the streets and squares of the city, and saw the scores of statues dedicated to the various pagan gods, he was both distressed and angered in his spirit.

The critics, as we might expect, have had a field day with Paul's Athenian ministry. Ernest Renan the French philosopher accuses him of being a cultural philistine, because he could not appreciate the fine works of sculpture, and called them idols. But Paul was not in Athens as a visiting tourist, to appreciate its works of art and its magnificent architecture. He was a missionary and a preacher of the gospel, and he was distressed to see such gifts of learning and artistic genius devoted to idolatry. For the truth was that, in spite of their philosophy and cleverness, the Athenians suffered from an intellectual restlessness and an emptiness of soul.

They knew nothing of the true and living God, and spent a great deal of their time in the market place and the city squares discussing the latest philosophy, and trading ideas on some new intellectual fad or novelty. 'For all the Athenians and the foreigners who were there spent their time in nothing else but either to tell or to hear some new thing' (Acts 17:21).

There are two insights here before we go any further. First, it tells us that human cleverness and knowledge, divorced from an understanding of who God is, can never fully satisfy the human spirit, hence the intellectual restlessness of the Athenians. They had no great moral or spiritual purpose to motivate them since their own philosophies had failed to give them an understanding of the true meaning of life. As Paul was to put it later: 'Where is the wise? Where is the scribe? Where is the disputer of this age? Has not God made foolish the wisdom of this world? For since, in the wisdom of God, the world through wisdom did not know God, it pleased God through the foolishness of the message preached to save those who believed' (1 Corinthians 1:20–21).

Second, the Athenians were interested in religion, but only as an academic exercise. They played with religious ideas in the way a small boy plays a game of marbles. It was not a matter of soul-searching for the truth. One still meets with people like that from time to time. They will discuss religion at the speculative level for hours on end. But they have no serious intention of seeking truth about the great realities of life, such as man's sin and his accountability to God as revealed in the Bible. Christians, too, can to a lesser extent get caught up with the latest spiritual fad or novelty on the evangelical scene—body ministry, inner healing, visual communication, dance and drama etc., all at the expense of growing in one's understanding of Bible basics.

The philosophers

Paul was so incensed with the obsessive idolatry of the Athenians that he determined to do something about it. 'Therefore he reasoned in the synagogue with the Jews and with the Gentile worshipers, and in the marketplace daily with those who happened to be there. Then a certain Epicurean and Stoic philosophers encountered him. And some said, "What does this babbler want to say?" Others said, "He seems to be a proclaimer of foreign gods", because he preached to them Jesus and the resurrection. And they took him and brought him to the Areopagus, saying, "May we know what this new doctrine is of which you speak? For you are bringing some strange things to our ears. Therefore we want to know what these things mean"' (Acts 17:17–20).

Who were these clever people who so contemptuously spoke of Paul as a babbler? The Epicureans were atheists since they did not believe in the one true God who is the creator of all things. They did however believe in the pagan gods, except that they were remote from men and had no interest in the world. Furthermore, everything that happened in the world was by chance rather than by any direct purpose and design. They also believed that the chief end of man was happiness and pleasure. The Stoics were pantheists, that is they identified God with the universe itself, and taught that men should seek to live in harmony with nature around them. They were also fatalists, believing that everything that happened in this life was pre-determined and had to be accepted without question. The result of this philosophy was to make men cold and hard in their hearts, and to destroy their finer feelings.

These were men who now invited Paul to the Areopagus, or Mars Hill, a kind of debating chamber where the members met to discuss religious and moral questions.

Paul on Mars Hill

'Then Paul stood in the midst of the Areopagus and said, "Men of Athens, I perceive that in all things you are very religious; for as I was passing through and considering the objects of your worship, I even found an altar with this inscription: TO THE UNKNOWN GOD. Therefore, the one whom you worship without knowing, him I proclaim to you"' (Acts 17:22–23).

Paul was never a man to miss an opportunity to preach the gospel, even when the congregation was made up exclusively of philosophers and intellectuals. He knew well enough that beneath their cloak of intellectualism they were hell-deserving sinners like everyone else. After all, he was no intellectual pygmy himself, and he needed salvation through Christ. He used the inscription to the unknown God as a point of contact, and goes on to show that the unknown whom they ignorantly worshipped is knowable through his own self-revelation. In this way Paul was also recognising that in all men there is the inward urge or instinct to worship, because man is a spiritual being. In outline the message itself falls into three parts.

In verses 24 and 25 he declares the fact of the Living God and his creative power in bringing the world and all mankind into being. As the maker of all things he cannot therefore be worshipped by anything the hands of man have made, such as the altars and images of the Athenians. Sad to say, modern man has still not learned this lesson and continues to worship the gods of his own making in the form of material things, money, sport, science, technology, pleasure etc. But these little deities of man's making have not given him the inward peace and fulfilment he is looking for, and as a result we do not find that people are happier or more content, or that our world is a better and safer place in which to live.

In verses 26–28 he declares that God has a universal and individual purpose for mankind. From the time that creation was brought into being God has been guiding history, and his hand is behind the rise and fall of nations. His purpose in this is that men 'should seek the Lord, in the hope that they might grope for him and find him, though he is not far from each one of us'. God's desire and purpose is that we should enter into a personal relationship with him, and enjoy the nearness of his presence. We have no need to sweat and struggle to find him, since he has come close to us, 'for in him we live and move and have our being'.

In verses 29–31 he declares the patience of God with sinful man. Over the centuries men and nations have gone their own way, relying on their own wisdom and understanding and worshipping the idols and gods of gold, silver and stone of their own making. God was very patient with this ignorant groping of mankind, but now the time of ignorance has past for he has revealed himself fully in the gospel of Christ. Men are not without excuse for not knowing God, and if they continue to reject the gospel they are faced with the prospect of God's judgement. The final proof that this will happen is seen in the manifestation of God's power in the resurrection of Jesus Christ from the dead.

The response

It was at this point when Paul mentioned the resurrection that there came a mixed response from his audience. 'And when they heard of the resurrection of the dead, some mocked, while others said, "We will hear you again on this matter". So Paul departed from among them. However, some men joined him and believed, among them Dionysius the Areopagite, a woman name Damaris, and others with them"' (Acts 17:32–34).

The reaction was threefold, and no different from the reaction any true evangelical preacher will get today. There were those who were openly contemptuous of the message. They found the whole experience faintly amusing and mock Paul's earnestness. The gospel for them was a fairy tale, and not to be taken seriously. The blood of those people is on their own heads, and one day they will answer at the judgement seat of God. There were those who treated the message seriously but wanted to speculate further, and so they put off making any definite commitment until a later time. But where salvation is concerned, and the destiny of one's soul, there is no room for delay. There may not be a tomorrow. Today is the day of salvation. But there were those also who believed the message and came to faith in Christ. That must always be the hope in our hearts when we preach the gospel, that God will have his hand on some member of the congregation who will cross over from the darkness of sin and ignorance into the light of Christ,

The church in Corinth

Read Acts chapter 18

The importance of this chapter lies in its account of the church in Corinth, a church that was to grow strong both in numbers and in the endowment of the most extraordinary spiritual gifts. Writing later to the members of that church Paul says: 'I thank my God always concerning you for the grace of God which was given to you by Christ Jesus, that you were enriched in everything by him in all utterance and all knowledge, even as the testimony of Christ was confirmed in you, so that you come short in no gift, eagerly waiting for the revelation of our Lord Jesus Christ' (1 Corinthians 1:4–7).

The city of Corinth was an important trading centre, rich, powerful, and pleasure loving. The very name Corinthians was a by-word for a debauched and lustful life-style. It was in that environment that Paul was to settle down for the next year and a half (Acts 18:11) preaching the gospel and establishing a church.

A Godly couple

'After these things Paul departed from Athens and went to Corinth. And he found a certain Jew named Aquila, born in Pontus, who had recently come from Italy with his wife Priscilla (because Claudius had commanded all the Jews to depart from Rome); and he came to them. So, because he was of the same trade, he stayed with them and worked; for by occupation they were tentmakers. And he reasoned in the synagogue every Sabbath, and persuaded both Jews and Greeks' (Acts 18:1–4).

Aquila and Priscilla are frequently mentioned in the New Testament, and always together. They were devoted to each other in marriage and in their desire to serve Christ. When Paul met with them they were more or less refugees, having been expelled from Rome, and he must have regarded it as a special providence since he knew no one in Corinth. They shared his trade of tent making and welcomed him into their home, which he made the base of his missionary operations. Later, in his letters, he refers to 'that church that is in their house' (1 Corinthians 16:19, Romans 16:5), and says that they 'risked their own necks for my life.

Clearly we have in Aquila and Priscilla a couple with open hearts and an open door, who believed that Christians can use their homes for purposes of evangelisation and worship. They represent in a sense all those ordinary believers in our churches today without whose faith and hard work the life of the local church would be much poorer.

Paul's vision

Corinth was a difficult place in which to testify to the gospel of Christ, and Paul soon came up against opposition. 'When Silas and Timothy had come from Macedonia, Paul was compelled by the Spirit, and testified to the Jews that Jesus is the Christ. But when they opposed him and blasphemed, he shook his garments and said to them, "Your blood be upon your own heads; I am clean. From now on I will go to the Gentiles"' (Acts 18:5–6). Reading between the lines it seems that, in view of the hostility he was up against, Paul had become somewhat down-hearted, for just when he needed it God spoke to him in a vision. '"Do not be afraid, but speak, and do not be silent; for I am with you, and no one will attack you to hurt you; for I have many people in this city". And he continued there a year and six months, teaching the word of God among them' (Acts 18:9–11).

We see from this that in the work of God's kingdom we all get our low moments when we need the word of encouragement. God spoke to Joshua when he took over the leadership following the death of Moses (Joshua 1:5); and to Elijah when he was in fear of his life from Jezebel, (1 Kings 19:11–18); and to the disciples in the upper room when they were feeling so low and dispirited following the crucifixion (Luke 24:36–49). That word of encouragement can come to us in different ways when we are in need of it. God will speak to us through his word in the Bible, through a sermon or address, in a Christian book or article, or through the word of a friend or colleague.

God told Paul he was to 'speak and not keep silent' (Acts 18:9). He was called to be a preacher and evangelist, and he was not to give up on that, however great the difficulties. When God gives us a task, he also gives us the strength to see it through. Was this, I wonder, why Paul urges Timothy to

'Preach the word! Be ready in season and out of season' (2 Timothy 4:2). That is, whether convenient or inconvenient the word must be preached. And the reason that Paul was not to give up preaching is given in the next thing God says to him: 'for I have many people in this city' (Acts 18:10).

In this simple statement we have two great truths concerning God's foreknowledge and election of those who are to be saved. It was God's intention to build a strong church in Corinth, and he would do it through the preaching of Paul. God knew—or set his heart in advance on—those who would respond to the word of salvation, whose names were written in the Lamb's book of life. 'For whom he foreknew, he also predestined to be conformed to the image of his Son, that he might be the firstborn among many brethren' (Romans 8:29). God describes these Corinthians as his people although at this time they still had not accepted the gospel, electing them to everlasting life.

Some are of the impression that to believe in the doctrine of election is to make preaching and evangelism unnecessary. But, as John Stott points out, the opposite is the case. 'It is only because of God's gracious will to save that evangelism has any hope of success and faith became possible. The preaching of the gospel is the very means that God has appointed by which he delivers from blindness and bondage those whom he chose in Christ before the foundation of the world, sets them free to believe in Jesus, and so causes his will to be done' (*Authentic Christianity*, p. 328).

Back in Antioch

As a result of the vision, and the encouragement it brought him, Paul remained in Corinth for eighteen months, and when his work was finished he began the long journey back to Antioch. 'So Paul remained a good while. Then he took leave of the brethren and sailed for Syria, and Priscilla and Aquila were with him. He had his hair cut off at Cenchrea, for he had taken a vow' (Acts 18:18). In all probability this was the Nazarite vow mentioned in Numbers chapter 6. It was undertaken in thankfulness for some blessing, and involved letting the hair grow and abstaining from wine and strong drink. Why Paul had taken such a vow we are not told, but it may have been in thankfulness for what God had done for him and through him in Corinth.

Vows can be easily made, and just as easily broken. But where God is concerned vows and promises made thoughtlessly can cause endless trouble. Broken marriage vows can bring great unhappiness, and create deep-seated feelings of guilt. When we become a church member, or get baptised, or have our children christened or dedicated, we make vows before God, and he will hold us responsible for their fulfilment.

From Cenchrea Paul made his way to Ephesus where he ministered in the local synagogue. 'When they asked him to stay a longer time with them, he did not consent, but took leave of them, saying, "I must by all means keep this coming feast in Jerusalem; but I will return again to you, God willing"' (Acts 18:20–21). Years ago Christians would often close a correspondence or take their leave by writing or saying the letters DV, Deo Volente (God wills). For Godly people this was not just a pious habit. They really believed God marked every step of their daily lives. We must of course distinguish between God's general will, revealed in the teaching and commands of scripture, and his particular will for each of us involving work, marriage, the use of money and so on. We must pray about these things, and if we cannot be specific we should tell God that we want, above all else, that his will should be done in our lives.

From Ephesus Paul continued his journey through Caesarea and Jerusalem, where he greeted the leaders of the mother church, and arrived finally at Antioch from where he had set out some three years before (Acts 18:22). This brought to a close the second missionary journey. In the next verse (23) the third missionary journey begins with Paul leaving Antioch and travelling through Galatia and Phrygia arriving once more at Ephesus. But what happened at Ephesus we must leave until chapter 19. In the meantime our present chapter closes with a new personality coming into the picture in the person of Apollos.

A deficient preacher

'Now a certain Jew named Apollos, born at Alexandria, an eloquent man and mighty in the Scriptures, came to Ephesus' (Acts 18:24). Alexandria boasted one of the greatest libraries of the ancient world, and was famous for its study of the Old Testament scriptures. Apollos came from this academic background and brought to his preaching his own gifts of learning and eloquence. Paul had a high regard for him as a preacher saying; 'I planted, Apollos watered, but God gave the increase' (1 Corinthians 3:6).

Apollos knew his Bible. He was 'mighty in the scriptures', and that is something we have the right to expect from any preacher. For if the preacher is not at home in the word of God, then he has neither the right nor the ability to teach it to others. And it is not only preachers who need to know their Bible, all Christians need to be familiar with it. The Bible is meant to be a workbook. We read and study it not only to inform us about God and his purposes, but also to give guidance on how to live our lives.

But for all his eloquence and learning, and zealousness in preaching, Apollos was deficient in one respect—he knew only the baptism of John and nothing of salvation through the saving work of Christ. What is more, it took that godly couple Aquila and Priscilla to put him on the right track. 'This man had been instructed in the way of the Lord; and being fervent in spirit, he spoke and taught accurately the things of the Lord, though he knew only the baptism of John. So he began to speak boldly in the synagogue. When Aquila and Priscilla heard him, they took him aside and explained to him the way of God more accurately' (Acts 18:25–26).

There are two things we learn from this. First, although Aquila and Priscilla were just two ordinary Christians they had the spiritual discernment to see that the scholarly Apollos lacked a true spiritual understanding of the gospel. This is something that is greatly needed among Christians today, for without discernment and the knowledge of God's word, all kinds of strange teachings and doctrinal aberrations can be preached from the pulpit.

Second, in defence of Apollos it must be said that he was a man of a humble and teachable spirit, since with all his scholarship he was perfectly willing to be instructed by these two ordinary Christians. For when we read in the closing verses that he went on to Achaia, he was no longer deficient in his understanding of the gospel, but 'he vigorously refuted the Jews publicly, showing from the scriptures that Jesus is the Christ' (Acts 18:28).

Strange happenings at Ephesus and Troas

Read Acts chapters 19 and 20

Chapter 19 is concerned wholly with Paul's missionary work at Ephesus where he stayed longer than at any other place, remaining there for three years (Acts 20:31). Ephesus was an important trading centre, but its fame throughout Asia lay in its being the guardian of the temple of the pagan goddess Diana. This is a chapter full of incident, beginning with Paul's strange experience when he meets with a group of Christian disciples.

Partial discipleship

'And it happened, while Apollos was at Corinth, that Paul, having passed through the upper regions, came to Ephesus. And finding some disciples he said to them, "Did you receive the Holy Spirit when you believed?" So they said to him, "We have not so much as heard whether there is a Holy Spirit." And he said to them, "Into what then were you baptised?" So they said, "Into John's baptism." Then Paul said, "John indeed baptised with the baptism of repentance, saying to the people that they should believe on him who would come after him, that is, on Christ Jesus." When they heard this, they were baptised in the name of the Lord Jesus. And when Paul had laid hands on them, the Holy Spirit came upon them, and they spoke with tongues and prophesied. Now the men were about twelve in all.' (Acts 19:1–7).

This is a difficult passage and raises some very complicated questions. Who were these disciples? Were they Jews? And where did they get their experience of Christianity? Was it under the preaching of Apollos when he knew only the baptism of John? And when Paul asked them: 'Did you receive the Holy Spirit when you believed?' was he referring to the gifts of the Spirit or the Spirit's work of regeneration in their lives? Calvin is of the former opinion. But for my own part I believe Paul was referring to the work of the Holy Spirit in salvation, since their answer clearly states that they knew only the baptism of John.

Paul does no criticise them for this, but he wants them to know that there is so much more to being a Christian than repentance such as John taught. There is the fullness of life through faith in Christ, and the indwelling of the Holy Spirit. Indeed, John himself had pointed to the coming Christ and said, 'I indeed baptise you with water; but one mightier than I is coming, … He will baptise you with the Holy Spirit and fire' (Luke 3:16). Having explained this to them, Paul baptised them in the name of Christ, and with the laying on of hands they received the Holy Spirit accompanied by the gifts of speaking in tongues and prophesying. This does not mean, as some understand it, that the visible gifts of the Spirit are for all who come to faith in Christ. As we saw earlier when dealing with Pentecost, the accompanying gifts were a special endowment for the general edifying of the church in its infancy.

One important lesson to emerge from this incident, is the vital necessity of experiencing true salvation through the regenerating power of the Holy Spirit in one's life, rather than having a form of godliness however sincere. For there is no doubt that people can be self-deceived in the matter of their salvation. They consider themselves saved because they believe in God, repent of their sins, attend church, pray, and live a morally good life—all with deep sincerity. Nicodemus (John 3), who was a good godly man, would have come into that category, and yet Jesus left him in no doubt that 'unless one is born again, he cannot see the kingdom' (John 3:3). This also means that a great responsibility rests on those of us who are preachers. For the failure on the part of some to understand the true nature of salvation is due in part to a lack of proper teaching from the pulpit. The issues can be so blurred that people are left confused and muddled about what salvation is, and how they are to obtain it.

Wasted effort

When Paul began preaching in the local synagogue he received a mixed reception. 'And he went into the synagogue and spoke boldly for three months, reasoning and persuading concerning the things of the kingdom of God. But when some were hardened and did not believe, but spoke evil of the Way before the multitude, he departed from them and withdrew the disciples, reasoning daily in the school of Tyrannus' (Acts 19:8–9).

Clearly Paul worked hard and conscientiously over a period of three months in seeking to persuade the Jews of the truth of the gospel. But when they rejected the message he then left them in their unbelief and directed his scene of operations elsewhere. This raises the question: is there a point when we leave people in ignorance of the gospel? To quote Calvin again it seems he is quite clear on this question. 'We are warned by this example that when we experience hopeless and incurable obstinacy, we must not waste our efforts any longer. For that reason Paul himself advises Titus (Titus 3:10) to avoid a heretical man after one or two admonishments. For the word of God has shameful insult inflicted upon it, if it is prostituted to pigs and dogs' (*Acts of the Apostles*, p. 154). Similarly Jesus instructed the seventy-two when sending them on an evangelistic mission to say to those who rejected the message: 'The very dust of your city which clings to us we wipe off against you' (Luke 10:11). And again he says, 'Do not give what is holy to the dogs; nor cast your pearls before swine' (Matthew 7:6).

We must be careful, however, not to make this a principle of universal application. People are different, and we must be discriminating in the way we witness to them. There will be those who wilfully and obstinately reject the truth, and it would be totally negative to continue with them when our witness might yield more positive results in another direction. In dealing with people we do not vary the truth, but we do vary the method of approach. The important thing is that we do not 'give up' on the possibility that the person who rejects the truth from us may, at some later point, be saved. We recall that Jesus said to the disciples: 'I sent you to reap that for which you have not laboured; others have laboured, and you have entered into their labours' (John 4:38).

An extraordinary ministry

When Paul left the synagogue and began operations in the lecture hall of Tyrannus, it was the start of a ministry that was to see extraordinary blessing. 'And this continued for two years, so that all who dwelt in Asia heard the word of the Lord Jesus, both Jews and Greeks' (Acts 19:10). We said earlier that Ephesus was an important trading centre. This meant that there was always a flood of visitors to the city to engage in buying and selling in the markets, and to worship at the temple of Diana. This in turn provided Paul with a great opportunity for evangelisation, for they would have heard of what went on in the hall of Tyrannus. Every day for hours on end he would discuss with them the things concerning the kingdom of God, and they would take the message back with them to their homes and districts. In this way 'all who dwelt in Asia heard the word of the Lord Jesus' (Acts 19:10).

But the ministry was not only extraordinary in the extent of its impact, but also in the extraordinary signs and wonders that accompanied it. 'Now God worked unusual (NIV extraordinary) miracles by the hands of Paul, so that even handkerchiefs or aprons were brought from his body to the sick, and the diseases left them and the evil spirits went out of them' (Acts 19:11–12).

We may wonder why the miracles are said to have been unusual or extraordinary when that is a description we would give to any miracle. I can only think that in this instance there was no direct contact between Paul, either by touch or the spoken word, and those who benefited from the power of God by means of the handkerchiefs and aprons. We have not come across this before in Acts, although we dealt with the question of miracles back in chapter 3.

We can only add a brief word to what was said above. First, the purpose of miracles in Acts was to authenticate the apostles as God's servants, and to give authority to the message they preached. As Paul says, 'Truly the signs of an apostle were accomplished among you … in signs and wonders and mighty deeds' (2 Corinthians 12:12). Second, miracles were given to mark special epochs in God's plan of redemption, and one of those epochs was Pentecost and the formation of the church. Third, as to the possibility of miracles today we must be open to God's power working through either natural processes or the miraculous.

Principalities and powers

'Then some of the itinerant Jewish exorcists took it upon themselves to call the name of the Lord Jesus over those who had evil spirits, saying, "We exorcise you by the Jesus whom Paul preaches". Also there were seven sons of Sceva, a Jewish chief priest, who did so. And the evil spirit answered and said, "Jesus I know, and Paul I know; but who are you?" Then the man in whom the evil spirit was leaped on them, overpowered them, and prevailed against them, so that they fled out of that house naked and wounded' (Acts 19:13–16).

In his letter to the Corinthians Paul says: 'I fought with beasts at Ephesus' (1 Corinthians 15:32). Was this encounter with demonic intelligences and the dark powers of the spirit world part of his thinking, I wonder? Ephesus was certainly a very pit of evil in that respect. That is clear from what followed when news of what happened to the sons of Sceva became known. 'This became known both to all Jews and Greeks dwelling in Ephesus; and fear fell on them all, and the name of the Lord Jesus was magnified... Also, many of those who had practised magic brought their books together and burned them in the sight of all. And they counted up the value of them, and it totalled fifty thousand pieces of silver' (Acts 19:17–19). This large sum of money indicates the wide and morbid obsession that people had in practices of the occult.

We have already considered the whole question of occult powers when dealing with Simon the sorcerer in chapter 7. We need only add a further brief word. Today it is unfashionable in the church to believe either in the reality of a personal Devil, or in the existence of demonic powers under his direction. For example, one modern commentator on the passage says: 'This is a vivid bit of local colour from the Ephesus scene', as though it were unthinkable that this kind of thing could happen today. And yet this passage clearly teaches that the demonic spirits themselves clearly recognised the authority of Jesus and of Paul his servant.

We must not allow our theological thinking in this matter therefore to be shaped or moulded by the trendy theologians, or by fashions in today's church, but by the clear teaching of the Word of God. And as this passage shows, on this occasion the powers of darkness were gloriously defeated and 'the word of the Lord grew mightily and prevailed' (Acts 19:20).

The Ephesian riot

This concluding passage of chapter 19 is long and detailed, but the main lines of thought are contained in the opening verses 23–28.

'And about that time there arose a great commotion about the Way. For a certain man named Demetrius, a silversmith, who made silver shrines of Diana, brought no small profit to the craftsmen. He called them together with the workers of similar occupation, and said: "Men, you know that we have our prosperity by this trade. Moreover you see and hear that not only at Ephesus, but throughout almost all Asia, this Paul has persuaded and turned away many people, saying that they are not gods which are made with hands. So not only is this trade of ours in danger of falling into disrepute, but also the temple of the great goddess Diana may be despised and her magnificence destroyed, whom all Asia and the world worship". Now when they heard this, they were full of wrath and cried out, saying, "Great is Diana of the Ephesians!"'

Disturbance

In our study of Acts thus far we have seen again and again that the preaching of the gospel caused disturbance. And that was certainly true in Ephesus where the disturbance involved the whole city, and might have had some very ugly consequences had not the town clerk intervened to diffuse the situation. But why does Christianity introduce this element of disturbance into people's lives and situations? Christ, after all, is set forth in the scriptures as the prince of peace. And did not he say in the beatitudes; 'blessed are the peacemakers for they shall be called sons of God'? (Matthew 5:9).

The truth is we have a paradox at the heart of the Christian faith namely, that it is precisely because he is a peacemaker that the Christian is also a disturber of peace and creates hostility in others. This happens because the Christian is different from other people. At Ephesus Paul did not directly attack the worship of Diana, nor did he criticise Demetrius and his fellow craftsmen for making silver images of the goddess. He simply preached the message of salvation and the need for men and women to be at peace with God through faith in the Lord Jesus Christ. But that in itself caused the disturbance because it portrayed a totally different way of life from the one people were already living. And that is what always happens. The Christian, said Jesus, is to be light and salt in the world, both of which make a difference to the medium they have contact with. Light exposes the evil things of darkness, and salt affects the food on which it is placed. All great causes introduce division and disturbance into people's lives, and there is no greater cause than the kingdom of God. One of the main lessons in our Lord's parable of the Yeast and the Dough (Matthew 13:33) is to show the unsettling and disturbing influence the gospel has in a person's life.

True and false religion

Another element in the Ephesian riot was the clash between Jesus and Diana, or between true and false worship. Demetrius himself made that distinction clear when he said to his fellow craftsmen; 'this Paul has persuaded and turned away many people, saying that they are not gods which are made with hands' (Acts 19:26). And that is the main feature of false religion in every age; it is the product of man's own mind and imagination. Millions today worship at the shrines of gods of man's own making, in as real a manner as the people of Ephesus venerated the silver shrines of Diana, made by Demetrius and his fellow craftsmen.

The images may no longer be made of silver, or wood or stone, but the essence of idolatry remains the same. It is that which is central in people's lives and to which they devote the loyalty and devotion, which rightly belongs to God alone. And that can include just about anything—money, sport, pleasure, politics etc. But in our multi-faith society church leaders have forgotten this, and wish to widen the ecumenical debate to include other religions in which icons and images are still objects of veneration and worship. The distinctive of Christianity on the other hand is not that it is one among other religions, but is a direct revelation of God in Christ and he alone is to be worshipped.

Vested interest

A third feature of the riot was that it brought to the surface the sinfulness and greed in the human heart. Demetrius and his fellow craftsmen pleaded the cause of religion with their slogan 'Great is Diana of the Ephesians', but the real motive for their hostility was that the preaching of the gospel had touched their pockets. Demetrius made that perfectly clear when he said to them; 'Men you know that we have our prosperity by this trade' (Acts 19:25). As more and more people turned to Christ, the sale of images was falling off. It was not any kind of faith, but finance, that was uppermost in the mind of Demetrius, and motivated his resentment.

And throughout history resentment has been sparked off whenever the truth of the gospel has come up against vested interest, even in the church itself. It was Martin Luther's attack on the moneymaking scandal in the sale of indulgences in the Roman Catholic Church that fired the first shot in the Reformation. It was William Wilberforce and the evangelical Clapham Sect that put the final nail in the coffin of the slave trade in this country, and cost the government twenty million pounds in lost revenue. And William Booth and his Salvation Army incurred great wrath with the big brewers by his preaching and attack upon the evils of the drink trade among the poorer classes.

The basic truth to come out of this passage therefore is that the gospel, either directly or indirectly, must have an effect upon the customs and habits of society as well as in the lives of individuals. In that sense we can never separate evangelism from social action.

As we move into chapter 20 it is perfectly evident from the first verse that there ought not to be any division at this point. 'After the uproar had ceased, Paul called the disciples to himself, embraced them and departed to go to Macedonia' (Acts 20:1). As we read the next verses (2–6), we follow Paul and his companions through Greece, back to Macedonia, and arrive finally at Troas where they remained for seven days.

The Christian Sunday
'Now on the first day of the week, when the disciples came together to break bread, Paul, ready to depart the next day, spoke to them and continued his message until midnight' (Acts 20:7). This is possibly the earliest reference to the official observance by the church of the first day of the week, Sunday, for the purpose of worship and communion. It is also one of the first accounts of what a Sunday service was like.

Back in Genesis we read that God 'rested on the seventh day from all the work which he had done. Then God blessed the seventh day and sanctified it' (Genesis 2:2–3). By the time of the Exodus the Sabbath had become a covenant obligation enshrined in the fourth commandment. 'Remember the Sabbath day to keep it holy' (Exodus 20:8). But when the New Testament church came into being, and more and more Gentiles were converted, the Jewish Sabbath was replaced by Sunday as the day for worship. The phrase 'first day of the week' is also mentioned in 1 Corinthians 16:2, and in Revelation it is called 'the Lord's day' (Revelation 1:10).

But although the day was changed, the principle underlying the institution of the Sabbath as a day set apart for worship remained. The Sabbath as a creation ordinance preceded the Mosaic commandment, and therefore has a permanent validity. Sunday was also the day of Christ's resurrection, and that is what made it so significant for the early Christians.

This verse also tells us something about the content of worship among the first Christians. The service included the preaching of the word by Paul, the sacrament of the Lord's supper, and the Agape or Love Feast. On this occasion Paul spoke for rather a long time since he was to leave them the next morning. Also his discourse would have included discussion as well as straight preaching. The expression 'break bread' is twice mentioned, the second time in verse 11 following the restoration of Eutychus. 'Now when he had come up, had broken bread and eaten, and talked a long while, even till daybreak, he departed'. The first breaking of bread was the sacrament, the second a proper meal to which all contributed, and was known as a love feast in which the believers enjoyed fellowship together, and discussed with one another. It signified the family spirit of the Christian community.

The remaining verses in this section, verses 8–12, contain the incident of the young man Eutychus who fell from the upper storey during Paul's lengthy preaching and discussion session. There is not a great deal here for the expositor, and we may wonder why Luke even includes it in his history of the church. It might be that he included the miracle, for that is what his restoration implies, because it illustrated the power of the gospel which Paul was preaching.

A sad farewell

When Paul left Troas he had it in mind to get to Jerusalem in time for the feast of Pentecost. In verses 13–16 we have the various stages of that journey as far as Miletus. From there he sent a message to the Ephesian elders inviting them to meet with him for a last farewell. 'From Miletus he sent to Ephesus and called for the elders of the church. And when they had come to him, he said to them: "You know, from the first day that I came to Asia, in what manner I always lived among you"' (Acts 20:17–18). What then follows is one of the most moving passages in all scripture.

The first part of verses 18–21 is highly charged with emotion as he describes his ministry among them '... serving the Lord with all humility, with many tears and trials, which happened to me by the plotting of the Jews.' We can understand the reference to a humble spirit and the trials and hostility of the Jews since we have come across all that often enough in Acts. But why tears? Clearly they were not because of his trials and sufferings. He wept because he had a true pastor's tender heart. Every pastor who takes his ministry seriously will have those occasions when he weeps before the Lord because of his concern for the spiritual needs of his people, and the care of their souls.

Verse 20, 'how I have kept back nothing that was helpful, but proclaimed it to you, and taught you publicly and from house to house'. He was not selective in his preaching, giving them only what they wanted to hear. He was fearless in his declaration of the gospel—even when the truth was hurtful. His concern was the well being of their souls. This may not have made him the most popular preacher, but he knew that one day he would have to account to God for his ministry, as we all shall.

Verse 21, 'testifying to Jews, and also to Greeks, repentance toward God and faith toward our Lord Jesus Christ.' His message was truly evangelical, stressing the need for repentance and not giving people the impression that God overlooks the ugliness of sin in the human heart. But he did not leave it at that. He showed that the problem of man's sin can be dealt with through faith in Christ's death on the Cross. That was the core of his message, and it is still the message the world needs to hear from the church today.

In the second part of verses 22–27 Paul speaks of what lay ahead. 'And see, now I go bound in the spirit to Jerusalem, not knowing the things that will happen to me there, except that the Holy Spirit testifies in every city, saying that chains and tribulations await me'. In the work of the gospel he felt himself under the constraint of the Holy Spirit. Driven by this inner compulsion he could face whatever lay ahead with confidence. Even the prospect of death held no fear for him. 'But none of these things move me; nor do I count my life dear to myself, so that I many finish my race with joy, and the ministry which I received from the Lord Jesus to testify to the gospel of the grace of God'.

There is a sense in which all believers should experience this inner compulsion of the Spirit to some degree, when it comes to making Christ known to others. Preachers especially require this holy passion when dealing with eternal issues, which for some are a matter of life and death. Richard Baxter once said, 'I did preach as never sure to preach again, as a dying man to dying men'.

Verses 25–27, 'And indeed, now I know that you all, among whom I have gone preaching the kingdom of God, will see my face no more. Therefore I testify to you this day that I am innocent of the blood of all men. For I have not shunned to declare to you the whole counsel of God'. Convinced as he was that he was speaking to them for the last time, Paul could look back on his ministry at Ephesus and derive great comfort from knowing that he had not diluted the gospel's content, or fed the people with an anaemic Biblical diet. He had given the whole counsel of God. Hence his expression; 'I am innocent of the blood of all men'. He may well have had Ezekiel 3:18ff in mind. For as preachers we do in fact participate in the guilt of those who are lost, if we fail to give the whole counsel of God. We must warn of hell, as well as give the promise of heaven, of God's wrath as well as speak of his love, of his judgement as well as offer his mercy.

In the third section, verses 28–31, Paul reminds them of their duties and responsibilities as pastors and shepherds of God's people. 'Therefore take heed to yourselves and to the flock among which the Holy Spirit has made you overseers, to shepherd the church of God which he purchased with his own blood. They were to care for their own souls first if they were to be fitted to care for the souls of others. I recall reading somewhere: 'The soil out of which all great preaching grows, is the pastor's own devotional life'.

Verses 29–31, 'For I know this, that after my departure savage wolves will come in among you, not sparing the flock. Also from among yourselves men will rise up, speaking perverse things, to draw away the disciples after themselves. Therefore watch, and remember that for three years I did not cease to warn everyone night and day with tears'. The local church is always open to attack by the Devil on two fronts. From without by 'savage wolves', and from within by members who, wittingly or otherwise, do the devil's work for him by causing dissension within the fellowship. The pastor must be on his guard against this deadly infection of the world, and he will do that best by warning, guiding, and instructing his people in the light of the scriptures.

In the last section, verses 32–35, Paul commends the elders to the grace of God and leaves them with an unforgettable word of the Lord Jesus. 'It is more blessed to give than to receive'. This saying of our Lord is not actually found in the canonical gospels, but it clearly breathes his spirit. Paul had himself given all that he possessed in the cause of Christ, and was willing, as we have seen, to give even his life as he faced an uncertain future. The true pastor will do the same. He will spend himself to the utmost in caring for the flock of God. He will not be sparing in giving of his time and energy, or be content to do only the acceptable in the eyes of others, but he will put his all on the altar for God.

The final picture, verses 36–38, is of Paul kneeling and praying with the elders who sadly feel the weight of his words 'that they would see his face no more'. The sails are set, waiting for the wind as they accompany him to the ship. He passes out of their sight, but never out of their lives. So it is with all the faithful in Christ Jesus. Our kinship is eternal.

'Blest be the tie that binds
Our hearts in Christian love;
The fellowship of kindred minds
Is like to that above.

When for a while we part,
This thought will soothe our pain,
That we shall still be joined in heart,
And hope to meet again.

From sorrow, toil, and pain,
And sin we shall be free;
And perfect love and friendship reign
Through all eternity'.

John Fawcett (1739–1817)

From Miletus to Jerusalem

Read Acts chapters 21, 22 and 23

Chapter 21 opens with Paul leaving his Ephesian friends at Miletus and continuing his voyage to Jerusalem. 'Now it came to pass, that when we had departed from them and set sail, running a straight course we came to Cos, the following day to Rhodes, and from there to Patara' (Acts 21:1). Various ports of call on the way are mentioned and the voyage ends at verse 14. It is not a detailed account since Luke is not writing a travel-guide, but is recording Paul's missionary progress. The best approach for the expositor therefore is to take an overview of this passage, and to touch on those points of special spiritual interest.

The first thing to notice is that at the various ports of call there were groups of believers with whom Paul and his friends were able to have fellowship. This happened at Tyre, verses 3–4, Ptolemais verse 7, and Caesarea verse 8. What this tells us is that in the Christian family wherever we travel we can always expect to meet up with those of like mind. We may find ourselves in a strange town or city and feel lonely and isolated; but once we seek out a church where the gospel is faithfully preached, we soon find ourselves accepted, and enjoying fellowship with those who shortly before were total strangers.

This is what it means to be brothers and sisters in Christ, and in verse 5 we have a wonderful picture of this very thing. 'When we had come to the end of those days, we departed and went on our way; and they all accompanied us, with wives and children, till we were out of the city. And we knelt down on the shore and prayed.' Here we see men, women and children all kneeling on the sand with Paul and his friends to send them on the next stage of their journey. It exemplifies, at its best, the love that members of the family of God have for one another, and reminds us of the words of Jesus: 'By this all will know that you are my disciples, if you have love for one another' (John 13:35).

A second thing to notice is how those who had a deep affection for Paul, and were concerned for his safety, tried to dissuade him from going to

Jerusalem. This happened at Tyre. 'And finding disciples we stayed there seven days. They told Paul through the Spirit not to go up to Jerusalem' (Acts 21:4). This raises a slight difficulty for some. We learned previously (Acts 20: 22–23) that Paul was led of the Holy Spirit to go to Jerusalem, knowing that prison and hardships awaited him. But it now appears that his friends, also by the Spirit, were seeking to prevent him doing so. Is there a contradiction here? I do not think so. The friends also knew through the Spirit of the trials in store for Paul and were saying in effect, 'If you are not prepared for this, Paul, then do not go to Jerusalem'. It was, in fact, both a warning and a test of his faith.

We have the same thing repeated by his friends at Caesarea. 'And as we stayed many days, a certain prophet named Agabus came down from Judea. When he had come to us, he took Paul's belt, bound his own hands and feet, and said: "Thus says the Holy Spirit, 'So shall the Jews at Jerusalem bind the man who owns this belt, and deliver him into the hands of the Gentiles'". Now when we heard these things, both we and those from that place pleaded with him not to go up to Jerusalem' (Acts 21:10–12). What Agabus prophesied did in fact come true, for at Jerusalem Paul was handed over to the Roman Gentiles. But he was not seeking to prevent Paul going there, he simply warned him of troubles ahead.

Now two things emerge from all this. First, we notice that it was out of love for him that his friends tried to dissuade Paul from carrying out God's will. And that happens still. Those who love us most can sometimes be the greatest hindrance to our Christian growth and obedience. Job's wife, out of love for him, became unwittingly the mouthpiece of Satan when she urged him to 'curse God and die'. But he would have none of it. 'You speak as one of the foolish women speaks. Shall we indeed accept good from God, and shall we not accept adversity?' (Job 2:9–10).

Paul's answer to his friends was the same as Job's. 'What do you mean by weeping and breaking my heart? For I am ready not only to be bound, but also to die at Jerusalem for the name of the Lord Jesus' (Acts 21:13). This brings us to the second thing here—the depth of Paul's conviction. He knew without any shadow of doubt that God had laid it on his heart to go to Jerusalem and face whatever lay in store for him. And it was this fire of conviction that strengthened him in his refusal to be deflected from his purpose.

That must surely speak to us as Christians today. For ours is an age in which people seem to lack conviction about anything of substance, whether in political life or social ideals, and certainly not in the things of the Spirit. They may have strong feelings about sport, or fashion, or moneymaking, but that is about as far as it goes for many. And the sad thing is that this flabbiness of thinking has infected the life of many Christians so that they lack the strength of conviction to withstand the pressures of society, The temptation arising out of the glamour and beckoning of the world's life-style they find hard to resist, and they drift into an acceptance of its worse features. A strong Christian character and unshakeable spiritual convictions are the result of a steady diet of prayer, the teaching of God's word, and worship, not with the flimsy values of our consumer society. That is why this passage ends with the words, 'So when he would not be persuaded, we ceased, saying, "The will of the Lord be done"' (Acts 21:14).

At Jerusalem

'And when we had come to Jerusalem, the brethren received us gladly. On the following day Paul went in with us to James, and all the elders were present. When he had greeted them, he told in detail those things which God had done among the Gentiles through his ministry. And when they heard it, they glorified the Lord' (Acts 21:17–20).

Clearly Paul was warmly received as a brother in Christ by James and the other leaders of the mother church, and they genuinely praised God when he told them of all God had done among the Gentiles. But as we continue reading about the meeting I cannot help feeling that there was a certain tension in the air connected with Paul's visit, he may even have proved something of an embarrassment to James and the elders. I say that because I find their attitude most perplexing, and I am not sure what conclusion to draw.

It seems that rumours had been circulating to the effect that Paul, on his missionary travels, had been encouraging Jews converted to the Christian faith to forsake the customs and traditions of the Mosaic Law. James the chief spokesman explained the position to Paul. 'You see, brother, how many myriads of Jews there are who have believed, and they are all zealous for the law; but they have been informed about you that you teach all the Jews who are among the Gentiles to forsake Moses, saying that they ought not to circumcise their children nor to walk according to the customs. What then? The assembly must certainly meet, for they will hear that you have come" (Acts 21:20–22).

Here was the old problem of ceremonialism raising its head again, and seemingly getting the sympathetic backing of James and the leaders of the Jerusalem church. The fact was, they were anxious to conciliate the Jewish believers because they were desperate to avoid causing a split in the church. The amazing thing is they were fully aware of Paul's insistence in the gospel of setting the Jews free from ceremonialism, especially the rite of circumcision, as contributing in any way to God's salvation, and yet they speak of it as merely a rumour, and want him to deny it. But he had preached often enough, 'circumcision is nothing' (1 Corinthians 7:19).

But further to that, they then suggest to Paul the following solution. 'Therefore do what we tell you. We have four men who have taken a vow. Take them and be purified with them, and pay their expenses so that they may shave their heads, and that all may know that those things of which they were informed concerning you are nothing, but that you yourself also walk orderly and keep the law' (Acts 21:23–24).

We need to look carefully at this compromise James and the elders were putting forward. This was the Nazarite vow mentioned in Numbers 6:2–12 and involved not merely shaving the head when the vow was completed—Paul himself had done that at Cenchrea (Acts 18:18)—but also the making of sacrifices before the priest; 'and the priest shall offer one as a sin offering and the other as a burnt offering, and make atonement for him ' (Numbers 6:11). The expenses Paul was being asked to pay therefore would be used to cover the cost of these sacrificial animals.

I find this attempt at compromise on the part of James and the elders quite deplorable, and the best construction I can put on it is to say that they were doing the wrong thing from the right motive. Their one concern was to keep the peace. I agree with A W Tozer: 'In a fallen world like ours unity is no treasure to be purchased at the price of compromise', especially where the truth of the gospel is involved. To some degree the Jerusalem church was compromising her faithfulness to Christ in failing to take a firm line with those zealous for the law.

The other equally perplexing thing in all this is that Paul seems to go along with it. 'Then Paul took the men, and the next day, having been purified with them, entered the temple to announce the expiration of the days of purification, at which time an offering should be made for each one of them' (Acts 21:26). Why did he do that? Calvin says; 'I do not deny that he was almost forced to concede this to the entreaties of the brethren' (*Acts of the Apostles*, p. 204). I agree with him. I believe Paul was pressurised into doing something he was deeply uneasy about in the depths of his heart. But who are we to criticise James, the elders or Paul? Have we never bent with the wind, and often from the best motives?

Paul's arrest

In the end the compromise attempted by Paul and the elders only complicated matters and led to a riot among the Jewish population. 'Now when the seven days were almost ended, the Jews from Asia, seeing him in the temple, stirred up the whole crowd and laid hands on him, crying out, "Men of Israel, help! This is the man who teaches all men everywhere against the people, the law, and this place; and furthermore he also brought Greeks into the temple and has defiled this holy place". (For they had previously seen Trophimus the Ephesian with him in the city, whom they supposed that Paul had brought into the temple)' (Acts 21:27–29). For Gentiles were not allowed in the temple.

As we continue reading down to verse 40 it is clear that the mob were so frenzied that they would have lynched Paul had not the commander of the Roman garrison arrested him for his own safety. But when he explained the situation, and added that he was a citizen of Tarsus, he was given permission to address the crowd. In chapter 22 Paul faces the mob howling for his blood and makes his defence.

Addressing the crowd

'"Brethren and fathers, hear my defence before you now." And when they heard that he spoke to them in the Hebrew language, they kept all the more silent. Then he said, "I am indeed a Jew born in Tarsus of Cilicia, but brought up in this city at the feet of Gamaliel, taught according to the strictness of our father's law, and was zealous toward God as you all are today"'(Acts 22:1–3).

Paul was wise to begin in the way he did. He was concerned to have a point of contact with his audience and he achieved this by speaking in their own language, stressing his Jewishness, his rabbinical training under Gamaliel, and his zealousness for the law. By mentioning these things he was more or less guaranteed a sympathetic hearing—'they kept all the more silent' (Acts 22:2). There is something here all preachers can learn. We must adapt our message, not in content but in approach, to the particular congregation we are addressing. Paul might have spoken in the cultivated Greek language, but not all would have understood him. Instead he used the common Aramaic which was the conversational language of the day. The preacher similarly will not address the Sunday morning congregation in the same way as he addressed a theological conference, or a youth meeting as he would a group in an Old People's Home. He will always be conscious of what one writer calls 'congregational overload'.

In the next section of Paul's address from verses 4–21 he speaks of his conversion experience on the Damascus road. We considered this in some detail in chapter 9 so we need not repeat what we said there, except to say that the argument from personal experience is the strongest of all, and cannot be refuted. Paul himself was well aware of this, since he repeats the same experience again at his trial before King Agrippa (Acts 26:12ff).

When a person's life has been changed out of all recognition by the power of God, it is a more forceful witness to the truth of the gospel than any form of words could ever be. We can spend weeks or even months debating with someone on the truths of Christianity and have no effect on them whatever. But let those words be backed up by a living, walking testimony to what Christ can do in a person and it is much more likely to be effective.

Indeed even with Paul his testimony seemed at first to be accepted by the mob, including the account of his conversion experience. But that was as far as it went. The moment he mentioned his God-given mission to the Gentiles the atmosphere changed and the anger and violence of the crowd flared up again. 'Then he said to me, "Depart, for I will send you far from here to the Gentiles". And they listened to him until this word, and then they raised their voices and said, "Away with such a fellow from the earth, for he is not fit to live!" Then, as they cried out and tore off their clothes and threw dust in the air' (Acts 22:21–23).

What stoked up their fury was not the fact that Paul *preached* to the Gentiles so much as *what* he preached to them. He was telling them they could enjoy all the rights and privileges accorded the Jewish race, but without accepting circumcision and the Law. In short he was preaching the gospel of God's free grace, and the Jews did not like it. They thought of salvation as their birthright as Jews, but here was Paul saying that it was for all men through faith in Christ.

The stumbling block for Jews was pride in their exclusiveness. And it is still the same where the gospel is concerned. Men in their pride still resist the idea that they themselves can have no part in their own salvation. Pride in their own ability, their own goodness, and their own powers of reasoning prevents them from acknowledging their sin, and bowing the knee in humble repentance before a holy God. And all our efforts and powers of persuasion cannot break down that pride without the convicting work of the Holy Spirit in a person's heart.

Paul's Roman citizenship

Once again Paul's life was in danger from the fury of the mob, and once again the Roman commander intervened to save his life. '... The commander ordered him to be brought into the barracks, and said that he should be examined under scourging, so that he might know why they shouted so against him. And as they bound him with thongs, Paul said to the centurion who stood by, "Is it lawful for you to scourge a man who is a Roman, and uncondemned?"... Then immediately those who were about to examine him withdrew from him; and the commander was also afraid after he found out that he was a Roman, and because he had bound him' (Acts 22:24–25 and 29).

'I know my rights'. That is an expression one is hearing more and more in our society today because we now have the United Nations Bill of Human Rights. And that is no bad thing, even if that legislation is appealed to at times for the most trivial of reasons. For the purpose of such a law is the protection of the rights of the individual in the way Paul claimed his rights and privileges as a Roman citizen. He had previously claimed that right when he and Silas had been unjustly treated by the authorities at Philippi (Acts 16:37–40). In this instance he was not simply standing on his dignity therefore. He was quite prepared to lay down his life for the gospel, as we have already seen. But when the interests of justice and the gospel required it, he was perfectly prepared to stand on his rights under the law and not recklessly throw his life away.

We learn from this that it is perfectly legitimate for the Christian to exercise his rights and privileges under the law when an injustice has been done. For scripture is clear that the rule of law is a divine provision for the good ordering of society, and for the protection of the individual. 'Let every soul be subject to the governing authorities. For there is no authority except from God, and the authorities that exist are appointed by God' (Romans 13:1).

The Roman commander was still totally confused what the riot had been about, and why his prisoner could stoke up such violence and anger among the crowd. He therefore decided that the only way to get to the bottom of the whole affair was to put Paul before the Jewish Sanhedrin. 'The next day, because he wanted to know for certain why he was accused by the Jews, he released him from his bonds, and commanded the chief priests and all their council to appear, and brought Paul down and set him before them' (Acts 22:30). We now move into chapter 23 where Paul once again has to defend his actions.

Before the Sanhedrin

There is little doubt that Paul could never have hoped to have a fair trial before the Jewish council after all that had happened. Its members were totally prejudiced towards him, and his rights under Jewish law counted for nothing in their eyes. Paul had hardly opened his mouth when steps were taken to silence him. 'Then Paul, looking earnestly at the council, said, "Men and brethren, I have lived in all good conscience before God until this day." And the high priest Ananias commanded those who stood by him to strike him on the mouth' (Acts 23:1–2).

That was a deplorable thing for the high priest to have done, and in that moment Paul knew that he had no chance of a fair hearing, and he re-acted very strongly, claiming once again his rights under the law. 'Then Paul said to him, "God will strike you, you whitewashed wall! For you sit to judge me according to the law, and do you command me to be struck contrary to the law?"' (Acts 23:3). Jesus made a similar claim for a fair trial under the law when he stood before Annas the high priest, but without re-acting as Paul had done (John 18:22–23). Although Paul did apologise when told Ananias was the high priest, it was more an apology to the office which he respected, than to the man. For Ananias was, as Paul described him, a wicked hypocrite notorious for his greed, and within a few years of this incident (AD 66) was assassinated by Jewish zealots.

It was at this point in the proceedings that Paul made an astute move, we might even call it his masterstroke. 'But when Paul perceived that one part were Sadducees and the other Pharisees, he cried out in the council, "Men and brethren, I am a Pharisee, the son of a Pharisee; concerning the hope and resurrection of the dead I am being judged!" And when he had said this, a dissension arose between the Pharisees and the Sadducees and the assembly was divided. For the Sadducees say that there is no resurrection— and no angel or spirit; but the Pharisees confess both' (Acts 23:6–8).

Paul knew full well that his strategy would divide the council and divert attention from himself, since there was no hope that he would get a fair trial. Nevertheless, there are those who feel that such a strategy was unworthy of him, and that in some way he was being evasive or shifty. But that was not so. Justice was being denied him, and his life was in great danger. When Jesus sent out the twelve to preach the gospel he said: 'Behold I send you out as sheep in the midst of wolves. Therefore be wise as serpents and harmless as doves' (Matthew 10:16). Paul was certainly among the wolves on this occasion and he was using wisdom, acumen, and shrewdness in the interests of the gospel. This is perfectly legitimate for the Christian.

On this point Hendriksen is right when he says that personal responsibility 'involves insight into the nature of one's surroundings, both personal and material, circumspection, sanctified common-sense, wisdom to do the right thing at the right time and place and in the right manner, a serious attempt always to discover the best means to achieve the highest goal... "How will it affect my own future, that of my neighbour, God's glory?"' (*Gospel of Matthew*, Banner of Truth, p. 461).

As Paul had anticipated the council was thrown into total disarray, and the Roman commander for the third time came to his rescue. 'Now when there arose a great dissension, the commander, fearing lest Paul might be pulled to pieces by them, commanded the soldiers to go down and take him by force from among them, and bring him into the barracks' (Acts 23:10).

God encourages Paul

After all that had happened to him since coming to Jerusalem, the dangers of mob violence, his imprisonment, the rescues, and the injustice of the council, Paul must have felt at a low point in his spirit. But just when he needed a word of encouragement God spoke to him in a very definite and positive way. 'But the following night the Lord stood by him and said, "Be of good cheer, Paul; for as you have testified for me in Jerusalem, so you must also bear witness at Rome"' (Acts 23:11). This word must have given a tremendous uplift to Paul's spirit.

Notice too that Paul's strategy in the council must have gained God's approval, else he would not have received this vision with its word of promise and encouragement. And when *we* reach a point in our spiritual lives when we feel low and discouraged, we ought not to feel guilty about it as if Christians ought never to feel this way. That will only lead us to dig ourselves even deeper into the hole of depression. The truth is we are not machines, or made of concrete, but human beings with feelings and emotions, and we are capable of being hurt by the harsh realities of life. And God knows that. After all he made us! We must not therefore allow the Devil to exploit these feelings and create in us a spirit of defeatism. On the contrary we must turn to God and seek his help. He will not disappoint us.

God's purpose will stand

Another point worth noticing is how God will not allow anything to prevent his purpose from being accomplished. His destiny for Paul was that he should preach the gospel in Rome, the heart of the empire and the Gentile world, just as he had already done in Jerusalem the centre of Judaism. This would be a clear evidence that the church really was on the move, and that the message of God's salvation was for all people. Everything that had happened to Paul since his arrival at Jerusalem was a step nearer to bringing that end about. But the trials were not over yet. In the rest of this passage (verses 12–22) we have a Jewish conspiracy against Paul and his attempted assassination.

'And when it was day, some of the Jews banded together and bound themselves under oath, saying that they would neither eat nor drink till they had killed Paul. Now there were more than forty who had formed this conspiracy ... So when Paul's sister's son heard of their ambush, he went and entered the barracks and told Paul. Then Paul called one of the centurions to him and said, "Take this young man to the commander, for he has something to tell him" ... So the commander let the young man depart, and commanded him, "Tell no one that you have revealed these things to me"' (Acts 23:12–13, 16–17 and 22).

God says through his servant Isaiah: 'My counsel shall stand, and I will do all my pleasure' (Isaiah 46:10). This passage confirms that. God's purpose was to bring Paul safely to Rome, and nothing that man and the forces of evil might devise would be allowed to thwart that purpose from being fulfilled. It may be that the devil, working through the malignancy and sinfulness of fallen humanity can frustrate God's plan in the short term, but ultimately God is in control, and the devil's stratagems will always fail. In the case of Paul neither the fanatical hatred of the mob, nor the contempt for justice by the Sanhedrin, nor the assassination conspiracy would determine the outcome, but only God himself.

It reminds us of those words in the second Psalm: 'Why do the nations rage, and the people plot a vain thing? The kings of the earth set themselves, and the rulers take counsel together, against the Lord, and against his anointed ... He who sits in the heavens shall laugh; the Lord shall hold them in derision' (Psalm 2:1,2,4). The agents of evil in the world may take their plottings seriously but their true significance is measured by God's derisive laughter at the futility of their efforts. So it was with the conspiracy against Paul. The plotters were serious enough, and even bound themselves with a religious oath. But God's contempt is seen in the instrument he used to defeat their plan: an obscure young lad. 'God has chosen the weak things of the world to put to shame the things which are mighty' (1 Corinthians 1:27).

Down to Caesarea

In view of the plot on Paul's life, the Roman commander arranged for him to be taken under military escort to Caesarea, the centre of Roman government, where he would be tried by the governor Felix. 'And he called for two centurions, saying, 'Prepare two hundred soldiers, seventy horsemen, and two hundred spearmen to go to Caesarea at the third hour of the night; and provide mounts to set Paul on, and bring him safely to Felix the governor' (Acts 23:23–24).

Paul's escort was virtually a small army and indicates how determined the commander was to prevent any ambush on the journey and to get his prisoner safely to Caesarea. God was still watching over his servant and was bringing him one step nearer to Rome. In the covering letter (Acts 23:27–29) the commander wrote to Felix, he expressed his own conviction that Paul was innocent of anything deserving imprisonment or death (verse 29), and having read it the governor kept Paul in custody until his trial under Roman law.

Paul before Felix

Read Acts chapter 24

In this chapter we get an account, not so much of a formal trial of Paul as a preliminary hearing, since no verdict was reached, and later (verse 27) the case had to be heard all over again. The purpose of the hearing was to allow the Jews the opportunity to state their charges against the accused, and for Paul to make his defence. But there were no witnesses present (Acts 24:18–19) as there would have been in a formal trial.

'Now after five days Ananias the high priest came down with the elders and a certain orator named Tertullus. These gave evidence to the governor against Paul' (Acts 24:1).

The speech of Tertullus

The hearing opened with Tertullus, a professional lawyer hired by the Jews, making a speech which was a mixture of the most nauseating flattery and falsehood, in order to gain the favour of Felix. 'And when he was called upon, Tertullus began his accusation, saying: "Seeing that through you we enjoy great peace, and prosperity is being brought to this nation by your foresight, we accept it always and in all places, most noble Felix, with all thankfulness. Nevertheless, not to be tedious to you any further, I beg you to hear by your courtesy, a few words from us"' (Acts 24:2–4).

Few things are more sickening than the empty words of the flatterer unless it is the flowery talk and insincerity of the person who simply loves to hear the sound of his own voice. Tertullus was well aware that the compliments he paid to Felix were totally untrue, as we shall see when we come to look at the character of the man. Insincerity is a temptation open to all who are engaged in public speaking, including preachers. And today we have plenty of it, in the lies and deceit that characterises so much of what goes on in public life. We have all become accustomed in a cynical way to the empty rhetoric of political speeches, the glib eloquence of the spin-doctors, and the lying and double-talk of the leaders in big business corporations and public institutions.

Words are both powerful and revealing, as the Bible clearly teaches. They are an index of character and mirror the state of the heart. 'For out of the abundance of the heart the mouth speaks' (Matthew 12:34). The character revealed in words is clearly seen in the contrast between the speech of Tertullus and that of Paul in his defence. The former was motivated by falsity, hatred and tawdry ambition; the latter by truth, sincerity, and clear conscience (Acts 24:16).

It was not for nothing that Jesus laid enormous stress upon the responsibility attaching to the words we speak. 'For by your words you will be justified, and by your words you will be condemned' (Matthew 12:37). The failure to guard what we say can so often cause tension and friction in personal relationships, destroy a person's character through malicious gossip, entice others into wrong-doing, or create disunity in a church fellowship. James was certainly right therefore to devote almost a whole chapter in his letter to the use of the tongue and the power of words (James 3).

Tertullus charged Paul as follows: 'for we have found this man a plague, a creator of dissension among all the Jews throughout the world, and a ringleader of the sect of the Nazarenes. He even tried to profane the temple, and we seized him, and wanted to judge him according to our law' (Acts 24:5–6). The accusation was threefold. Paul was an insurrectionist, the ringleader of a dangerous revolutionary sect called the Nazarenes, and the desecrator of the temple.

Paul's defence

In his defence Paul refuted all the charges brought against him and challenged Tertullus and the Jews to bring forward witnesses to prove their case. 'Nor can they prove the things of which they now accuse me' (Acts 24:13). He made it clear that he was no insurrectionist, and had come to Jerusalem for the peaceful purpose of worship. '…because you may ascertain that it is no more than twelve days since I went up to Jerusalem to worship. And they neither found me in the temple disputing with anyone nor inciting the crowd, either in synagogues or in the city' (Acts 24:11–12). On the second charge he readily confessed that he was a follower of the Way of Jesus, but denied that it was any kind of revolutionary or dangerous sect.

On the contrary he readily pointed out that he held much in common with the Jews themselves. 'But this I confess to you, that according to the Way which they call a sect, so I worship the God of my fathers, believing all things which are written in the Law and in the Prophets. I have hope in God, which they themselves also accept, that there will be a resurrection of the dead, both of the just and the unjust' (Acts 24:14–15).

As to the third charge, that he had desecrated the temple, the very opposite was the case. He had come up to Jerusalem to bring gifts for the poor, and was in the temple worshipping when the riot broke out. He powerfully added that those who started the riot should be present at the hearing to put their case. 'Now after many years I came to bring alms and offerings to my nation, in the midst of which some Jews from Asia found me purified in the temple, neither with a mob nor with tumult. They ought to have been here before you to object if they had anything against me' (Acts 24:17–19).

Clearly Paul's defence made a strong impression upon the mind of Felix, since he adjourned the hearing to a later date (Acts 24:22).

The role of conscience

Underlying the whole of Paul's defence is his emphatic assertion that in all he had said and done he had acted with a clear conscience. 'This being so, I myself always strive to have a conscience without offence toward God and men' (Acts 24:16). He had made the same statement in his trial before the Sanhedrin (Acts 23:1).

The New Testament has a lot to say about conscience, it is mentioned some thirty times, and frequently occurs in Paul's letters. But what is conscience, and why is it so important in the Christian life? To begin with everyone has a conscience, and we can appeal to it whenever we preach or witness to people of Christ (2 Corinthians 4:2). It is part of the moral equipment of the soul, which God gave to man at his creation, and which sets him apart from the animals. Indeed, so important is it at the moral and spiritual level, that those who have never heard the gospel will be judged according to how they have obeyed its dictates (Romans 2:14–16).

The conscience is intended to act both as a judge of our behaviour and as a guide to our conduct. But in the psychological culture of today this is ignored, and people are encouraged to suppress any guilt feelings they may have for bad behaviour since this, they are told, will damage their self-esteem. Instead they must see themselves as the victims of circumstances—a poor upbringing, a broken home, stress, emotional trauma etc. They must not blame themselves therefore because they are not wholly responsible for their behaviour. Such advice is pernicious, and the very antithesis of the Bible's teaching.

Even as a guide to behaviour the conscience will fail us if it is not disciplined by the higher authority of God's word. If we ignore its warnings long enough it will lose its sensitivity to wrongdoing, and will become unreliable as a guide of conduct. Since we are all influenced by what we read, the programmes we watch on TV, the company we keep and the places we go to, the information fed into our minds, if it is of the wrong kind, can easily cripple the conscience and make it ineffective. If we want to keep our conscience to be strong and reliable then we must feed it with the right information by the reading of God's word, by prayer, worship and the fellowship of other believers.

What about Felix?

Since Paul had not been convicted of any wrongdoing Felix adjourned the proceedings and put his prisoner under a form of house arrest. 'But when Felix heard these things, having more accurate knowledge of the Way, he adjourned the proceedings and said, "When Lysias the commander comes down, I will make a decision on your case". So he commanded the centurion to keep Paul and to let him have liberty, and told him not to forbid any of his friends to provide for or visit him' (Acts 24:22–23).

In this final section of the chapter we are told something about the character of Felix. He played an important part in Paul's life over a period of two years (Acts 24:27). So what kind of man was he? Before we deal with that we must ask in what sense did he have a 'more accurate knowledge of the Way'? (Acts 24:22). Does this mean that he had an understanding of the gospel? I do not think so. We can only suppose therefore that having been governor of Judea and Samaria for six years Felix would have picked up a considerable amount of information about the Christian church. Furthermore, his wife Drusilla was a Jewess and he would probably have learned from her something of the relations existing between Jews and Christians.

Now let us look at the relevant verses 24–26. 'After some days, when Felix came with his wife Drusilla, who was Jewish, he sent for Paul and heard him concerning the faith in Christ' (Acts 24:24). We saw earlier that Tertullus in his speech had paid Felix the most flattering compliments, but he knew well enough that this did not square with the man's true character. Josephus the Jewish historian, and Tacitus the Roman historian, both describe him as an unprincipled and corrupt government official. Indeed his greed is perfectly evident from verse 26 where he appears open to a fat bribe. 'Meanwhile he also hoped that money would be given him by Paul, that he might release him'. As to his moral life, he had married three times, and his present wife Drusilla was in fact living in adultery with him, since she was already married at this time to Azizus, king of Amesa. The Jews hated him because of his excessive cruelty, but eventually it all came to an end when he was dismissed from his post and recalled to Rome. Such was the man who now stood in judgement on the apostle Paul.

But what are we to make of the fact that later 'he sent for Paul and heard him concerning the faith in Christ' (Acts 24:24), and also that over a period of two years 'he sent for him more often and conversed with him?' (Acts 24:26). He reminds us of Herod with John the Baptist. When Herod heard John, he was greatly puzzled; yet he liked to listen to him (Mark 6:20). Felix was a mixed up pathetic kind of man. In spite of his licentious and cruel life-style he might well have had a wistful longing for God that would break through whenever he was in the presence of a godly man like Paul.

He would not be the first to react in that way. I have no doubt that many people, even the most depraved, have those sober moments of reflection when they ponder deeply on questions relating to God and the eternal world. Speaking of mankind in general the writer of Ecclesiastes says: 'He has put eternity in their hearts, except that no one can find out the work that God does from beginning to end' (Ecclesiastes 3:11). He means that man has a spiritual dimension to his being, and he will never understand himself, or begin to penetrate the mystery and meaning of life, until he finds peace with God. As Augustine put it: 'Our hearts are restless, until they find their rest in thee'.

Not only was Felix a mixed-up man, he was also a man with a sense of foreboding and fear. At one of their meetings Paul 'reasoned about righteousness, self-control, and the judgement to come'. At that point, 'Felix was afraid and answered, "Go away for now; when I have a convenient time I will call for you"' (Acts 24:25). One wonders if his past life of cruelty, greed, and licentiousness did not flash through his mind at that moment and cause him to tremble (AV) inwardly as Paul spoke of the judgement to come.

In the church's preaching today, do we ever make people afraid of meeting God at the judgement? Do they ever tremble? Or is it all so pleasant and comfortable that the thought of accounting one day to God never even crosses their mind. Has the church gone 'soft' in its message? Is it a case of not wanting to make the members of the congregation feel any discomfort, or upsetting them in any way, because they may not want to come back again? If that is the case then we have already lost them in a much deeper sense, since we have neglected to give them the whole counsel of God.

But the really sad thing about Felix, it seems to me, is that he missed the opportunity to get his life right with God through repentance and faith in Christ. When he was inwardly afraid as Paul spoke of righteousness and judgement to come, it was because the Holy Spirit was convicting him. But instead of yielding to the movement of God's Spirit, he hardened his heart and put off the thought of God until a more 'convenient time'. But in his case it seems the more convenient time never came. What a grave warning that is to all those who have moments when they are made to think seriously about the needs of their souls, but never do anything about it. Always they put it off until a more convenient time.

But the only time that is convenient is 'now'. 'Behold, now is the accepted time; behold, now is the day of salvation' (2 Corinthians 6:2).

Festus, Paul and Agrippa

Read Acts chapters 25 and 26

D uring his earthly ministry Jesus had warned his followers: 'but beware of men, for they will deliver you up to councils and scourge you in their synagogues. You will be brought before governors and kings for my sake, as a testimony to them and to the Gentiles' (Matthew 10:17–18).

That prophecy was certainly fulfilled in Paul's experience, for his ordeal was not yet over. He had already appeared before the Jewish Council and before Felix the governor. Now in these chapters we shall see him appearing before yet another governor—Festus, and also before King Agrippa. Chapter 25 opens with yet another conspiracy by the Jews to assassinate Paul.

'Now when Festus had come to the province, after three days he went up from Caesarea to Jerusalem. Then the high priest and the chief men of the Jews informed him against Paul; and they petitioned him, asking a favour against him, that he would summon him to Jerusalem— while they lay in ambush along the road to kill him' (Acts 25:1–3). But God's providence was watching over his servant, for Festus decided instead to travel down to Caesarea for the hearing. 'And when he had remained among them more than ten days, he went down to Caesarea. And the next day, sitting on the judgement seat, he commanded Paul to be brought' (Acts 25:6).

Paul's defence on this occasion was virtually the same as he had made before Felix, except for one very important difference, which was the question Festus put to Paul. 'Are you willing to go up to Jerusalem and there be judged before me concerning these things?' (Acts 25:9). Paul knew full well that he could never expect a fair trial before the Jews, and so once again he claimed his rights as a Roman citizen and appealed to be judged before Caesar. 'So Paul said, "I stand at Caesar's judgement seat, where I ought to be judged. To the Jews I have done no wrong, as you very well know." Then Festus, when he had conferred with the council answered, "You have appealed to Caesar? To Caesar you shall go!"' (Acts 25:10 and 12).

The final step was now taken, and Paul would shortly be on his way to Rome, as God had said.

Who was Festus?

Before we go any further we need to look a little more closely at Porcius Festus and his attitude towards Paul. He was very different from Felix, his predecessor in the governorship. He was neither corrupt nor oppressively cruel, and had a much deeper concern for Roman justice. He was cultivated and cultured, a typical sophisticated pagan, but where spiritual matters were concerned he was totally ignorant. Later the opportunity came to confer with king Agrippa about Paul, and he says to him: 'When the accusers stood up, they brought no accusation against him of such things as I supposed, but had some questions against him about their own religion and about a certain Jesus who had died, whom Paul affirmed to be alive. And because I was uncertain of such questions, I asked whether he was willing to go to Jerusalem and there be judged concerning these matters"' (Acts 25:18–20).

It was as if he said to Agrippa: "You know Agrippa, I had not a clue what the man was on about, and I am at a complete loss how to deal with him. Frankly, I could not care less about their religious disputes, but when he goes to Rome I will have to make out some kind of report on his case". He then went on: 'I have brought him out before you, and especially before you, King Agrippa, so that after the examination has taken place I may have something to write' (Acts 25:26).

This lack of any spiritual interest or understanding on the part of Festus can also be seen in his hysterical reaction to Paul's testimony: 'At this point Festus interrupted Paul's defence "Paul you are beside yourself!" he shouted, "Much learning is driving you mad"' (Acts 26:24). From his point of view Paul was suffering from some kind of religious mania, for in his crass manner of thinking anyone who could get excited and enthusiastic, like Paul, about God's power to raise the dead through Christ, must necessarily be dismissed as a crank.

And there are plenty of people today who think just like Festus. Like him they can be cultivated and cultured, sophisticated and urbane, but are totally rooted in the things of earth, and suffer from an inability to comprehend anything of a higher spiritual nature. Often they are charming and interesting people, intelligent and morally upright, but have a closed mind where religion is concerned. They are like those people Jesus likened to the seed that fell on the pathway in his parable of the Sower. They think it is perfectly all right to get excited and enthusiastic about sport, or politics, or holidays, but not about God, the soul and salvation.

The God of this world

Anyone who has attempted to speak to a modern day Festus about spiritual matters will know that he or she will look at you in total bewilderment, as though you were from another planet. They cannot understand what interest there can be in dealing with things which, as they see it, are irrelevant to real life, such as their golf handicap, or education, or market trends etc. The terrible seriousness of their lost condition means nothing to them.

We must ask why that is, for we have to deal with these people in the interests of the gospel. It is because they are the victims and prisoners of the 'god of this age'. Paul puts it like this: 'But even if our gospel is veiled, it is veiled to those who are perishing, whose minds the god of this age has blinded, who do not believe, lest the light of the gospel of the glory of Christ, who is the image of God, should shine on them' (2 Corinthians 4:3–4).

It is not so much that these people *will* not see the truth, but they *cannot* see the truth, because Satan has blinded their spiritual and intellectual perception of the truth. They may be highly enlightened in their minds concerning other branches of knowledge, politics, mathematics, medical science etc, but are incapable of grasping spiritual truth.

How to deal with Festus

The temptation when dealing with a modern Festus is to become irritated or frustrated because he appears to be so dense in failing to understand those spiritual truths that seem so clear to us. But we must resist that feeling, else we shall give up on such people, and we must never do that. Remember what we are told of Jesus when he saw the people who had come to hear him preach? 'But when he saw the multitudes, he was moved with compassion for them, because they were weary and scattered, like sheep having no shepherd' (Matthew 9:36). At the spiritual level we must try to see these people like that—as the dupes and victims of the devil who has blinded them to the truth. We must pray for them therefore as Paul prayed for the Ephesians: '... that the God of our Lord Jesus Christ, the Father of glory, may give to you the spirit of wisdom and revelation in the knowledge of him, the eyes of your understanding being enlightened; that you may know what is the hope of his calling, what are the riches of the glory of his inheritance in the saints, and what is the exceeding greatness of his power toward us who believe, according to the working of his mighty power' (Ephesians 1:17–19).

To adopt this attitude calls for great patience on our part, especially if we have been praying for someone for a long time only to find that they remain as hard and obdurate as ever. After all, someone probably prayed for us until our hard heart was broken.

A complex personality

'Then Agrippa said to Paul, "You are permitted to speak for yourself."' (Acts 26:1). To my mind Agrippa is a strange and complex character, and very different from Festus who we described as a sophisticated pagan. Agrippa on the other hand was a Jew, and deeply religious, with a good working knowledge of the Old Testament and of Jewish customs and traditions. Paul himself acknowledges all that in his opening statement. 'So Paul stretched out his hand and answered for himself: "I think myself happy, King Agrippa, because today I shall answer for myself before you concerning all the things of which I am accused by the Jews, especially because you are expert in all customs and questions which have to do with the Jews. Therefore I beg you to hear me patiently"' (Acts 26:1–3).

But although he was deeply religious, there is good reason to suppose that Agrippa's lifestyle did not match up to his convictions. According to Josephus, the Jewish historian, there was a strong rumour at the time that his sister Bernice was living in an incestuous relationship with him (*Antiquities* book 20, chapter 7). Be that as it may Paul, in his speech before the king, asserts that Agrippa believed the message of the Old Testament prophets concerning the coming of Christ the Messiah. 'Now as he thus made his defence, Festus said with a loud voice, "Paul, you are beside yourself! Much learning is driving you mad!" But he said, "I am not mad, most noble Festus, but speak the words of truth and reason. For the king, before whom I also speak freely, knows these things; for I am convinced that none of these things escapes his attention, since this thing was not done in a corner. King Agrippa, do you believe the prophets? I know that you do believe"' (Acts 26:24–28).

Clearly Agrippa was no stranger to the truth of God's word, but it seems it went no further than the level of his mind. In this respect he was totally different from Festus, who was altogether ignorant of the truth of God. Agrippa therefore was in a worse position since he knew the truth, knew what the Old Testament taught about God and the prophecies concerning the coming of Christ, and yet rejected it outright. That that was in fact his position is clear from his response to Paul. 'Then Agrippa said to Paul, "you almost persuade me to become a Christian"' (Acts 26:27).

Agrippa's response

Among Bible commentators there is a certain disagreement about Agrippa's reply to Paul because of the ambiguity of the language. The NIV reads: 'Do you think that in such a short time you can persuade me to be a Christian?' The RSV: 'In a short time you think to make me a Christian!' J B Phillips: 'Much more of this Paul ... and you will be making me a Christian!' So how are we to interpret the response of Agrippa—was it serious, contemptuous, or frivolous? However we take it one thing is certain, Agrippa did not become a believer. Paul confirms that. 'I would to God that not only you, but also all who hear me today, might become both almost and altogether such as I am, except for these chains" (Acts 26:29). But let us look at the different responses.

If it was serious: 'You almost persuade me to become a Christian' (NKJ), then there is a deep sadness at the heart of it. In the depths of his soul Agrippa realised the profound implications of what Paul was saying, but he lacked the decisiveness to act upon it. He 'almost' believed, but could not take the final step of faith. There are many like him. They believe and want to take it further, but always there is something holding them back—the seductions of the world, what others might say, or the personal cost in terms of money, time and effort.

If it was contemptuous: 'Do you think that in such a short time you can persuade me to be a Christian?' (NIV), we sense the resentment and sarcasm as if he thought it a downright cheek for Paul, a prisoner, to try to convert him in front of his pagan friend Festus. After all, was he not a king? Pride is the darling sin and the greatest obstacle to the penetrating truth of God's word. Thousands, like Agrippa, feel they have no need of what they contemptuously describe as the 'religious crutch' of the gospel of Christ.

If it was said frivolously: 'Much more of this Paul, and you will be making me a Christian' (J B Phillips). Paul was speaking out of the depths of his heart about the great issues of life and death, and all Agrippa could do was trivialise it. So many do the same thing, they are light-minded, pleasure loving people whose philosophy of life is 'eat, drink, and be merry, for tomorrow we die'. But the day of judgement is coming when they will wake up to the fact that you cannot trivialise God.

Paul's defence

There is not a great deal we can comment on in Paul's speech, since much of what he says we have already covered in the account of his conversion (Acts 9:1-9), his speech to the mob (Acts 22:1-21), and his speech before the Sanhedrin (Acts 23:1-10). There is however one point worth noticing. In verse 18 Paul gives a marvellously concise description of the mission of the gospel which God has given to the world. '...To open their eyes, in order to turn them from darkness to light, and from the power of Satan to God, that they may receive forgiveness of sins and an inheritance among those who are sanctified by faith in Me'. Five things are mentioned which we must convey to others concerning the gospel.

To open blind eyes. We looked at this when dealing with the life of Festus, and we have no need to repeat what we said then except to say that we can never, by our own reasoning or eloquence, open blind eyes to the truth of God's word. ' But the natural man does not receive the things of the Spirit of God, for they are foolishness to him; nor can he know them, because they are spiritually discerned' (1 Corinthians 2:14). What we must do therefore is pray as we bring God's word to people that the Holy Spirit will open their blind eyes to discern the truth.

To turn from darkness to light. Modern man ridicules the idea that the world is in darkness. He points to the progress mankind has made in the fields of medicine, genetics, engineering, space technology and travel, etc, as clear evidence that the world is no longer the victim of darkness and ignorance. Man is an enlightened individual. And it would be foolish to deny that we have indeed benefited tremendously from the advance of human knowledge. But at the moral and spiritual level the world seems to have made little headway, and is still in darkness. Nations still cannot live together in peace and harmony, evil and wrong-doing still flourishes in our towns and cities, and covetousness and hatred continue to bring pain and suffering to millions of people.

And the reason the world is in darkness is because it is estranged from the God who created it and brought it into being. 'God is light and in him is no darkness at all' (1 John 1:5). Our task in the church, and as preachers, is to enable people to turn from darkness to light by being reconciled to God through faith in Christ.

From the power of Satan to God. Evil in the world is not a vague abstract force, as liberal theology would have us believe. It is concentrated and personalised in the sinister figure of Satan who is behind all the violence, rape, drug trafficking, child abuse and war that afflicts our modern world. He is immensely powerful, highly intelligent and utterly unscrupulous, always strategizing and scheming his opposition to God's kingdom of light and truth. Jesus spoke of him as the 'prince of this world' (John 12:31), and Paul describes him as the 'ruler of the power of the air' (Ephesians 2:2).

He binds men to himself in their sin and disobedience, and it is only God's greater power in the gospel that can set them free.

That they may receive forgiveness of sins. To be set free from the bondage of Satan is what the New Testament means by the term Salvation. This is a comprehensive term relating to God's forgiveness for the past, present and future. Through faith in the sacrifice of Christ, God forgives our past wrong-doing, and we are saved from the penalty of sin.

But because here and now we live in a sinful world, we constantly fall into sin and need God's forgiveness every day. We are being saved therefore, in the present, from the power of sin in our lives.

Even so, our salvation as a forgiven people is not yet complete for we still live in our corrupt bodies. Only when Christ comes again, and when at the resurrection morning we change corruption for incorruption, will God's forgiveness reach its triumphant conclusion in our future life in heaven when sin will be no more.

An inheritance in heaven. As believers in the Lord Jesus Christ we have a future inheritance that is greater and more glorious than anything we can possibly comprehend.

'Eye has not seen, nor ear heard,
Nor have entered into the heart of man
The things which God has prepared
For those who love him' (1 Corinthians 2:9).

This inheritance involves all the negative joys of heaven—no more hunger or thirst, no more pain or suffering, no more tears or sadness, no more sin, sickness or death. Peter adds something further. He says it is 'an inheritance incorruptible and undefiled and that does not fade away, reserved in heaven for you, who are *kept* by the power of God...' (1 Peter 1:4–5). We need not fear therefore that we might not make it—to heaven I mean. God will *keep* us and bring us to our heavenly home at the last.

Following Paul's defence the chapter closes (verses 30–32) with Agrippa, Festus and Bernice discussing the hearing, and there is no doubt that Paul had made a solid impression on both the Jews and the Romans, for Agrippa concluded: 'This man might have been set free if he had not appealed to Caesar'.

The voyage to Rome

Read Acts chapters 27 and 28

A t last Paul is on his way to Rome. Chapter 27 records the actual voyage and the shipwreck, and chapter 28 the three months spent on the island of Malta, and the final journey to the imperial capital. The account of the voyage is both thrilling and dramatic, but since it is largely descriptive it provides little scope for the expositor by way of spiritual insights or lessons. Some Bible commentators overcome this by spiritualising the account and treating it more or less as allegory.

For example one writer sees Paul's voyage as representing the voyage of life. The ship itself is this world, the two hundred and seventy-six passengers and crew symbolise humanity in all its variety and complexity, and the raging storm and shipwreck point to the dangers and trials we all have to face in this life from time to time. Now there may be some spiritual value in this approach, but for my own part I find it more helpful to treat it as a straightforward historical account of a stormy and dangerous voyage. That is not to say that there are no points of interest which do have a spiritual significance, and which call for comment.

Paul's influence

The one really important truth that shines out through the whole narrative is the calm and authoritative manner in which Paul carries himself when everyone else is in turmoil and on the verge of despair. He is a prisoner and has no knowledge of seamanship, and yet he speaks and acts with authority. 'Now when much time had been spent, and sailing was now dangerous because the Fast was already over, Paul advised them, saying, "Men, I perceive that this voyage will end with disaster and much loss, not only of the cargo and ship, but also our lives"' (Acts 27: 9–10).

It is possible that the centurion and the captain had consulted Paul, since he was a seasoned traveller and—according to 2 Corinthians 11:25—had experienced shipwreck on three occasions. The centurion and the captain must later have deeply regretted that they had not heeded Paul's warning.

Be that as it may, when the storm was at its height and everyone was now at the point of despair Paul, once again, surrounded by soldiers, passengers and crew, shows a spirit of great calm and confidence as he assures them that whilst the ship is doomed no life would be lost. 'But after long abstinence from food, then Paul stood in the midst of them and said, "Men, you should have listened to me, and not have sailed from Crete and incurred this disaster and loss. And now I urge you to take heart, for there will be no loss of life among you, but only of the ship"' (Acts 27:21–22).

If the people were wondering how he could speak with such positive certainty they soon got their answer. His confidence was in God. 'For there stood by me this night an angel of God to whom I belong and whom I serve, saying, "Do not be afraid Paul; you must be brought before Caesar and indeed God has granted you all those who sail with you." Therefore, take heart, men, for I believe God that it will be just as it was told me' (Acts 27:23–25). This had a profound effect and put new life into them. That is evident from what we are told next.

'And as day was about to dawn, Paul implored them all to take food, saying, "Today is the fourteenth day you have waited and continued without food, and eaten nothing. Therefore I urge you to take nourishment for this is for your survival, since not a hair will fall from the head of any of you". And when he had said these things, he took bread and gave thanks to God in the presence of them all; and when he had broken it he began to eat. They were all encouraged, and also took food themselves' (Acts 27:33–36). This is a deeply moving and dramatic picture, which we cannot easily get out of our minds. The whole ship's company listen quietly as Paul speaks, then he takes the bread and prays, and we get the feeling that a deep sense of calm comes upon everyone.

The influence of Paul's presence and words upon the others on the ship reminds me strongly of an incident John Wesley records in his journal, which occurred on his voyage to Georgia in 1736. This was before his conversion experience. In the middle of a terrific storm he was deeply affected by the calm and serenity of spirit shown by a group of German Christians at worship. It is so strongly similar to what we have been saying about Paul that it is worth quoting in full. It begins with Wesley describing the spirit of these German Christians.

'And every day had given them occasion of showing a meekness which no injury could move. If they were pushed, struck, or thrown down, they rose again and went away; but no complaint was found in their mouth. There was now an opportunity of trying whether they were delivered from the spirit of fear, as well as from that of pride, anger and revenge. In the midst of the psalm wherewith their service began, the sea broke over, split the mainsail in pieces, covered the ship, and poured in between the decks, as if the great deep had already swallowed us up. A terrible screaming began among the English. The Germans calmly sung on. I asked one of them afterwards, "Was you not afraid?" He answered, "I thank God, no". I asked, "But were not your young women and children afraid?" He replied mildly, "No; our women and children are not afraid to die."

'From them I went to their crying, trembling neighbours, and pointed out to them the difference in the hour of trial, between him that feareth God, and him that feareth him not. At twelve the wind fell. This was the most glorious day which I have hitherto seen' (*Journal*, vol 1, p. 11).

The only explanation for the serenity of Paul and the Germans, and its effect on others, was their confidence in God. It speaks volumes for the way in which Christians should meet the adverse circumstances of life. How do we meet trouble, grief, sickness and disappointment? Is it evident to others that we are drawing upon some resource of inner power and strength that is not our own? And are we as ready to give the same explanation as Paul— 'the God to whom I belong and whom I serve', and the German Christians when they said, 'our women and children are not afraid to die'.

Before leaving this section we must notice one other thing. Throughout Acts we have become accustomed to associating Paul with visions and direct communications from God. But we must not overlook the fact that he was also an intensely practical man with his feet firmly on the ground. We see this when the storm was at its height and the sailors planned to abandon the ship and leave the passengers to their fate. 'And as the sailors were seeking to escape from the ship, when they had let down the skiff into the sea, under pretence of putting out anchors from the prow, Paul said to the centurion and the soldiers, "Unless these men stay in the ship, you cannot be saved". Then the soldiers cut away the ropes of the skiff and let it fall off' (Acts 27:30–32).

Paul was shrewd enough to see what the sailors were really up to and he was quick to frustrate their plan. He knew that God had promised there would be no loss of life, but that did not mean they themselves had no part to play. The sailors with their knowledge of seamanship would be needed if they were to be saved. Another example of Paul's practical approach is his appeal to the passengers and crew to eat in preparation for the ordeal ahead. 'Therefore I urge you take nourishment, for this is for your survival, since not a hair will fall from the head of any of you' (Acts 27:34). He could see they were all exhausted by the events of the past fourteen days and the lack of food, and he also knew that if they kept up their physical strength they would be in much better shape to save their own lives.

We learn from this that in our Christian experience God's purpose and man's instrumentality go hand in hand. Or, to put it another way, God not only ordains the end, but also the means to that end. In any situation what we ourselves can do, *has to be done,* for God will not do, by way of miracle, what we ourselves can do by the practical application of sanctified common sense.

Unexpected kindness

'Now when they had escaped, they then found out that the island was called Malta. And the natives showed us unusual kindness; for they kindled a fire and made us all welcome, because of the rain that was falling and because of the cold' (Acts 28:1–2).

It is generally agreed by Bible commentators that it was around the end of October or the beginning of November when Paul and the other passengers and the crew landed on the island. It was not the best time of year to be shipwrecked, and physically they must have been in a bad way being exhausted by their ordeal, and wet and cold, with rain adding to their misery. We can imagine how their spirits must have been raised therefore by the gracious welcome they received from the islanders who kindled a fire to warm their frozen bodies and dry their clothes, and probably provided them with food and shelter. Luke describes it as 'unusual kindness', and we see it again in the action of Publius, the chief man of the island, 'who received us and entertained us courteously for three days' (Acts 28:7). And as if that were not kindness enough Luke says further: 'They also honoured us in many ways; and when we departed, they provided such things as were necessary' (Acts 28:10).

And all this came from people who knew nothing whatever of the gospel of Christ, and who could expect nothing in return for their kindness since Paul and the others had lost everything in the shipwreck. I wonder if that is why Luke describes it as 'unusual' kindness? Was it a case of these islanders doing by nature the very thing Jesus asked of his followers? '...Do good, and lend, hoping for nothing in return' (Luke 6:35). For it clearly shows that those who have not been regenerated by the Holy Spirit can nevertheless exhibit kindness and goodness in their lives. True, man can not save himself by his kindness and goodness and can only be put right with God through the righteousness of Christ. But at the same time we must be careful in the way we understand man's fallen nature. He was created in God's image, and although that image has been defaced and overlaid by sin, it has not been completely destroyed. As Paul says: '...for when Gentiles, who do not have the law, by nature do the things in the law ... who show the work of the law written in their hearts' (Romans 2:14–15).

Commenting on this Hendrikson writes: 'To be sure, man is by nature "totally depraved" in the sense that depravity has invaded every part of his being: mind, heart, and will. If he is to be saved it is God who must save him. Man cannot save himself. This however does not, and cannot mean that he is *absolutely* depraved, as bad as he can be, as bad as the devil himself. Did not also Jesus teach that there is a sense in which even the unconverted "do good?" (Luke 6:33)' (Hendriksen *Romans*, p. 100).

When we preach and evangelise therefore, we can take heart from knowing that man still has this spiritual dimension to his nature that we can appeal to, and with the help of the Holy Spirit he is able to respond positively to that appeal in acceptance of the gospel.

Paul and the viper

'But when Paul had gathered a bundle of sticks and laid them on the fire, a viper came out because of the heat, and fastened on his hand. So when the natives saw the creature hanging from his hand, they said to one another, "No doubt this man is a murderer, whom, though he has escaped the sea, yet justice does not allow to live". But he shook off the creature into the fire and suffered no harm. However, they were expecting that he would swell up or suddenly fall down dead. But after they had looked for a long time and saw no harm come to him, they changed their minds and said that he was a god' (Acts 28:3–6).

It is difficult, to my mind, to be certain whether this was a miracle God performed on Paul's behalf. I say that because we are not actually told that he was bitten by the viper, although it is implied by the reaction of the islanders who expected him to fall down dead. We must also keep in mind that God had already promised that Paul would go to Rome, and that would not be possible if he had died of poisoning. But whichever way we take it, we can say with certainty that it shows clearly the over-ruling providence of God on behalf of his servant.

When the islanders see the viper clinging to Paul's hand they think he is a murderer escaping justice, but then when he does not die they regard him as a god. This means they were clearly idolaters, although we do not know what gods they worshipped, but they also had the sense of a divine power above and beyond themselves, ruling over all things. Moreover, they also had a moral sense of divine retribution, of right and wrong. All this therefore simply reinforces what we said earlier, that although the image of God in man has been overlaid and defaced by sin it has not been totally destroyed.

This section ends with Paul healing the father of Publius, and others on the island. 'And it happened that the father of Publius lay sick of a fever and dysentery. Paul went in to him and prayed, and he laid his hands on him and healed him. So when this was done, the rest of those on the island who had diseases also came and were healed' (Acts 28:8–9).

It seems strange that no mention is made of Paul preaching the gospel during his three months stay on Malta. Strange, because he never seems to have lost an opportunity of making Christ known to others. But a simple explanation might be that there was a language problem, which made communication difficult. But the power of God was nevertheless made known in other ways. The incident of the viper would have made a profound impression on the islanders and made them aware of the divine presence in Paul. And this healing ministry equally would have made them aware that the power of God was moving among them. This too was preaching, but of a different kind. And sometimes our actions can speak louder than our words.

Rome at last

We are now coming to the climax of our story. When he arrived at the outskirts of the city Paul was met by a company of believers from the church in Rome to whom he had written some three years earlier expressing his hope to one day visit them. And now he was there! '…When the brethren heard about us, they came to meet us as far as Appii Forum and Three Inns. When Paul saw them, he thanked God and took courage' (Acts 28:15).

We can well understand Paul's sense of thankfulness and joy. God had promised: 'You must also bear witness at Rome' (Acts 23:11). And now, in spite of the hatred and conspiracies of the Jews, the two years imprisonment at Caesarea, and the disastrous voyage and shipwreck, here he was at last among the Roman brethren who loved and welcomed him. The word of God had gloriously triumphed over all the powers of sin and darkness.

Within days of arriving Paul arranged a meeting with the Jewish leaders. His purpose was to explain that, although he was a prisoner, he had committed no crime against Israel or the Jewish faith. 'Men and brethren, though I have done nothing against our people or the customs of our fathers, yet I was delivered as a prisoner from Jerusalem into the hands of the Romans, who, when they had examined me, wanted to let me go, because there was no cause for putting me to death. But when the Jews spoke against it, I was compelled to appeal to Caesar, not that I had anything of which to accuse my nation. For this reason therefore I have called for you, to see you and speak with you, because for the hope of Israel I am bound with this chain' (Acts 28:17–20).

By 'the hope of Israel' he means the Jewish expectation of the coming Messiah as foretold in the Old Testament, and was thus encouraging them to enquire about the Christian Messianic hope. And that is exactly what they did. 'But we desire to hear from you what you think; for concerning this sect, we know that it is spoken against everywhere' (Acts 28:22). This was Paul's opportunity, and he took full advantage of it to preach the gospel in the light of the Old Testament prophecies and promises. 'So when they had appointed him a day, many came to him at his lodging, to whom he explained and solemnly testified of the Kingdom of God, persuading them concerning Jesus from both the Law of Moses and the Prophets, from morning till evening' (Acts 28:23).

The result was a mixture of acceptance and rejection. 'And some were persuaded by the things which were spoken, and some disbelieved' (Acts 28:24). It was this hardness of heart that led Paul to speak his last and final word of warning to the Jews: 'The Holy Spirit spoke rightly through Isaiah the prophet to our fathers, saying,

"Go to this people and say:
'Hearing you will hear, and shall not understand;
And seeing you will see, and not perceive;
For the hearts of this people have grown dull.
Their ears are hard of hearing,
And their eyes they have closed,
Lest they should see with their eyes and hear with their ears,
Lest they should understand with their hearts and turn,
So that I should heal them.'"' (Acts 28:26–27).

In this final word of Paul to his fellow Jews there is something both sad and glad. In the words of Isaiah the Jews had deliberately closed their hearts and ears and eyes to the gospel, so that even when it was explained to them as clearly as Paul had done, they failed to understand it. That is always sad in any person. But, as Paul saw it, even this rejection was within the overruling purpose of Almighty God, and a cause for gladness, for the door which the Jews had closed, was opened to the Gentiles. 'Therefore let it be known to you that the salvation of God has been sent to the Gentiles and they will hear it!' (Acts 28:28).

For the next two years Paul remained a prisoner in his own rented house, but he was able to continue his evangelistic ministry, 'preaching the kingdom of God and teaching the things which concern the Lord Jesus Christ with all confidence, no one forbidding him' (Acts 28:30–31).

The story ends there, and we do not know whether Paul was eventually executed or released from his imprisonment. But we can praise God for the part he had in the story which began thirty years earlier in Jerusalem, and which continues to unfold today in the church which is still on the move.